THE ETHICS
of
GIVING AND RECEIVING

The mission of the Cary M. Maguire Center for Ethics and Public Responsibility at Southern Methodist University is to heighten ethical awareness throughout the campus and the Greater Dallas community, and, when appropriate, among members of the global society. The Center serves as a forum for the exploration of issues bearing on the public good. At its conferences, the Center brings together people on important social issues and provides opportunities and resources for ethical reflection. But these sometimes exciting contributions tend to be limited to the participants gathered for an occasion. The purpose of the Center's books and other publications is to capture these contributions in a more permanent form and to make them available to a wider audience. In this way, we hope to make available to leaders and concerned citizens knowledge about issues in ethics of interest to them so that they might reach more informed judgments. In so doing, the Center hopes to make a lasting contribution to the greater public conversation on ethics.

RICHARD O. MASON, DIRECTOR
Maguire Center for Ethics and Public Responsibility

The Ethics
of
Giving and Receiving

Am I My Foolish Brother's Keeper?

EDITED BY
William F. May and A. Lewis Soens, Jr.

INTRODUCTION BY
William F. May

THE CARY M. MAGUIRE CENTER FOR
ETHICS AND PUBLIC RESPONSIBILITY

and

SOUTHERN METHODIST
UNIVERSITY PRESS
Dallas

Requests for permission to reproduce material from this work should be sent to:
Rights and Permissions
Southern Methodist University Press
PO Box 750415
Dallas, Texas 75275-0415

Library of Congress Cataloging-in-Publication Data
The ethics of giving and receiving : am I my foolish brother's keeper? / edited by William
F. May and A. Lewis Soens, Jr. ; introduction by William F. May.—1st ed.
    p. cm.
    Includes bibliographical references and index.
    ISBN 0-87074-452-6 (alk. paper)
    1. Charities—United States. 2. Social service—United States. 3. Church charities—
United States. I. May, William F. II. Soens, A. L. (Adolph L.), 1931–

HV91.E783 2000
361.7'0973—dc21   00-026740

Jacket photograph by Bernard Safran, © Estate of Bernard Safran

Jacket and text design by Tom Dawson

Printed in the United States of America on acid-free paper
10   9   8   7   6   5   4   3   2   1

To Cary M. Maguire
and
Laura Lee Blanton
(1928–1999)

whose generosity and expectations
have set a high standard for giving and receiving.

A covenant exists . . . between all the citizens of a democracy when they all feel themselves subject to the same weakness and the same dangers; their interests as well as their compassion makes it a rule with them to lend one another assistance when required.

ALEXIS DE TOCQUEVILLE

Contents

Acknowledgments

ary M. Maguire, a member of the board of trustees of Southern
Methodist University, generously endowed the Maguire Center for
Ethics and Public Responsibility at the University in June 1995. Mr.
Maguire and fellow trustee Laura Lee Blanton established university-wide
chairs in ethics at Southern Methodist University in 1985. These early gifts
made the eventual establishment of the Maguire Center possible. Ms.
Blanton served as a charter member of the Ethics Center Advisory Board
until her death in August 1999.

In the second year of its operation, the Maguire Center, with the substantial program support of an anonymous donor, sponsored two conferences
on "Entrusted with Giving and Receiving." The first conference examined
philanthropic foundations; the second, voluntary communities. This volume
on *The Ethics of Giving and Receiving* grew out of the two conferences and
benefited from the continuing, keen interest that Cary M. Maguire, Laura
Lee Blanton, and Richard O. Mason, the current Director of the Maguire
Center, have shown in the project.

We are hugely indebted as well to Renee Rivers, David Halleen, and Professor Lonnie Kliever. As former Associate Director of the Maguire Center,
Ms. Rivers helped conceive and plan the conferences and negotiated with

authors on the preparation of their manuscripts for publication. As current staff associate for publications at the Maguire Center, Mr. Halleen has provided indispensable help in bringing this project to its completion. Professor Kliever, a member of the Faculty Advisory Committee to the Maguire Center, gave valuable suggestions for the ordering of the chapters. Our thanks go as well to the distinguished authors who attended the conferences and eventually contributed chapters to this volume.

Preface

America has relied heavily upon voluntary communities (and the foundations that support them) for its flourishing as a nation. Alexis de Tocqueville, as far back as the 1830s, referred to the vigor of voluntary communities as the distinctive feature of American society. John Nason aptly referred to board and staff members of foundations and voluntary communities as "public servants." That characterization may surprise those who prefer to describe such groups as the "private sector," reserving the term "public" exclusively for officials on the government's payroll. But leaders of foundations and voluntary communities, along with business leaders and government officials, cumulatively wield immense public powers and help shape the fate of millions of people. After government and business, voluntary communities (and the foundations that support them) constitute what Nason and others have called the "third sector."

The government traffics in making and enforcing laws, the marketplace in buying and selling, and the third sector in the no less important tasks of giving and receiving as these exchanges spread beyond the confines of the family.

However, most institutions in the third sector today feel hard-pressed, underfunded, and overloaded. The government has withdrawn from many of the social responsibilities it carried through the 1970s. Voluntary communities and various philanthropic organizations wonder whether they can take up the slack and supply some basic goods to the needy or support the "higher" goods of research, education, and the arts.

Nongovernmental institutions that support these various social goods vary greatly and sometimes compete fiercely for support. The nonprofits often compete with each other for the same dollars. Donors thus must decide to what cause or organization they should make a large contribution while fending off others with a token pledge or nothing. One's alma mater? One's church or synagogue? The American Cancer Society? The local food bank or the local symphony orchestra? Flood victims in Bangladesh?

Competing for the same dollars and driven by the differing commitments and enthusiasms of their volunteers, leaders of these varying institutions do not often meet to share problems and solutions. A splendid patron of the arts in Dallas confessed that she finds herself very uncomfortable when she appears on the same panel with advocates for the needs of the hungry and the homeless. Her high cause seems to pale before the needs of the poor. To spare themselves such awkwardness, various leaders and communities in the third sector tend to go their separate ways, except for the tactical collaborations in fund-raising through the United Way.

But, at the same time, these competitors share common problems, which this book seeks to address:

- Identifying the warrants for and understanding the psychology of giving;
- Identifying the responsibilities of receiving;
- Coping with the scarcity of time and treasure;
- Addressing the vexing issue of setting priorities;
- Accommodating the sometimes conflicting fiduciary responsibilities of donors, boards, staffs, and beneficiaries;
- Mapping the interface of voluntary communities with the other great players in our common life especially, the government;
- Balancing the always difficult-to-settle tensions between charity and solidarity; and

• Responding to the challenge of those who fear that welfare encourages
  irresponsibility—am I my foolish brother's keeper?

As preparation for dealing with these and similar issues, the Maguire
Center for Ethics and Public Responsibility held two conferences in 1996
and 1997 on "Entrusted with the Task of Giving and Receiving." The first
examined the Ethics of Philanthropy and Trusteeship, especially in the world
of foundations; the second, Ethical Issues Facing Voluntary Communities.
We did not invite authors to the conferences to conduct a social laboratory
experiment from which one might draw conclusions. Nor did we call them
together as a legislative assembly or a deliberative body, to make a set of
recommendations. The book presents not a compendium of conclusions
and recommendations, but a symposium (richer in its insights than the introduction to this volume can convey) whose voices will help trustees, staff
members, and others reach their own conclusions and recommendations. No
book, however wise on the subject of giving and receiving, can relieve them
of those tasks.

WILLIAM F. MAY

Introduction

WILLIAM F. MAY

I deally, philanthropy embodies a love of humankind that issues in concrete deeds of service to others. This service can take the form of goods,
time, or money. Such gifts either meet basic needs (for food, clothing,
shelter, and medical care) or foster beneficiaries' excellence (by supporting art,
culture, research, parks, museums, public buildings, and education). These
two levels of service reflect an important distinction in human life between
the goods necessary for existence and the goods that enhance developed existence. Philanthropy envisages dual responsibilities: to care for the being of
others and to foster their well-being.

From antiquity, religious traditions of charity largely directed gifts to
relieve or console those in misery; that is, they enjoined distributing to the
needy the goods of bare existence (feeding the hungry, giving drink to the
thirsty, caring for the sick, visiting the imprisoned). Without exception, the
Abrahamic religions of Judaism, Christianity, and Islam called believers to
such works of mercy. In contrast, modern managers of philanthropic foundations have largely (although not exclusively) concentrated their resources on
fostering excellence in the lives of beneficiaries. They believe that supporting
human excellence, through, for example, research and education, will ultimately help prevent and eliminate some of the structural causes of human

misery. The early efforts of the Carnegie Endowment and the Ford Foundation helped develop this strategy. To attack the problem of too little food in the Third World, one must not simply feed the hungry but develop technologies that will increase the food supply. Thus, while distributing some of the goods of developed existence, philanthropic foundations addressed some of the deeper causes of human misery. They tried to avoid merely treating symptoms.

Historically, a variety of institutions have served as the medium of aid. In traditional societies, the family, kinship groups, castes, or extended clans helped needy members. The sacred writings of Jewish, Muslim, Buddhist, Confucian, and other religious traditions provided warrants for, and cultivated the habits of, giving (see the essays by David Smith and James Wind). Sometimes these traditions fostered specialized institutions offering hospitality and aid. In classical Western society, the church, which at one time possessed one-third of the usable land in Europe, supplemented the aid to the needy distributed by families and feudal allegiances. In the colonies of the New World, voluntary communities and religious congregations distributed most of the aid that met welfare needs (see the essay by Curtis Meadows). Indeed, settlers in the new land developed practical ways of helping one another, long before they formed governments and worried about the abstract principle of the separation of church and state. Voluntarism has persisted and flourished as a distinctive feature of American life. By 1982, philanthropic giving reached a total of $60 billion, by 1995, $103 billion, and in 1998, according to the estimates of the *Chronicle of Philanthropy*, $175 billion.

However, in the modern world, the welfare state (which had its proximate origins in Bismarck's Germany, its remote precedent in ancient Rome, and its more immediate derivation in the legislation of the Franklin Roosevelt and Lyndon Johnson presidencies) has increasingly assumed philanthropic functions. The state accepted responsibility not simply for security (protection against fire, theft, murder, and foreign invasion), but also for social welfare by creating a safety net that partly protects citizens from the damages inflicted by the accidents of nature, the harshness of the marketplace, and their own mistakes. The state also expanded funding for the high goods of research and education and, to a lesser extent, the arts. Since the emergence of the welfare state, the term "philanthropic" has come to refer more narrowly to giving by private donors, voluntary communities, or incorporated foundations rather than to giving within the reciprocities of family life or to the legislative largesse of the state.

Across the last two decades, a reaction set in against extended government support and services. Libertarian advocates of a minimal state (the Reaganites in the U.S. and the Thatcherites in the U.K.) sought to divest the national government of its welfare functions (derisively criticizing the "nanny state") and to limit its responsibility for supporting education, research, and the arts. They would return these responsibilities altogether either to local governments or, preferably, to voluntary communities.

A. Voluntary Communities: Overloaded and Criticized

The proposal to meet human needs and to foster excellence exclusively through voluntary giving poses a variety of difficulties. First, very practically, voluntary communities depend for their continuing vitality on their members who contribute treasure and time. Prolonged inflation through the 1960s and '70s, however, eroded the financial base of churches, synagogues, and service organizations. Further, the women's movement, sometimes in combination with the pressures of inflation on family income and low wages for men and women in service jobs, propelled women into the workforce and thus reduced the number of people free to contribute time. Just as the Catholic Church relied heavily for its service mission on the donated time of priests and nuns, now in dwindling supply, other churches, synagogues, and organizations in this country depended on women volunteers, increasingly in short supply. In losing the spouse and mother, moreover, congregations tended also to lose the rest of the family.

Justice forbids turning the clock back on the women's movement. But clearly churches, synagogues, and other voluntary communities will need to enlist the services of economists, sociologists, anthropologists, and theologians to address this major personnel problem that will affect their work over the next forty or fifty years. Where will "free" time come from? From the elderly? From a renegotiation of the length of the work day, the work week, or the work year? Or, failing these personnel resources, by replacing volunteers with paid professional staff members? Voluntary communities face a problem of sustaining themselves precisely at a time when the government has abruptly reduced many of its traditionally accepted welfare responsibilities. J. Cook, chief program officer for the Communities Foundation of Texas, testifies in this book to the overload that foundations currently face because of diminished government funding.

A society that depends heavily on voluntarism faces some further difficulties. Modern communities have so organized themselves as to segregate the rich from the poor. The affluent crawl past the poor sections of town on gridlocked and elevated superhighways. Private charities often fail to reach out beyond the limited circle of the donor's experience. One corporation sponsoring a grant program matching the charitable contributions of its employees discovered that it made entirely too many grants to Little League, since many of its middle-aged worker/fathers heavily invested their time with that organization. This corporate matching program simply reflected the natural altruism of the workers whose sympathies didn't reach much beyond family enthusiasms. As one of the leaders of volunteerism in the Reagan administration once conceded, there are just so many Louisville Sluggers one can make use of in a given suburb. A society that relies too heavily on voluntarism to meet basic needs finds its distributions too parochial, too episodic, too dependent upon the moral imagination of its affluent members. In a finely balanced sentence, Robin Lovin observes, "If compassion often leads us into imprudence by moving us to waste resources on those who cannot use them or do not deserve them, it can also lead us into injustice by obscuring the true character of suffering when that suffering just happens to be very unlike any that we are apt to experience."

Further, the ideal of philanthropy traditionally tends to see the human race as two species: relatively self-sufficient benefactors and needy beneficiaries. It tends to presuppose a unilateral or one-way transfer from giver to receiver. This assumption of asymmetry dominated not only private giving, but also the self-interpretation of America as philanthropist amongst the nations after World War II. Americans modified somewhat this image of themselves in the last ten or fifteen years with the nation's trade and budget deficits and its default on its UN pledge, but previously Americans viewed themselves chiefly as benefactors and others as beneficiaries. Similarly, the American churches saw themselves as patrons to the churches in the Third World. Further, idealists in the helping professions, such as law, medicine, and ministry, tend to define themselves asymmetrically as expert givers offering remedies to their needy clients, patients, and parishioners.

Surely this idealist's picture of a social world divided into givers and receivers morally surpasses the cynic's outlook that justifies callous neglect or that reduces all human relationships to self-interested marketplace transactions. But sensitive participants in giving also recognize that the idealist's picture sometimes encourages a conceit. It does not acknowledge that the benefactor receives as well as gives. A two-way street of giving and receiving marks the entire human community, not merely the family. Long before Americans devised the Marshall Plan for Europe, Europe gave the Colonies much of their heritage. The philanthropic nation has received bountifully from other nations; the American church, from other churches; and philanthropic professionals, from their clients, patients, and students.

Voluntarism is a distinctive, attractive, and, indeed, indispensable feature of American life (it is difficult to imagine the American character without it). But a society that relies too exclusively on voluntary giving can fall into a series of moral traps, some of which derive from the fiction of the self-sufficient giver. Donors can become too overbearing or too demeaning or too given to covert control or too insensitive to long-range negative side effects of their well-meaning interventions, too given to monumentalism, too oriented to their own glory, and, sometimes, comically inflexible or narrow. (One donor gave funds to provide a baked potato at each meal for each young woman at Bryn Mawr.)

Finally, that favorably disposed but shrewd nineteenth-century critic of philanthropy Charles Dickens warned against the vice of what he called "inconstancy." A philanthropist usually gives out of surplus. He does not want to mire down in the life of the beneficiary. (Recall the rich man in Charlie Chaplin's *City Lights*. The tramp enjoyed his benefactor's favor as long as the rich man was drunk; but as soon as the rich man sobered up, the tramp was out on his ear again.) Philanthropy often espouses a doctrine of love without ties. The philanthropist wants to give, but not to end up entangled in the toils of the receiver. Consequently, giving can deteriorate into the episodic, the fitful, the too easily discouraged.

A twentieth-century foundation sometimes reinforces this inconstancy when it insists on supporting only the novel, the innovative. Staff members grow restless with the old. They are fearful of establishing a "dependency relationship." They look for "pilot projects," "multiplier effects," and "catalytic proposals." They sometimes succumb to an overstimulating environment. Applicants for money, consultants on how to spend it, and star professors, performing at conferences and high-level seminars, keep them instantly abreast of the latest. Staff members become masters of the quick study. New ideas arouse their interest; but other applicants rapidly copy them; and these new ideas and their daughters quickly age overnight. The pressure to achieve a breakthrough adds to this fickleness. In the hopes of achieving the definitive reform, the benefactor becomes fearful of any and all constant ties.

In addition to these more internally generated moral criticisms, philanthropic organizations have faced attack from political movements on the left, center, and right. Each political attack, of course, appeals to its own (not always unassailable) moral principles. A long-standing criticism from the center and left argues that a society must shoulder a much stronger duty to its vulnerable citizens than the vagaries of beneficence and charity can fulfill. Food in the mouths of infants, beds for the decrepit, and medicines for the sick should rank as duties of justice within the regularities of a tax system; they should not depend wholly upon the occasional inspirations of charity. These burdens of support, moreover, ought to exert a claim evenly upon well-to-do citizens through a tax system rather than depend wholly upon a system of voluntary giving, which, as David Smith points out in his essay, fails to net the freeloader. Some liberals on the left have argued that an impersonal tax system respects the freedom of the recipient better than the paternalism that creeps into personal giving. With an eye to the practices of other industrial nations, other critics on the left have argued that the citizenry (through their government or through government-supported independent councils) owe a greater and more sustained support for the arts and other higher goods than ticket sales, TV pleas, and publicized lists of patrons currently generate in America.

Still more radical populist critics have complained that both private charity and state-supported welfare tend to flow downward through established institutions and professional staffs from the powerful to the powerless; they leave the most vulnerable and unorganized in the society perhaps fed, but still disorganized and disempowered and therefore not as well served as they should be.

From the opposite direction, the political right suspects that philanthropic foundations and other "third sector" communities aid and abet the basic agenda of the welfare state. By their grants, the foundations support intellectuals and artists on the left, radical causes, the UN, and internationalism. In this vein, the journal *Foundation Watch* attacked the MacArthur Foundation, despite the presence of ABC's Paul Harvey on the MacArthur Foundation Board.

More seriously, conservatives, including the revisionist historian Christopher Lasch and Leon Kass, whose essay "Am I My Foolish Brother's Keeper?" appears in this volume, have asked whether we have let compassion lead us astray both in our legislation and in the forms of our charity. In giving, have we not often enfeebled rather than strengthened the recipient's sense of responsibility for his own life and well-being? To this degree, have we not, in attempting to do good, in fact done harm? These critics also ask whether, to the detriment of individuals and the society at large, our sense of justice based on need has eclipsed our sense of justice based on desert. However one decides these issues, the proponents of giving must face the question of the standards by which they give and the standards to which receivers may be held.

Recently, a literature has begun to emerge on the subject of philanthropy and trusteeship (for example, by the Council on Foundations and by the Indiana University Center on Philanthropy at Indianapolis). This literature derives from the work of historians, sociologists, political scientists, and other academic advisors to foundation staffs, and from thoughtful practitioners in the art of responsible giving and receiving.

However, we have not seen a modern literary treatment of the relations of benefactors to beneficiaries to match the critique that surfaced in the dramatic literature of the sixteenth to eighteenth centuries or in the novels of Dickens and Trollope in the nineteenth century. Perhaps the official egalitarianism of the U.S. accounts for a dearth of this literature in America. The U.S., at least officially, prizes the notion that all persons are created equal. It grows uncomfortable with the discussion of permanent inequalities of rank, so readily conceded by aristocratic societies. It has not fully acknowledged the vast inequalities in income and power, which Dickens and Trollope perceived in Great Britain as that country moved from an aristocratic to a hierarchically organized industrial nation.

Americans—once rid of slavery—tended to view poverty and huge inequalities in wealth as temporary, passing bad luck, or a way station for immigrants who would eventually get ahead in the land of opportunity. Only in the last two decades of the twentieth century has the country appeared to move into huge and ever increasing inequalities of wealth. According to the conservative political advisor Kevin Phillips, 70 percent of the increase in the national product in the 1980s went to the upper 1 percent of Americans, the top 10 percent of households controlled approximately 68 percent of the nation's wealth, and "downward mobility emerged as a real fear in the American workplace."[1] Despite these increasing and sometimes permanent-looking inequalities in wealth which the term "underclass" reflects, the public rhetoric of the country remains egalitarian.

Thus the country has not developed the criticisms of asymmetrical relationships which the Restoration comedians and the satirists among the nineteenth-century novelists noted with a clear eye: the vanity, pretensions, condescension, overbearingness, and shortsightedness of the donor and the obsequiousness, hypocrisy, manipulativeness, irresponsibility, and deviousness of the recipient. However, Dr. Roy W. Menninger contributes to such a literature in our time with his essay on the psychology of giving and receiving money. As a psychiatrist and foundation head, he notes the tangle of motives that can accompany giving (sometimes narcissistic, sometimes guilt-ridden, sometimes altruistic) and the varied and often dark motives that beset practitioners and beneficiaries (feelings of inadequacy, compensatory aggressiveness, flattery, latent resentfulness, and proud disdain). Good psychiatrist that he is, Menninger believes that naming and recognizing the dark side of things can help a little—in this case, help both givers and receivers of money attain a greater "sense of participation and value" in the cause that brings them together. Such matters need ventilation, not to dismiss and discredit giving and receiving but to strengthen them and to keep them honest.

Still, the satirists did not deal with the deeper problem which philanthropy itself poses, that is, the denial of human solidarity that gifts often imply. As suggested earlier, philanthropy establishes a gulf between giver and receiver deeper than the condescension of any particular patron or philanthropist. It divides humanity into benefactors and beneficiaries. The very act of giving, which attempts to achieve solidarity between the haves and have-nots, also strains solidarity at its deeper levels. David Smith shrewdly points out that taxes affirm the solidarity of "We the people" by saying, "We are all in the same boat." Awkward philanthropies, on the other hand, can remind us of the distinction between first class and steerage.

An earlier literature, embedded in the religious tradition of the West, sought to deal with this issue by putting the imperative to give into a narrative, which overcomes some of the gulf between giver and receiver. This narrative endows the imperative to give with a moral force stronger than the gentle nudges of the modern principle of beneficence; justice itself commands us to give. Even as we have received, justice calls us to give to others, and to give generously.

B. THE WARRANTS FOR GIVING

The Western Scriptures provide powerful injunctions to give, but always within the setting of a primordial receiving which binds together the giver and receiver in a final equality of need before God. The Jewish farmer, for example, in harvesting his crops, should not glean his fields too clean. He should leave some fallen grain for sojourners, for he himself long ago received as a sojourner in Egypt. The passage does not describe the Jewish farmer simply as a benefactor. It reminds him that historically and primordially he was and is a beneficiary. Whatever benefactions he offers flow from that original gift. Similarly, the Christian's love, from beginning to end, only responds to primordial *caritas*. "Herein is love, not that we love God, but that God first loved us. . . . Since God so loved us, we also ought to love one another" (1 John, 4:10,11, ASV). The trivial gifts that humans give, from the widow's mite to a Rockefeller's fortune, take place within a transcendent receiving. These gifts function as a small sign of the huge mercy which the givers have not themselves produced. Cosmically we have all received; and our petty benefactions derive from this huge gift.

Further, few people have sacrificed to meet genuine human need or to foster human excellence who have not discovered that they themselves have received in the transaction and distribute benefits as stewards, not owners. The venerable notions of stewardship and trusteeship describe us as stewards entrusted with what we have received. The traditional, aristocratic ideal of noblesse oblige partly recognizes this status and charge. However, the phrase does not find a sympathetic hearing today. "Noblesse oblige" evokes the weary, condescending patron. But the ideal underlined a very important point. Members of the nobility could harbor no illusion that they created the wealth and power which they wielded. They inherited it; they received it; and the inheritance carried a responsibility to others.

Self-deception and moral danger lurk in the alternative which we have adopted for ourselves, the myth of the self-made man or the self-made woman. No sensitive person can go through the school system of a nation and through its institutions of higher learning and think of himself or herself as self-made. An enormous social investment helped each and obliges each to make some small return on that investment to serve the common good. In acknowledgment of this indebtedness, the professions traditionally emphasized the importance of *pro bono publico* service, service rendered for the public good.

The tradition of stewardship and trusteeship at its best supplied a powerful incentive to expend time and treasure through the institutional setting of voluntary communities. A society should not, for all the reasons already cited, try to solve its welfare needs exclusively through voluntary communities, but little platoons of locally organized benevolence among us amplify the capacities of a community to serve the needs and enhance the excellences of its members in ways beyond the resources of family and state alone.

Indeed, we may be moving into a period in which we need to sustain two types of social organization that parallel the two types of art forms that flourished at the time of the construction of the Egyptian pyramids. First, the huge bureaucracies of state and corporation supply us with the organizational equivalent of the pyramids—massive, formal, geometrical, and hierarchical. But, second, we also need small-scale, informal, and spontaneous communities that can counterbalance the bureaucracies; just as the Egyptians developed spontaneous, lyrical art forms to compensate for the impersonal, massive forms of the pyramid. These small-scale, informal, and flexible communities among us depend especially, but not exclusively, for their support upon religious communities and the foundations.

Smaller communities of volunteers serve several indispensable functions in supplementing the work of professionalized bureaucracies. First, they offer supplementary and often more targeted and personally nuanced services than the bureaucracies can provide. Personal interaction with recipients also can help generate in the latter responsibility and accountability. To expect small-scale voluntary communities to bear the full burden of care is naïve. Several contributors to this volume—David Smith, James Wind, Trey Hammond, and Carl Trovall—have noted that one cannot realistically look to local philanthropies to take up the slack if the government withdraws support. The government already contributes, either directly or indirectly (through the grant of tax exempt status), a substantial portion of the funds which voluntary communities and congregations distribute in their philanthropic work. However, to neglect what these communities can do to supplement (and often do better than) the government wastes an opportunity. Small-scale institutions, such as churches and synagogues, may better build a local community and inspire recipients of aid with a stronger sense of responsibility than can a distant faceless bureaucracy. Wind explores such synergism at work between the public and the voluntary sectors in coastal cities; Trovall and Yohn, in the rural Southwest; and Hammond, on the specific issue of housing, both in Dallas and nationally.

Second, volunteers provide a critical check on the bureaucracies when amateurs frequent the halls of professional institutions and elect representatives to institutional boards. Professional bureaucrats can drift from their mission and lapse into protective self-serving. To stay focused, bureaucrats need the responsible outside amateur trustees who dare to ask basic questions.

Further, and more positively, voluntary communities can help nourish and support service bureaucracies. Nineteenth-century idealism created huge institutions, such as mental hospitals, chronic care facilities, and prisons, to take care of various communities of need and desert. However, in time, funding dwindled, and these institutions collapsed into the custodial bins in which we sequester "inmates" today. Only as outside amateurs enter hospitals, prisons, schools, and nursing homes and offer their services there will we create an ethos within the society at large more favorable to their support at a humane level.

Finally, voluntary communities can and should experiment. They need not only to work within existing institutions to supplement, criticize, and support them, but also to create alternative responses to human need, responses proleptic of social worlds to come. Earlier I pointed to the danger of inconstancy—the mind-set of those who are ever on the prowl for a creative breakthrough or a multiplier effect. But we also need bold experiments. Cumbersome bureaucracies often cannot redo themselves. They have invested too much in the status quo. They need the prod of successful experiments before they will lurch into motion. Thus society needs its smaller, spontaneous, informal communities to sortie into the future and prepare for the day when the great institutions among us, which look so permanent as ways of meeting needs and fostering excellence, will crack and decay.

C. DUTIES IN RESPONSIBLE GIVING

If we agree that trustees and staff members of foundations and leaders of voluntary communities in the third sector serve also as public servants, then we must concede that they face at least two basic kinds of moral problems: temptations and quandaries. Temptations present clear distinctions between right and wrong and tempt us to do the wrong thing. Obviously, politicians betray their public identity when they wield power and money for private advantage. Shakespeare's Henry V recognized and rejected this temptation when he took up the public duties of the crown and broke with his old friend Falstaff, who would have treated the crown as a convenient windfall enriching without disturbing their private life together as cronies. Similarly, prohibitions in trustee ethics against self-dealing, cronyism, or acting on uncriticized preferences (making decisions without the test of competition from other proposals) follow from the need to sustain the public integrity of the enterprise.

Trustees of foundations also betray their public mission when they serve the company from which the foundation initially derived its resources at the expense of their duties as foundation trustees. At one time, creating a foundation provided some wealthy families with a device for maintaining covert control of a corporation that inheritance taxes would otherwise have eroded. Transmitting to the foundation the great bulk of family stocks in the company of origin relieved heirs of the need to sell off their holdings (and thus forfeit much power) to pay huge taxes. As foundation board members voting the stock, they could continue to control the original company. This strategy, of course, conflicted with a board's fiduciary responsibility to ensure the security of the foundation's assets, a purpose which the board could not well serve without diversifying its portfolio. Other foundation boards yielded to the temptation to limit severely the number and size of their grants in order to retain and increase the foundation's assets and power at the expense of its stated philanthropic purposes. The federal government intervened to curb both of these institutional conflicts of interest.

Other conflicts of interest emerge for the trustee who serves simultaneously on a foundation board and on the board (or as an administrator) of another institution that may be applying for funds. Nielsen and Wheatley have highlighted these problems in the history of the Carnegie Foundation. Some early trustees treated the Foundation as a cash cow to meet the needs of another institution which they led. Requiring public disclosure helps guard against some of these abuses. The trustee's sense of public responsibility tends to strengthen to the degree that his actions may face public scrutiny.

Staff and board members face a second and larger range of moral problems which I would characterize as quandaries. A quandary, as opposed to a temptation, does not confront us with a clear choice between right and wrong, but with an unavoidable conflict between competing goods or evils. Any choice forfeits or curtails some good or imposes some evil.

In attempting to resolve quandaries (dilemmas, hard cases, or moral binds), we usually appeal to one or more moral principles. In the field of applied ethics today, many writers emphasize the importance of the principles of beneficence (doing good or preventing evil), nonmaleficence (doing no harm), justice (varyingly defined as distributing benefits and burdens according to need, or desert, or social contribution, or entitlement), and respect for autonomy (respect for personal or institutional self-governance).

In philanthropic endeavors, the principle of beneficence, that is, the principle of doing good, looms as especially important. However, the principle hardly of itself lays to rest the question of what one must do. Trustees and leaders of voluntary communities must decide which of many competing goods they will support. Will they attempt to supply the urgent goods of existence (necessities such as food, clothing, shelter, and health care) or the high goods of a developed existence (such as education, art, culture, and communal values)? If they decide simply to meet urgent human needs, which needs? Should a society at large attempt to relieve all the misery in its precincts before it begins to enhance excellence?

Leon Kass, in his essay, worries that a contemporary "ideology of compassion" threatens to override the principle of doing good for humankind. An ideology of compassion tends to sacrifice the "high to the urgent," both in the decisions of the government and in voluntary giving. In reply, Charles Curran, a Christian ethicist, argues for policies that make a "preferential option for the poor." However, he notes that "preferential" does not mean an "exclusive" option; one must leave room for philanthropies other than works of mercy.

This volume explores at greatest length the tensions in making decisions between the principles of beneficence and the three other principles of justice, respect for autonomy, and nonmaleficence. Leon Kass in his essay "Am I My Foolish Brother's Keeper?" argues that philanthropic giving today melts down into an indiscriminate compassion and thus tends to ignore justice. Lacking the constraints of justice (which Kass chiefly links with desert) an "ideology of compassion" undercuts the beneficiaries' sense of responsibility. Treating them as victims, rather than as responsible persons, it expects nothing of them. To this degree, it fails to respect them as self-governing persons, and it ultimately harms them. It corrupts them by turning them into permanent wards of the government or a charity. Thus indiscriminate compassion violates not only the principle of justice, but the principles of autonomy and nonmaleficence. In ignoring desert, indiscriminate compassion fails to grant recipients responsibility, and thereby disenfranchises and damages them.

For varying reasons, Kass does not propose a principle of strict responsibility. Time and chance happen to us all; not all risk-taking is bad; not all failure results from folly or vice; second chances can pay off; and fate deals people very different cards in talent, intelligence, life experience, and family opportunity. Further, he concedes that "a decent community will try to care not only for those who are worse off than others through no fault of their own, but even to bear some of the costs of helping those who are partly responsible for their own troubles." A society ought to "improve upon justice in the direction of generosity and self-care," he advises, both for the sake of the common good and for the sake of the self-affirmation which acts of generosity bring to benefactors. But Kass chiefly argues for discriminate giving, giving that exacts from recipients responsible receiving. Compassion without standards and limits eventually ends up with too limited a view of the good that we can serve—the urgent at the expense of the high—and it shortchanges recipients themselves in that it expects nothing from them and thus does not encourage their own full development.

The responses to Kass take two forms—direct and indirect. The three direct responses come from the ethicists, Steven Sverdlik, Robin Lovin, and Charles Curran. Sverdlik concedes the importance of personal responsibility but warns that if we attempt to fit giving entirely to desert, we will have to conduct a quasi-legal search to determine responsibility as we allocate or withhold aid. Further, even when we can determine fault, we may damage the innocent by withholding help. For example, we may damage the innocent, unliable child in the course of withholding charity from the liable mom. Charity in such cases justifiably serves as damage control. Finally, Sverdlik argues, compassion can create constructive change; it does not inevitably corrupt. While he does not appeal to it, Scripture supports the philosopher in this perceptive empirical judgment.

Robin Lovin gives a partly historical account of the importance of norms or principles. He agrees with Kass that compassion, merely as a passing sentiment, will not suffice; it is insufficiently just, wise, or even benevolent. But he differs in diagnosing the chief problem of contemporary philanthropy: ". . . under the social conditions that we have created in our modern America, our compassion will reveal its limitations as well in not caring enough about certain kinds of suffering as in caring unwisely." The landscape of the modern city reflects his diagnosis. The derelict areas in our cities suffer less today from the overbearing presence of the nanny state, the paternalistic corporation, and indeterminately sentimental charities than from their absence. The city suffers less from the presence of saccharine parental love than from cold, impersonal indifference and neglect.

Curran presses for further thought about the content and scope of the principles of autonomy and justice. We think too individualistically if we limit respect for autonomy to an insistence upon personal accountability and individual self-governance. Autonomy must include the encouraging of self-governing communities and institutions. Curran then notes that beneficiaries do not always willingly surrender their autonomy for dependency. Benefactors sometimes curtail or eliminate their support for beneficiaries who display too much independence. They do not want to lose control, particularly of communities whose goals begin to diverge from the recognizable values to which the patrons subscribe. Yet, in their better moments, philanthropists will recognize that we cannot always have it both ways: we cannot both hope that individuals and grass roots communities will show initiative and yet expect them to seek only the goals we set them.

Curran also asserts that we operate with too limited a view of justice if we equate it exclusively with rewarding desert and penalizing delinquency. A fully realized notion of justice must include distributions according to need and contributions proportionate to ability to pay. The moral and political tradition has developed technical terms that correspond roughly to these additional dimensions of justice: "distributive and contributive justice." The state acknowledges (or ignores) the claims of distributive and contributive justice chiefly through its budgets and its tax system. As it exacts fair contributions through taxes and makes fair distributions through its budgets, the state mounts a platform of justice beneath the charitable work of voluntary communities. Some of the better institutional collaborations between the government and the third sector conjoin distributive and contributive justice with benevolence.

Wind, Yohn, Trovall, and Hammond supply indirect responses to Kass's provocative essay. They illustrate the ways in which a society, through collaboration, can compensate for the blindness of the government and the weakness of voluntary communities. The government can provide some of the resources voluntary communities lack; and voluntary communities can provide the local discernment and personal interaction that bureaucracies cannot easily arrange. We need the responses and sometimes the collaboration of both institutions to help meet human need, encourage accountability, and promote excellence.

Undoubtedly, collaboration poses dangers. It can lead congregations and voluntary groups to surrender the critical distance they need to fulfill their prophetic role in relation to the government. Religious congregations may also try to divert funds, earmarked for service to the common good, to their own ends and purposes and, then, shield themselves from charges of the abuse of power by appeal to the principle of separation of church and state! However, such dangers can be anticipated and addressed. Meanwhile, congregations and other voluntary groups have demonstrated, in such areas as housing, food, and health care, that they can sometimes serve the common good more efficiently and imaginatively than the government can acting alone.

To cite one instance: A friend in the pastorate, whom I had not seen in thirty-five years, insisted that I stop by his church basement in the course of a professional trip to San Francisco. At first glance, I saw only a conventional instance of charity—elderly people, stranded in a not very good neighborhood, were getting a daily square meal and a chance to meet acquaintances. But then I noticed a not so conventional feature—the people serving food at the cafeteria line and bussing the tables were themselves a community of need, what the politically correct in their earnest way call "mentally challenged." My friend (and his colleagues at five other congregations, Jewish and Christian) had imaginatively put together two communities of need, each serving the other; one, in need of a balanced diet and the nourishment of friends and community; the other, in need of meaningful work. However, even by pooling their resources, the city congregations could not possibly have funded the project. They needed money from the government to make the project work; just as the government needed the congregations, who supplied the idea, the institutional presence, the space, and the collateral staffing, to make the government's money work effectively.

In the foregoing review of the principles and goods germane to the work of foundations, congregations, and other voluntary groups, I have emphasized the points at which these principles conflict with one another. The term "hard case" refers to just such quandaries; and, unfortunately, duties do not conveniently arrange themselves in a permanently valid hierarchy to resolve such conflicts. I do not know any ethicist who can claim: "this principle or good should always trump that principle or good; and the second should always trump a third, on down the list." No moralist possesses such a table of principles that would conveniently relieve decision-makers of the burden of deliberation and judgment in resolving a quandary.

Thus board members will need not only to appeal to principles but also to bring to the table some virtues needed to resolve disputes. Practical wisdom surely heads the list. Givers need the gift and discipline of wisdom both to make good on doing good and to determine which principle or set of principles takes precedence in a particular conflict. No set of abstract criteria for making decisions will do more than set one along the path. Givers need a wisdom that will open itself patiently to the specifics of a case rather than operate deductively and repetitively from a favorite idea. Giving wisely also requires enough humility not to blow the bagpipes too loudly and self-righteously for one's own cause, as well as enough charity towards an opposing colleague at the table to recognize that some dignity attaches to being honestly wrong. The resilience of an organization also depends upon maintaining civility between advocates of competing proposals as controversy rises through the organization to its board.

D. INTRAMURAL ETHICS: THE RELATIONS OF DONORS, BOARDS, AND PROFESSIONAL STAFFS

This volume does not, and could not, attempt to cover the widely varying forms of governance and intramural life that inform voluntary communities and congregations. But it offers essays on the more limited world of foundations and their donors, trustees, and staff members. Foundations came into being, not to last forever, but to span the generations; they provide a partial response to the inescapable fact that all men and women, donors included, must die. Donors cannot rule from the grave, but they hope through wills, charters, and boards of trustees to set the courses of the institutions they entrusted with the task of serving the causes that prompted their original gifts.

However, what is the role of trustees? Should they adhere strictly and literally to original intent? Or should they exercise discretionary power as they attempt to fulfill an intent that does not follow the donor into the grave? Bruce Jennings of the Hastings Center has borrowed from Edmund Burke's famous distinction between two competing views of political representation to define the fiduciary responsibility of trustees. In one view, elected representatives must reflect and vote strictly the views of the constituents who put them in office: fidelity requires literal adherence to constituents' expressed wishes on particular subjects. Analogously, board members must reflect and extend the will of the donor, living or dead. In the second view, voters elect representatives for their good judgment and entrust them with the task of reaching decisions in changing circumstances. Faithful service does not permit them to ignore the views of their constituents, but they must also interpret, not merely reflect, those views as they deliberate and reach judgments. On the whole, it seems, Smith and Meadows hold to this second view of a board's fiduciary responsibility to donors. Faithful trusteeship requires that board members give a prima facie weight and priority to the donor's intent; however, that intent may call for interpretation, not simply strict and literal adherence in the discharge of one's responsibilities.

Waldemar A. Nielsen in his essay "The Ethics of Philanthropy and Trusteeship" and Steven C. Wheatley in "The Natural History of Foundation Management" have traced historically the conflicts and tensions that have emerged in the growth of foundations. Nielsen explores the history of the Carnegie Foundation, which, despite the careful design of its great donor, went through four successive stages: betrayal, slump, muddle, and renaissance. In ironic key Nielsen draws lessons from the century-long chronicle of the Foundation in the form of multiple questions rather than conclusions. What can the history of the Carnegie Foundation teach us?

- That a foundation's purposes over time will inevitably change and diverge from original intent, and that the donor should realistically understand and accept that fact?
- Or that a donor should try to tie down the objectives of his foundation so tightly and specifically that no board or administration can abandon or subvert them, ever?

- Or that if the foundation of a donor as wise and experienced as Carnegie can encounter such grave problems for decades at a stretch, then the foundations of donors who are more ordinary mortals face even worse prospects?
- Or that time has proven the wisdom of Andrew Carnegie's faith that over the long term, and despite periods of decline, "the perpetual foundation will have a new birth of usefulness and service"?

In his essay, Steven Wheatley shows how the intramural development of the trustees and staffs of foundations bears on the question of their political status in the U.S. He also finds an irony. Foundations emerged in the U.S. because Americans mistrusted state power. However, powerful foundations eventually became themselves the targets of populist mistrust. Donors compounded the political problem by giving most of their attention to the formation of continuing bodies of trustees who paid little attention to developing professional staffs. Donors often appointed trustees who ran their own institutions that looked to the foundation for support. Thus the foundation effectively isolated itself from the wider public. The later development of staffs with expertise meant that foundations eventually opened to a wider range of applications for grants. As they broke out of their circles of cronies, foundations created for themselves wider public support. Less isolated, they began to fit into the emerging ecology of institutions in the society at large.

E. RESPONSIBLE RECEIVING

Fiduciary responsibilities come with gifts. A gift usually carries with it a charge to put it to good use. Critics and authors in this volume have given most of their attention to the responsibilities of the needy and forlorn to make good use of charity and welfare payments. We have already noted how Christopher Lasch and others, best represented in this volume by Leon Kass, took liberals to task for their failure to hold recipients to moral standards. By ignoring the question of the beneficiaries' performance, liberals were guilty of an ultimate condescension: they excluded recipients from moral community by expecting nothing from them.

However, the distinguished heads of institutions, not simply the lowly recipients of charity, can ignore the promises implied in their acceptance of support funds. During the manic expansion of our universities, many of them indiscriminately accepted gifts, especially new buildings and programs, without thinking through the cost of making good on their promises. The vice president of a major public university told me that he said "Yes" as often as he could, and "No" as seldom as possible. Obviously, he liked to be liked. However, eighteen-year-old women quickly learn that always saying "Yes" is not a wise principle on which to conduct one's life; and mature academic administrators from the '80s forward finally found it painful to undo the foolish yea-saying of an earlier decade.

Passive board membership can also encourage irresponsibility in beneficiaries. If one serves on the board of trustees of a church, a synagogue, or an educational institution and ignores the question of its performance, one treats the institution as an avocational toy. Board membership merely serves personal vanity if one evades the hard ethical choices the institution faces in allocating its energies and funds.

However, we need to keep in mind several traps in the process of assessing recipients. First, if foundations make grants exclusively upon the basis of past performance, they may find it difficult to venture into the territory of the most vulnerable, resourceless, and disempowered in the society. America faces the growth of an underclass, a proletariat—those who are *in* the society but not *of* it, those who have no stake in its life. Venturing effectively into the world of the disempowered and the unorganized requires a level of discernment and discretion that cannot easily submit itself to the conventional standards by which we judge performance. Yohn, Trovall, Wind, and Curran post warnings on these difficulties.

Second, we also need to recognize a couple of hidden metaphors that govern our understanding of the task of evaluation. (A metaphor, I take it, allows us to see one thing as if it were another.) The conventional metaphor for assessment derives from manufacturing and engineering. Recipients must turn out a specific product which others can assess. Foundations invest money pointed toward outcomes. Well and good. The metaphor, however, may be a little too neat, too tidy, too constricting. I prefer the metaphor, not of engineering, but of dirt farming. Voluntary boards serve more as dirt farmers than as engineers. The metaphor has a muddy flexibility to it, which suits other important human enterprises as well—among them marriage and parenting. Mates and parents who think of themselves as engineers producing a product to specification let themselves in for a terrible letdown. Neither children nor spouses respond to machining as well or tidily as one anticipates. Teaching also is a species of dirt farming. The metaphor lies buried in our words "seminar" and "seminary" (from Latin for seeds). Teachers who plan to mass-assemble students as precisely machined products discover that all sorts of contingencies get into the gears. At best, in marriage, parenting, and teaching, one tills the ground a bit, broadcasts a little seed, and prays for a little sun, rain, and luck.

Broadcasting some seed doesn't mean that one is irresponsible and indifferent to the harvest. But evaluating often depends upon more subtle insight than the mechanical weighing of outcomes permits. Recall the evidence available at the beginning of the twentieth century in comparing two major competing modes of transportation, the automobile and the horse. The car offered two great advantages over the horse: it was faster, and it polluted less. The judgment about pollution, however, looks odd today. At least what the horse produced was biodegradable.

A memorable trip to the Caswell Center in Kinston, North Carolina, where I spent three days at a campus for the retarded, reminded me of the dangers of simple quantification. A vocational therapist there noted that federal money came to institutions like Caswell from 1963 forward to help the retarded develop skills. However, in order to prove to the government that they were not simply warehousing residents, institutions emphasized training that would yield obvious, statistical data. They taught the retarded how to put round pegs into round holes in order to demonstrate quantitatively their progress. But in retrospect the therapist observed: "You know, some of our retarded needed not the development of manual skills, but rather more elusive social skills. However, we could not find a way of quantifying and demonstrating in our reports that we had developed those social skills; thus we tended to neglect them. Still other of our residents were so retarded that they derived more benefit, humanly, by being touched and held; but again the benefits in this case couldn't be measured or quantified."

I do not want to suggest by these comments that one renounces all efforts at assessment. Indeed the metaphor of dirt farming points toward the notion of a harvest. "By their fruits, ye shall know them." One hopes that, when measured by that biblical standard, neither foundations nor voluntary communities nor the communities they serve will be found wanting.

PART I

A Contemporary Challenge

Am I My Foolish Brother's Keeper?

Justice, Compassion, and the Mission of Philanthropy

LEON R. KASS

These are critical times for philanthropic and voluntary associations, as they are for the nation at large. With the federal government cutting back funding for social services and programs, private philanthropy is being asked to take up the slack and is considering how to meet the challenge. But, in my view, we should first consider a prior question: Whether philanthropy *should* meet this challenge. In particular, should private philanthropy adopt for itself the goals of the Great Society and other social programs, programs that have not succeeded in the hands of Uncle Sam but that might succeed better in the nimbler hands of private philanthropy and its grantees.

Most of these programs, like them or not, sprang from a humane compassion for the less fortunate among us—the poor, the sick, and the needy; the ill-fed, the ill-housed, and the ill-educated; the deprived, the despised, and the disabled. Caring for the unfortunate has always been part of the mission of private charities, especially those connected to religious organizations. Thus, the adoption by the charitable sector of the government's compassion-driven programs might seem to restore the *status quo ante*, before the Great Society or even the New Deal. But times have changed, and we should think carefully before reaching this conclusion. Much depends on whether com-

1

passion is today the necessary and sufficient operating principle for philanthropic action.

I begin with some reflections on the spirit of philanthropy. For some people, especially on the left, the heart of the philanthropic spirit is compassion. One recent commentator even defines philanthropy as "compassionate action on behalf of other human beings." But this is a partial and narrowed view. In its root sense, philanthropy means the love of mankind, practical goodwill towards human beings in general, the disposition to promote the happiness and well-being of one's fellowmen—not just the relief of their miseries. The first English usage occurs in Francis Bacon's essay "Of Goodness and Goodness of Nature" (1607): "I take Goodness in this sense, the affecting of the weal of men, which is that the Grecians call *Philanthropia*." Bacon adds that "this of all virtues and dignities of the mind is the greatest; being the character of the Deity: and without it man is a busy, mischievous, wretched thing; no better than a kind of vermin." Indeed, philanthropy once meant explicitly God's love—specifically, Christ's love—of man. Joining these two meanings, *human* philanthropy would seem to be the godlike disposition to love all mankind, *in imitatio Dei.*

But for the Greeks who coined the term, *philanthropia* was nothing so exalted. Plato and Aristotle did not even number it among the human virtues, and the one man-loving god, Prometheus, was punished as a traitor to his kind, a fool who cared overmuch for mere mortals, who are too lowly to deserve divine love. The loves celebrated by the Greeks were more focused and circumscribed: *eros*, for one's beloved; *philia*, for one's good friends; *philopatria* or *philopolis*, for one's fatherland or city. No Athenian cared a fig for the well-being of Spartans or Corinthians, much less even conceived the notion of the weal of all humankind. Indeed, for the Greeks, *philanthropia* seems to have been but one of a whole family of such fondnesses: *philodendrists* liked trees, *philippists* liked horses, *philomachists* liked battle, and *philanthropists* liked human beings—just as, today, *philatelists* like stamps and *bibliophiles* like books.

Philanthropy probably acquired its modern meaning—the disposition to promote human well-being in general—because of the influence of Christianity and its emphasis on universal love of neighbor or charity, a term often used as a synonym for philanthropy. It is through philanthropy's connections to charity that compassion becomes a leading candidate for philanthropy's ruling spirit.

Charity, in early English usage, meant Christian love—both God's love for man and man's love for both God and his human neighbor, friend and foe alike. Even when secularized, charity meant love, kindness, and a feeling of benevolence toward one's neighbors, most especially to the poor, as well as the practical beneficence that issues from this feeling: charity as almsgiving or as public poor-relief. Thus "a charity" became any bequest, foundation, or institution established for the benefit of others, especially of the poor or helpless— hospitals, asylums, homeless shelters, and charitable trusts promoting health, education, and welfare.

Christian charity is clearly the ancestor of charity as the compassion-driven distribution of money and services to the needy. For unlike our natural loves, which are inspired by the beautiful or the virtuous, Christian love is unconditional and unmerited. Indeed, it stands out for its capacity to love the naturally unlovable—not only the poor, the weak, the deformed, and the crazed, but even the wicked and vicious. Though, one imagines, God's love for man goes beyond His wish to relieve poverty or to cure illness, it is no accident that charity—both Christian and secular—has come to mean primarily benevolence and beneficence toward the lowliest among us, those who are unable to help themselves. If this is the heart of charity, and if charity is regarded as synonymous with philanthropy, we can easily see why compassionate humanitarianism comes to be seen as philanthropy's proper guiding nerve.[1]

This brief foray into the meanings of philanthropy and charity raises some troublesome questions: First, *toward whom* shall we practice philanthropy? Humankind is an abstraction, hard to love and certainly hard to love well. Even "one's fellowmen" is a rather obscure object for goodwill and love. For which human beings should philanthropists exercise their benevolence and beneficence? In particular, should it matter if some of the proposed beneficiaries have brought their troubles on themselves? Should it matter if they are unwilling or unable to benefit from the philanthropist's offerings?

Second, *how* do we properly love those we seek to benefit? Philanthropy, strictly speaking, describes only a condition of our will or inclination or intention: having a good will toward one's fellowmen. But does the *desire* to promote the good of others necessarily carry with it *true knowledge* of that good, what it is, and how to obtain it? Are good intentions or goodwill sufficient? Is love or compassion enough?

Third, if philanthropy should be broader than charity, if the generous love of human beings goes beyond, and aims higher than, the alleviation of human suffering, how will the goals and works of philanthropy be confined should compassion increasingly command its ship? How should philanthropy seek to balance the competing claims of the high and the urgent, the promotion of excellence versus the demands of necessity? If the high is always being sacrificed to the urgent, what kind of a society will we be creating?

Let me address each of these three questions in turn.

I. WHOM SHOULD PHILANTHROPY SERVE?

First, whom to serve? Private philanthropy has always seen as part of its charge the care of those who are badly off through no fault of their own. But for several decades, we as a society have been increasingly asked, encouraged, and sometimes even compelled to come to the aid of those who refuse to take care of themselves, who live dangerously, foolishly, and self-destructively, incurring great risks not only to life and limb, but also to the economic, psychic, and social well-being of those around them as well as themselves. I mean those engaged in heavy drinking, drug abuse, gangs, reckless driving, treacherous amusements, unsafe and irresponsible sexual activity, excessive gambling, excessive borrowing and spending, and refusal to make good on ordinary obligations in school or on the job.

In a free society, people will be free by and large to run these risks; the question is to what extent should everyone—or anyone—else bear the cost of the resulting harms.

Our Judeo-Christian tradition teaches us that each of us is his brother's keeper. To deny responsibility for one's brother is, tacitly, to express indifference to his fate, and in this sense to be tacitly guilty of all harm that befalls him: in the extreme, to say yes even to his death.

But this moral lesson is both far from clear and far from complete. For who exactly is my brother—which is to say, for how many human beings do I bear such fraternal responsibility? More importantly, what does it mean to be someone's keeper? Does the duty to guard and protect against outside dangers extend also to dangers one's brother poses to himself? What if he chooses to court disaster, whether from vice, weakness of will, foolishness, or ignorance? Does guarding your brother mean picking up after his stupidity? Am I my *foolish* brother's keeper?

Consider an example. My entire liver has been damaged in an auto accident. My brother is the most suitable donor for a partial liver transplant. Have I a claim on his liver? Not at all. Should my parents—or anyone else—put pressure on him to donate? I believe not. But what does our brotherliness require of him? Should his decision to donate be influenced by the fact that I was responsible for the accident, that I had been speeding on icy roads and not wearing a seat belt? Or what if my need of a liver transplant were due not to a one-time auto accident but to a lifetime of alcoholism? Should my brother be obliged to help? Does my promise to stop drinking and join Alcoholics Anonymous make a difference? Should our public policy regarding donation (or health insurance) be influenced by whether and how people have brought their troubles on themselves and whether they intend to reform?

There can be, of course, no simple or set rules for answering these questions. Much will depend upon the particulars. For example, we will be more inclined and expected to alleviate harm caused by foolishness or weakness of will than by vice, by a single or occasional episode of folly than by chronic foolhardiness, by bad judgment stemming from depression than from insolence, and so forth. These qualifications aside, any prima facie obligation to help will surely be limited and perhaps even overturned, first, when we do not know what real help is; second, when assistance will be useless because it is refused or squandered; or third, when there are better or more urgent outlets for one's beneficence, including competing obligations to others.

For these reasons, among others, there are many times when it is surely foolish to come to the rescue of foolishness. Moral obligation cannot mean that the remedy for someone else's foolishness is to match or surpass it with our own. The obligation to be even our blood brother's keeper cannot be absolute and unqualified.

Much as we may love our brothers, and much as we should endeavor to care for our neighbors, we also love and care for what is good and right. Indeed, the beginning of morality is the subordination of unqualified self-love and love of one's own to the standards of good and bad, justice and injustice. We are taught to do what's right. We are taught not to make exceptions in our own case. We are taught to accept responsibility for our own lives and conduct, and to expect others to do the same.

Most Americans, in fact, believe in the importance of accepting and fostering personal moral responsibility. Most of us see that human action is based on human freedom, human freedom is manifested in choice, and human dignity in action resides in making our choices in full cognizance that we are the sources of our deeds and responsible for their effects. Self-conscious choice tacitly cheers for justice, for a world in which people get what they deserve. And while we all know that the world is far from wholly just, all societies and institutions and most human lives work on the premise that the world makes sense. Moreover, by our responsible practices and by our praise and blame we contrive to have the world make even more sense. We read children stories like "The Little Red Hen," to teach them that it is just that those who work for their food should get to eat and those who refuse to work should not. People are pleased when hard work and fair play are rewarded; and at least until recently we did not take kindly to whiners, complainers, and those who blamed others for their own failures. A man who pleaded drunkenness as an excuse for his violence was doubly punished; a woman who went to a man's bedroom and then got drunk with him could not escape bearing some responsibility for what happened next. America grew strong because people acted in the spirit of the maxim, "By the time a man is thirty, he is responsible even for his face."

But what then about compassion? The claims of compassion might seem to oppose the claims of justice and lead us always to our foolish brother's assistance. Yet if compassion is rightly understood, this turns out to be at best only partly true. In fact, compassion as experienced sentiment—rather than as ideological principle—is somewhat allied with justice. The point was noted already by Aristotle, in his account of pity:

> Pity is a certain pain at manifest or apparent badness, destructive or painful, *hitting one who is undeserving*, which one might expect oneself or someone of one's own to suffer (emphasis added).

Pity, or what we now call compassion, is not indiscriminate sympathy for suffering. A judgment of whether the badness suffered is deserved is implicit in the feeling of compassion.

This is not to say that everyone judges well whether the suffering is deserved; racists think all suffering of the despised race is somehow appropriate, while bleeding hearts are willing to overlook blatant fault—even rape, murder, and terrorism—in those whose suffering they have privileged, sometimes by designating them generically as society's victims. But most people, given half a chance and adequate information, will pity fittingly, which is to say justly. They feel more pity for crack babies than for their mothers, more pity for a man if his liver failure be caused by tainted blood transfusion than if it be the result of chronic alcoholism, more pity for the homeless person who is mentally ill than for the one who for years has refused to work.

Compassion as sentiment is not, in principle, at war with a concern for justice. Yet modern life and modern political thought have done much to distort the normal operation of compassion, even while elevating it to political principle. Powerful visual images of suffering—horror without context—are television's daily fare, tugging at our heartstrings, which are already overstretched far beyond the capacity for normal response. The media's exploitation of visual images of suffering corrupts compassion by demanding instant and unqualified sympathy, without knowledge or judgment. It moves us toward what one might call a merely medical view of the world, more precisely, the emergency-room view of the world, with its amoral and no-fault approach to all troubles and its justice-neutral brand of compassion—a point to which I will return.

Add to this the political hegemony of compassion as the first proof of public virtue, and we see how we have created a world in which victims are more honored than heroes. Indeed victims are lionized for their suffering— and, more to the point, despite their own culpability in coming to harm: Do more people think Magic Johnson is a fool for living dangerously than think he is a hero for going public as a victim? Sympathy and fellow feeling are of course precious and praiseworthy, but an indiscriminate compassion that is deaf to judgment can hardly be the basis for a morally sound philanthropy.

Yet there are other reasons, beyond the inadequate claims of our new breed of compassion, why the principles of strict responsibility and giving to each his just deserts, however suitable as a starting point, cannot be the whole story. Given the unpredictabilities of life, it is presumptuous to believe that one can live with perfect forethought and planning, immune to bad results. Besides, there is frequently much virtue in risk-taking: many of society's greatest benefactors have gambled on their ability to make good in the absence of guarantees. Needless to say, not all failure is the result of folly or vice. In recognition of this fact, society prepares partial safety nets to catch those who fall while trying to climb. We abolished debtors' prisons, permit people to declare bankruptcy, and in many other ways embody our sound belief in the rightness of second chances. America is internationally famous as the home of the second chance.

But for even more profound reasons, the principle of strict responsibility cannot be the sole standard for assessing the misfortunes of our foolish brethren. For not everyone starts out with a full deck when it comes to living prudently. Differences in rearing and life experience create differences in each person's ability to choose, in the choices we make, and in our capacity to stick by our better choices. The mysterious yet nigh universal phenomenon of moral weakness—that is, knowing the good but not doing it—accounts for much of what we call foolish conduct; and, repeated, it is habit-forming. Children are maimed for responsibility both by indulgent parents who shelter them from learning from the consequences of their mistakes and by negligent parents who fail to teach them the importance of avoiding them in the first place. Inborn influences, no less than environmental ones—neither of them of our own making—predispose to success or failure in the battle for self-command. About these things science still knows very little, but enough to suspect that some aspects of intractable and self-harming behavior probably have a partly genetic foundation. And, perhaps most important, there are inborn differences in intelligence. One can say to one's child, "Be sensible," but one cannot say, "Be intelligent." Yet if, in this increasingly complex world, it takes more and more intelligence to figure out what "being sensible" requires, lots of people are going to be playing the game of life with severe but invisible handicaps. And regarding their economic independence, it is sad but true that hard work and the best intentions will still leave many people at the bottom of the heap, increasingly so in our hypertechnological age in which a strong back and a willingness to work are not enough to enable you to prosper.

This does not mean that we stop teaching the young to brush their teeth, do their schoolwork, avoid bad companions, and stay away from drugs, tobacco, and motorcycles. We should still demand and foster personal responsibility and publicly speak as if it were possible for all—at least at some basic level. We should continue to insist on the importance of obeying the law and to hold people accountable for criminal misconduct. But we would do well to remain modest (rather than proud) if we happen to be—at least for now—less foolish than some of our brothers.

On the basis of arguments like these, one might suggest that a decent community will try to care not only for those who are worse off than others through no fault of their own, but even to bear some of the costs of helping those who are partly responsible for their own troubles. This is not so much a matter of justice or of rights or even compassion; people have no right or claim to receive from life better than they deserve. It is rather a matter of the common good. We care for our fellow citizens because we are all in this together. The fortunate and less foolish among us have every reason not to be limited by such strict proportionality. We can, not least for our own sakes, improve upon justice in the direction of generosity and care. Acts of benefi-cence contribute to the common good not only by the benefits they bestow; they contribute also because they are manifestations of virtue and as such are central to the flourishing of the benefactors—and, indeed, of the whole society. Rightly understood, philanthropic deeds are not self-sacrificing but self-affirming and self-fulfilling, and a society that is generous beyond what is strictly owed must be counted among humanity's finest achievements. Thus, if our brothers need defense against themselves even more than against outsiders, we should be willing—in principle—to offer it, not least for our own goodness's sake.

II. HOW TO SERVE?

This then brings me to the second dilemma: *How* should we care for them?

The difficulty for philanthropy turns out to be not one of intention but of knowledge: What does it really mean to help and to keep? The present hegemony of no-fault compassion is to be blamed not so much for its implicit willingness to care but for its failure to understand what care really means. For one does not really keep one's brother by helping him in ways likely to increase his foolishness. On the contrary, help aimed at undoing the harms caused by foolishness is insufficient if it is unaccompanied by help aimed at fostering the benefit of assuming moral and personal responsibility.

This is not easily done, not by anyone, certainly not by distant do-gooders. A desire to help does not translate readily into sensible policy or grant proposals. Compassionate measures aimed at *preventing* foolish behavior are often difficult to devise; it is notoriously difficult to get people to do what is good for them without tyrannizing them. And measures aimed at *remedying* the harm afterwards may remove disincentives for abandoning prudent self-restraint. For example, we have compassionately spared illegitimate children the opprobrium they once had to bear, but, as a result, many more of them are sired out of wedlock and abandoned with impunity.

More generally, the availability of an ounce of cure drives out pounds of prevention. Worse, remedies can even change our view of whether risky behavior is in fact foolish. Not so long ago, a man who had contracted syphilis was, by and large, not an object of pity, and this quite apart from the question of his likely immorality. For he had almost certainly consorted with the wrong sort of woman, and carelessly to boot; he knowingly brought his troubles on himself. Today, in the age of antibiotics, many sufferers from sexually transmitted diseases overlook their own responsibility; instead they even blame their miseries on society's failure to provide a cure. Increasingly, the privileged status of suffering, of being a victim, makes it almost impossible to see this as self-induced harm, one that clamors less for a miracle drug, more for decent and responsible conduct.

This points toward the forgotten crux of compassion. Most deserving of our sympathy and compassion is not our brother's bodily suffering but his inability or unwillingness to stand in the world with freedom and dignity, which is to say, as a responsible source of his own conduct ready and willing to be held accountable for himself and for his actions. Just as the sentiment of compassion-rightly-experienced is natively not immune to judgments of past responsibility, so the exercise of compassion-rightly-practiced is centrally concerned with enabling the recipient to become more willing and able to choose better and to accept responsibility in the future. True compassion, especially toward the remediably foolish, is synonymous in the current lingo with "tough love."

How this is to be accomplished is, of course, a tricky matter, varying case by case. There are no set rules, no single strategy. It is never easy to shift effectively from individualized strategies for the interpersonal cases to the necessarily statistical approaches of public policy for larger populations. But the sound moral principle of tough-loving prudence is the same in every case, regardless of scale, and regardless of whether the benefactor is Uncle Sam or a private foundation: to foster personal responsibility and a world that approximates justice in which people get what they deserve; and, at the same time, to foster fellow feeling and a world in which people are inclined to be generous—and especially generous in helping people morally and spiritually so that they will eventually no longer need such generosity.

Unfortunately, institutional philanthropists, public and private, often enjoy nurturing dependency, for they too are needy creatures, with a great need to be needed. By labeling their beneficiaries as "victims," and by some-times whipping up hostility toward nonvictims and normal society, they degrade the objects of their compassion and encourage further dependence. They seem too often to forget that "the proper aim of giving," as C. S. Lewis put it, "is to put the recipient in a state where he no longer needs our gift." This means attaching demands and inducements for change of behavior to offers of outright aid in relief of self-induced harm; it also means not destroying the public will to generosity with excessive and unreasonable demands upon our compassion or with unrealistic programs built on unrea-sonable hopes borrowed from utopian dreams.

III. THE LIMITS OF COMPASSION

Thus, finally, to the third question: Should philanthropy sail increasingly under the flag of compassion?

Compassionate humanitarianism, the guiding light of the welfare state, is arguably the most powerful idea of modernity. It is certainly at the root of the modern scientific-and-technological project, begun in the seventeenth century and growing exponentially in our own time, a project whose explicit purpose was from the start the conquest of nature for the relief of man's estate. Facing a world seemingly tragic for all human aspiration, our rationalist fore-bears—like Bacon and Descartes—set out to conquer fate and fortune on the basis of the scientific understanding of nature. They set the stage for the vast modern utopian project, in principle comprehensive and complete: by rational means, to banish all human misery and misfortune—and perhaps even death—and to remake the world according to human aspirations.

We all are the grateful beneficiaries of science and technology, including its perhaps finest fruit, modern medicine. Yet these increasing benefits come at increasingly heavy costs. For one thing, we now suffer from a radically "medicalized" view of life: because illness is beyond guilt or innocence, because suffering is suffering, it demands attention. Even bad behavior often comes itself to be treated as illness (e.g., alcoholism or rage-behavior) or sometimes as an inborn, hard-wired predisposition that one must not judge in moral terms (such as a penchant for pederasty). The medical view of life not only focuses on the ills of the body to the neglect of the soul; it seeks bodily causes for all psychic and moral phenomena.

Drunk on its remarkable successes in analyzing and treating acute infectious disease, modern medicine is confident that its materialistic approach to life will unlock all the secrets of heart and mind and will permit for the first time a rational and successful approach to all the troubles of the human condition. The fault, dear Brutus, is not in ourselves but in our genes that we are underlings—which is to say, there is no fault or responsibility, only the misalignment of matter. It is stunning how the outlook of the present day pays tribute to the dreams of Descartes, who saw in his newly invented science the possibility of human mastery of nature and through it the relief even of man's psychic and moral troubles:

> For even the mind depends so much on the temperament and disposition of the bodily organs that, if it is possible to find a means of rendering men wiser and cleverer than they have hitherto been, I believe that it is in medicine that it must be sought.

Psychophysics, not praise and blame or moral self-command, is, as Descartes predicted, the wave of the future. It is no longer "God helps those who help themselves," but rather "Mankind through a scientific medicine helps everyone regardless."

The successes of the modern project have materially improved our lives, but they have not made us more content. On the contrary, all residual failure and suffering now become increasingly unacceptable. We have come to expect technical solutions for all our ailments, and we demand that society provide them.

While science forges ahead toward the goal of complete mastery, the continuing presence of personal misery and misfortune becomes primarily the responsibility of society, often of the state. Compassion is "elevated" from natural human sentiment to necessary political principle. Society becomes one big hospital, government one big healer. The technological approach to life—rational mastery through methodical problem-solving—finds its political expression in bureaucracy and the welfare state. We go slowly but surely from "Uncle Sam Wants You" to "The Doctor Is In." No longer is the main goal of statesmanship to make the citizens good and obedient to the laws (as in classical republicanism) or to make secure against interference the natural rights of life, liberty, and the pursuit of happiness (as in modern liberalism), but rather to guarantee universal day care, health care, and hospice care.

Driven partly by guilt for its own good fortune, the utopian elite takes up the cudgels for the least fortunate, demanding a politics of compassion on behalf of society's victims. This is ironically a politics that blithely victimizes those hardworking and morally responsible Americans who do not have the margin to be very generous to strangers and who are not yet aboard the train to utopia.

Another irony of this project for the rational medical-cum-political conquest of fortune is that it leaves most of us less, rather than more, in control of our own attempt at a prudent life. Science's materialistic ideas about human life undermine our belief in human freedom and morality; our technologies (and their accompanying bureaucracies) in myriad ways make many of us actually more dependent and helpless in our daily lives. Even through its very successes, compassionate humanitarianism may pave the way to dehumanization, as Aldous Huxley brilliantly showed in his *Brave New World*.

The bureaucratic enforcement of compassion saps most of the impulse to care for another. For to look on every man as brother, and on every stranger-brother as guiltless victim for whom I am responsible, eventually produces a condition in which I feel myself victimized by the burdens of care, and therefore seek to excuse myself even from my primary duties to those who are nearest and dearest.

The utopian project for mastery of fortune through rationalized technique is thus in danger of bringing about the very tragedy it willfully sought to prevent. For to produce a herd of people who don't care for themselves and who consequently have to rely on unreliable and ineffective powers that are only capriciously responsive to their needs is to re-create the ill-fated and fatalistic world against which modern science first took up arms, a world that today is returning to our inner cities.

IV. A HEALTHIER WORLD VIEW

Fortunately there is another world view, between an irresponsible surrender to indifferent fate and an unreasonable belief in human mastery, one still within hailing distance of our collective memory. It was the reigning world view of the West until the coming of the Enlightenment and its newer nihilistic descendants, and it remains the insufficiently defended view of most decent and hardworking Americans and the source of our residual moral good sense. It is the sensible, moderate, but hope-filled world view of human freedom and dignity under the rule of law, both encouraged and demanded by divine providence. It champions personal morality and responsibility, duties as well as rights, genuine neighborhoods and communities, hard work, fair play, and the pursuit of excellence.

Organized philanthropy, if it is truly to promote human flourishing, must come to the aid of this now beleaguered world view. Concretely, this means supporting strong family life, rigorous schools, and all sorts of religious and other voluntary associations capable of renewing our moral and spiritual capital. It means flying the banners of decency, justice, liberty, reverence, and truth, as well as the banner of compassion. It means supporting those individuals and groups who can combat the relativism, cynicism, and decadence purveyed in our best colleges and universities and our worst popular culture, who can reinvigorate our belief in everything good, beautiful, and holy. Anything less will be a betrayal of true philanthropy, of the wise love of humankind.

NOTES

1. To be sure, philanthropists also act from other motives and serve not only the needy. They also contribute heavily to colleges, museums, and symphonies. But when they do so, they are vulnerable to the charge of elitism and are often made to feel guilty for not doing more for those who are down-and-out. In contrast, one who works with single mothers or dying patients or AIDS victims is immediately seen as justified and noble: Compassionate philanthropy, with purity of motive, sets the standard for what it means to be genuinely and sensitively a good and caring person. "I feel your pain" has even become the first prerequisite of popular statesmanship.

Compassion and Responsibility

A Response to Kass

STEVEN SVERDLIK

D r. Kass addresses two main concerns in his stimulating essay. First, he argues that our society tends to limit "philanthropy" to "charity," or the relief of suffering, and, second, that we undertake such philanthropy in a "medicalized" or no-fault spirit that ignores issues of personal responsibility. Dr. Kass quite correctly, in my view, stresses that compassion, operating properly, does not ignore a person's responsibility for her own condition. Thus, we do not feel the same degree of compassion for a person who we believe has brought on her own suffering as we do for one who has not. It is "tricky," however, as Dr. Kass also notes, to turn this important reaction into policy, whether governmental or charitable. In these comments I will limit myself to exploring this issue a little further, and I will not discuss the larger issues about the trends in modern culture and the relations between science and ethics that Dr. Kass also brings up. I offer my remarks as a sympathetic but cautious commentator who believes that the qualifications that we need to make to turn compassion into a policy that recognizes responsibility may all but undo the policy in practice. However, Dr. Kass is grappling with very serious issues, and I hope he and others will find my comments constructive.

Dr. Kass mentions some considerations that argue *against* structuring charities in such a way as to insure that assistance corresponds to a person's responsibility: life is unpredictable, some risk-taking is reasonable and even welcome, humans differ genetically in their intelligence and ability to manage their impulses, and we exercise some virtues in helping others when they do not deserve it. About these particular considerations I would only add one comment: depending upon which kinds of behavior we regard as reasonable or even welcome, the meaning of the term "responsible" shifts. When we speak of "responsibility" for the suffering a careless driver endures, the term implies that we blame the driver's behavior. But if we regard certain investments as risky but reasonable, we will speak of the investor's "responsibility," if any, for her losses, in a different sense. To use the terminology of H. L. A. Hart, we have moved from "liability responsibility" to "causal responsibility."[1] In other words, people who suffer as a result of bad luck with regard to reasonable risk-taking may be said to have *caused* their own woes, but they cannot be said to be *blameworthy* for doing so. In the rest of my comments I will limit my attention to "liability responsibility," that is, to cases where wrongful or foolish behavior has brought about someone's own suffering. But it bears emphasizing that we do not always find it easy in particular cases to separate the reasonable but risky from the foolish and blameworthy. To mention a few examples, consider bungee-jumping, hang-gliding, professional boxing, and investing in derivatives.

Some further points should be mentioned in considering how philanthropies might devise policies that incorporate the "tough love," or compassion molded by a sense of justice, that Dr. Kass rightly seeks. One point is straightforward. An ounce of prevention is worth a pound of cure. It would be preferable, other things being equal, that people not engage in irresponsible behavior in the first place. Thus, we would all prefer that people not smoke cigarettes rather than smoking and then suffering as a consequence. Philanthropies can help prevent the suffering by disseminating information about the risks of various behaviors, and thereby counteracting to some extent the allure attached in the media and advertising to such things as smoking. At another level philanthropies can develop programs that enhance the general powers of "self-command" that Dr. Kass briefly mentions. Activities such as scouting, camping, and sports, when properly conducted, can teach children how to deal with challenges, temptations, and ridicule in a mature way, and how to develop self-respect. Finally, philanthropies could sponsor programs targeted at developing specific skills for managing temptations such as gambling. It would be a bit odd to speak of such programs as motivated by compassion, since we tend to think of that emotion as reactive. Suffering that one perceives or learns about elicits compassion. The proactive measures I am now referring to seek to avert the need for compassion by helping people develop the skills and maturity they require to take care of themselves and others.

Unfortunately, some people will behave irresponsibly. They will smoke cigarettes, take drugs, engage in unsafe sex, bear children out of wedlock, drink to excess, and so on. If we disseminate the relevant information and teach people the skills of self-command, we may confidently predict that the amount of irresponsible behavior in our society will decline. Paradoxically, however, those who do engage in such activities will be all the more responsible for their own suffering, precisely because of the availability of information. So we do need to think about how to respond to such individuals. But we ought not to suppose that we now have in our society the ideal availability of information about risks, or training in the skills of self-control. There still seem to be, for example, deplorable pockets of ignorance about safe sex. And if the distribution of wealth concerns one, one may worry that the poorer members of society encounter stronger temptations to engage in certain risky activities than do the affluent. One suspects that relatively few well-off people pursue careers in boxing, for example. It is an interesting exercise in utopian thinking to ask ourselves, how should an ideally just and supportive society respond to irresponsible behavior? In More's *Utopia* he writes that "the Utopians . . . deal more harshly with their own people than with the others [slaves and foreign residents], feeling that their crimes are worse and deserve stricter punishment because, as it is argued, they had an excellent education and the best of moral training, yet still couldn't be restrained from wrongdoing."[2] But I assume that most of us would not characterize our society as already ideally just. More realistically then: how should our imperfect society and our charities respond to behavior that is at least *somewhat* due to the irresponsibility of the people needing care? We can think of this question as asking, also, what can we do to make our society *more* just than it now is?

At this point I find myself somewhat at odds with what I understand as the thrust of Dr. Kass's remarks. He worries about a "no-fault" or "medicalized" approach to the relief of suffering, and he wants our society and our charities to insist on responsible behavior. I take him to suggest that charities, for example, ought in some cases simply to refuse to treat people who are responsible for their own suffering. We might remember that the institution that is designed to determine responsibility accurately is the law, especially criminal and tort law. Thus, it seems fair to say that Dr. Kass is proposing that we "legalize" medical and social services. This we might do either by incorporating within the guidelines of a treatment program standards that make levels of care inversely proportional to the degrees of irresponsibility on the patient's part, or else by requiring caregivers themselves to judge the responsibility of the patient. However we imagine the details, clearly such determinations of responsibility will become adversarial, as indeed they should. If, for example, whether a doctor operates hinges on whether a patient is responsible for her own condition, it seems only fair to allow her the opportunity to argue that she was not responsible for it. We can easily imagine the need for trained advocates. And notice how such proceedings will give patients a strong incentive to lie about their past behavior. How far down such a road do we wish to go?

We often hear it said that virtue is its own reward. Less often do we hear that vice is its own punishment. But usually it is. Thus many of the irresponsible people who concern Dr. Kass and me do not escape from all of the consequences of their own choices, even if a safety net of some sort protects them. Drug addicts, smokers, and heavy drinkers often suffer because of their habits. And in the most extreme manifestations of these behaviors, I doubt that such people feel as though they are just as well-off after their treatment as they would have been had they never developed bad habits in the first place. A smoker who has lost a lung to cancer and then quits probably earnestly wishes she had never taken up smoking. Of course, some people will not give up smoking even after such an operation. But my point is that our sense of justice, which Dr. Kass rightly sees as involved in compassion, need not fear that a charity which treats such a person completely lets her escape the costs of her irresponsible behavior. She will suffer a good deal, even if she does receive care.

Dr. Kass made clear to me in a private communication that in writing his essay he was concerned with behaviors that strongly affect the well-being of others, especially in the realm of sex and the family.[3] For instance, we cannot say of a teenager who bears a child out of wedlock that her behavior affects only herself, and that her vice is its own punishment. This important point brings out the complexity that exists in the realm of "irresponsible" behavior. Some irresponsible behavior, such as smoking, overeating, and excessive drinking, mainly affects the agent. Other types of irresponsible behavior—for example, careless handling of firearms—largely affect others. Indeed, one could reasonably argue that intentional criminal wrongdoing is "irresponsible." Of course, no irresponsible behavior affects only the agent or only others. Drinking, for instance, can affect both agent and others. Speaking generally it seems that we can only say that behaviors that mainly affect the agent lie on one end of a continuum ending at the other end with behaviors that tend mainly to affect others. Clearly, strategies that are appropriate and effective with one sort of irresponsible behavior will not be either appropriate or effective with others.

Let me turn, then, to the topic that interests Dr. Kass most: irresponsible behavior with regard to sex and the family. I suspect that one of his main worries is childbearing out of wedlock, especially by teenagers. In any case, the topic illustrates the relationship between compassion and responsibility. Such irresponsible behavior deeply affects others. I take it that we agree that such young women should not have children, especially if they are unmarried and still in school. And we probably agree that the behavior of the young women and men who bring these children into being is to some degree irresponsible in the sense that we are interested in. What should decent charities, animated by just compassion, do with such mothers and fathers? Education and training of various sorts might avert the problem beforehand. Moreover, the mothers will suffer as a result of their irresponsibility, even if the shaming reactions of old have largely disappeared. Should charities threaten to withhold the benefits they confer, or could confer, to deter such irresponsibility and, if the threat fails, limit their compassion for the irresponsible by carrying out the threat? For example, a religious school might threaten to expel any student who bears a child out of wedlock. Or a camping program might refuse to enroll unwed mothers. (A charity might find it impossible to know of, and respond to, the irresponsible behavior of the father.) Once again I would note that even if the issue were not the provision of a medical service, we would hope and expect some "legalization" here, to wit, an inquiry into whether the woman was indeed responsible for her pregnancy. It could, after all, have been due to rape.

Consider two further points about what we can call "just compassion" as it might operate in such circumstances. First, measures that withhold goods from the mother tend also to diminish the well-being of her child. This consideration apparently finally persuaded Congress not to adopt proposals to withhold welfare from women already in the program who have more out-of-wedlock children. (Note that withholding payments would work hardship not only on the child and its mother but also on all the other children, since five people, for example, would have to live on an income formerly serving four.) For the same reason, expelling a mother from school penalizes the child, whatever effect we may wish on the mother. Thus, one of the vexing difficulties in the area of teenage pregnancy is fashioning policies that can be seen as responsive to the mother's irresponsible behavior but that do not unfairly punish or harm her child. It is true that the vices of sexually irresponsible young men and women do not harm only themselves, but it is also true that limits on our compassion for the mother tend to work hardships on her children.

The second concern involves another sense of the term "responsible." (We are touching on all four of the senses that Hart analyzes in his classic treatment.) The issue is the "capacity responsibility" of teenagers. By this phrase, Hart means the ability of a normal person to understand the morally relevant features of her environment and to choose to act rightly in accordance with them. Our society believes that certain persons lack this ability—for example, infants and senile adults. It is a subtle and difficult question to say how much capacity responsibility teenagers of a certain age have, or how responsible an individual teenage mother or father is. Clearly our society is changing its views on these issues to some extent, as the trend toward imposing adult punishments (such as imprisonment) on ever-younger lawbreakers shows. Yet we can hardly be said to have a consistent position in our laws as a whole since we do not allow teenagers below age eighteen to vote or even to enter into binding legal contracts! This ambivalence reflects our personal reactions to teenagers. I suspect that a given piece of wrongdoing evokes stronger indignation or resentment in us when an adult, rather than a teenager, commits it. (The sort of reasoning the Utopians used is at work here.) This reaction suggests that we should mitigate our reactions to teenage parents even when we can precisely focus our responses on only the parents and spare their children.

I want to consider an objection to my essay that someone might wish to make. Imagine a charity with limited resources which restricts its help to people who do not display self-destructive habits that would undo the help the charity can provide. (This returns us to examples of "irresponsible" behavior that mainly affects the irresponsible person.) One can imagine a hospital that runs a liver transplant program instituting a policy that denies transplants to alcoholics. Or, on a less urgent level, one can imagine a community loan program that excludes compulsive gamblers or repeated bankrupts from qualifying for loans. Are such exclusions morally objectionable? While these policies might seem to exemplify "just compassion," they could also be seen as simply *prudent* compassion that will not squander scarce resources. Obviously in a case like the repeated bankrupt, "just compassion" and "prudent compassion" will roughly coincide. But in some cases, they diverge. For instance, a formerly irresponsible person might reform. One way to understand the justice involved in just compassion is that it is entirely "backward-looking," that is, focused only on the past behavior of the individual. Such a sense of justice might prompt us to withhold goods from the formerly irresponsible even if they have reformed themselves. A more "forward-looking" compassion might be prepared to disregard past irresponsibility so long as the help it now provides will be properly used, not wasted. Here, interestingly enough, one could see a need for some "legalization" if a charity is going to be willing to disregard a person's responsibility: one would need some hard evidence that the beneficiary really has reformed. I wonder how Dr. Kass would advise charities to act in such a case.

These reflections have emphasized the complexities in our ideas about responsibility, and the burdens that come with taking them seriously. I want to reemphasize that I have not intended to question the basic claims that Dr. Kass has so vigorously put forward about compassion and justice. My aim was to pursue his thinking about their connection in a little more detail. I am confident that we agree that our time will have been well spent if we have done something to assist those engaged in philanthropy in carrying on their critical work with a deeper understanding of its moral basis.[4]

NOTES

1. H. L. A. Hart, "Postscript: Responsibility and Retribution," in *Punishment and Responsibility* (New York: Oxford University Press, 1968), 211–30.

2. Thomas More, *Utopia*, ed. George M. Logan and Robert M. Adams (Cambridge, England: Cambridge University Press, 1989), 80. Plato's *Republic*, in contrast, seems to have no institution of punishment at all, presumably because in its ideal conditions no one will ever do anything wrong!

See Mary Margaret Mackenzie, *Plato on Punishment* (Berkeley: University of California Press, 1981), 41, n. 39.

3. I am grateful to Dr. Kass for sending me a very detailed and thoughtful response to my earlier comments. It has been a pleasant challenge for me to come to grips with his ideas.

4. I am indebted to Bill May for his invitation to participate in the conference that formed the basis of this volume.

Compassion and the Norms of Philanthropy

A Response to Kass

ROBIN W. LOVIN

hanging political attitudes toward human need generate important changes not only in public policy, but also in society's understanding of our moral obligations to assist those in greater need than most, or whose vulnerabilities render them unable to help themselves. A decade or two ago, the moral arguments centered on questions of justice, on the claims that needs make on the resources of the whole society. The question then was about distributive norms that weigh the claims of the least well off against the counterclaims of those who claim special merit or unusual contributions to the common good.[1]

By contrast, more recent discussions of poverty and welfare emphasize the limits of distributive justice and pay new attention to the rights and interests of those who provide assistance through taxation or through voluntary contributions.[2] Today's commentators stress the inefficiency of government programs and the limited tax dollars available to support them. They place new hope in private charity and in private, corporate, and religious philanthropy,[3] which often seem to provide better results at lower cost.

Precisely because these new discussions place less emphasis on assistance programs viewed as recipients' entitlements, they focus attention on the motives and interests of those who give the aid. If society limits the moral

26

authority or the political will of the government to tax its citizens, what role does private or corporate philanthropy play in making up the difference between government resources and social need? If individual recipients cannot claim their aid as an entitlement, how should the donor choose among the many voices clamoring for assistance? More to the point, if society does not mandate aid, why should a donor give at all?

The shift from a discourse based on distributive justice to one based on the choices of the donors may create the impression that charity has become voluntary in the contemporary understanding of that term, namely that we give because we want to. Those who have should give when they feel so moved, and wanting to give is the only good reason for giving.

Compassion for those in need will inspire some voluntary giving, and agencies that deal with social needs have understandably stepped up their efforts to tell the human stories of those left stranded by welfare reform and other policy changes. Nevertheless, the new discourse about charity and philanthropy cannot be reduced to a problem of social psychology. Leon Kass's essay, "Am I My Foolish Brother's Keeper? Justice, Compassion, and the Mission of Philanthropy," reminds us that compassion is a norm, as well as a feeling.

This link between norm and feeling was more clearly developed in eighteenth-century British moral philosophy. Terms such as "charity" and "benevolence," which we use roughly as synonyms, carried more nuanced and specific meanings, rooted in Christian theology and piety, which the eighteenth-century authors sought to articulate. These philosophers emphasized a form of fellow feeling or compassion they called "benevolence." This form of love for others is conditioned neither by their utility to my own interests, nor by the beauty of their person or their character. Rather, Jonathan Edwards described it as "that affection or propensity of heart to any being, which causes it to incline to its well-being, or disposes it to desire and take pleasure in its happiness."[4] Benevolence in this sense differs markedly from the more common feeling which eighteenth-century writers called "complacence." Complacence is the love we feel for others because they have proved themselves useful to us, or simply because their particular endowments of body, mind, or skill excite our admiration.[5] Complacence is love for particular persons for specific reasons. Benevolence moves us to want the best for everyone.

Benevolence is a virtue, a habitual way of feeling that we should cultivate. Benevolence should control our choices and actions, especially when we are inclined to feel vengeful, selfish, or indifferent. In the eighteenth-century discussion, Edwards and other Christian writers argue that benevolence is the form of God's love for us. God wants being, beauty, and happiness for us, not because we deserve them, but because it would be good for us to have them.[6] Other moral philosophers still broadly informed by Christianity, but more liberal or secular in their thinking, make benevolence an "instinct," or a "determination of our nature."[7] They identify concern for the well-being of others as a norm, perhaps the most basic of all norms. Benevolence leads us to care for the needs of others, without consulting our own self-interest.

The problem is that benevolence is not the only norm. Self-love, a concern for one's own well-being, is also appropriate. (If God desires being, beauty, and happiness for all, I cannot fail to desire these things for myself, too.) In particular cases, self-love and benevolence can dictate choices that seem hopelessly opposed. Self-love may urge that I do good by elevating my sensitivities and enhancing my capacity for understanding by reading good literature or attending a performance of great music. Benevolence requires that I help a homeless person find a hot meal and a responsive volunteer at a shelter. Both are good, but limited time and resources often make it impossible for me to achieve both of them at the same time.

The conflict between the norms of benevolence and appropriate self-love is often immediately felt, but other norms that may limit benevolence only come into play after a calculation of more remote consequences. Prudence requires me to consider not only the goodness of the intended results of my action, but also the likelihood that they will come to pass. Is it prudence, or a failure of benevolence, that leads us to refuse the panhandler with alcohol on his breath who asks for a dollar for something to eat?

Justice, likewise, may conflict with benevolence, and not just in the narrow, retributive sense that those in need deserve exactly what they get. If resources are limited, justice may lead us to devote more to persons whose needs result from genetic weaknesses over which they had no control than to those whose deliberate choices of risky behaviors caused their health problems.

Such considerations quickly become complex, as the negotiations surrounding the public health costs of smoking illustrate, but the basic point for our purposes is simple: Benevolence is not just a feeling that may motivate us to contribute to the needs of others. Benevolence is also a norm, part of a complex normative system that we use to determine how we should expend our energies and our resources. Because benevolence is a feeling, its immediacy may spark our thinking about our obligations to others in need, but we cannot let the reflection end there.

The discussion of benevolence in eighteenth-century moral theory sheds light on our twentieth-century confusions about the role of compassion in our decisions about charity and philanthropy. While theological and philosophical literature during this century has thoroughly explored the concept of social justice, this literature offers little guidance for the new role that society calls upon religious institutions and private philanthropy to play in meeting the needs of the poor. Indeed, we may find ourselves ignoring questions of effectiveness and long-term results out of a sense that compassion provides a motive for philanthropy that we cannot question. If that happens, philanthropic efforts to meet human needs will be even less efficient than government programs of social welfare, because we will leave policy choices to the feelings of those who control the philanthropy. The more important our philanthropic choices become to the meeting of human need in our society, the more certainly we must raise the normative discussion of compassion to the same level of conceptual clarity and detail that we have given in previous decades to the discussion of distributive justice. Ironically, this new emphasis may mean that the formation of a social philosophy for the twenty-first century will have to incorporate some of the nuances of eighteenth-century moral philosophy that utilitarianism drove from the public square after the publication of Bentham's "Principles."[8]

The ethicist, then, must reconnect what Leon Kass calls "compassion as experienced sentiment" to compassion as a norm, understood in relation to other norms such as justice and prudence. In order to do this difficult task well, we must attend to all of the dimensions of the experience. Compassion as a norm resembles the eighteenth-century notion of a benevolence that encompassed all persons, and indeed all creation, but compassion as "experienced sentiment" is not always so generous. Ethics, as Kass suggests, guides philanthropy by testing the scope of an initial, emotive urge to give against a system of norms that includes both the other claims on our resources and a normative understanding of the obligations to others that our feelings for them impose on us. On that key point, I entirely agree with him. I think it is important to recognize, however, that compassion as experienced sentiment may need expansion, as well as constraint, if we use it as a normative guide to charity and philanthropy.

Kass emphasizes that compassion as sentiment leads us to want to relieve suffering indiscriminately, so that to follow compassion as a norm, we have to build connections between this felt urge to help others in need and the requirements that justice and prudence impose on our giving. We must highlight the ways that our emotions of pity respond not just to suffering, but especially to *undeserved* suffering. Professor Kass takes us back to Aristotle, noting his definition of pity as the pain we feel when evil befalls someone who doesn't deserve it.

But Aristotle's pity is touched by self-interest, as well as justice, and we must recognize that touch of self-interest in our experience of compassion in order to understand the limits of "compassion as experienced sentiment." "Pity," says Aristotle in the passage that Kass quotes, "is a certain pain at manifest or apparent badness . . . hitting one who is undeserving, *which one might expect oneself or someone of one's own to suffer*" (emphasis added). We feel compassion not just when bad things happen to people who do not deserve them, but when they are the sorts of bad things that might happen to us, too.

Aristotle's canny observation about the element of self-interest that tinges our experience of pity must modify our assessment of the limits of compassion as a guiding principle for philanthropy. If we should not let our feelings of compassion drift loose from their moorings in justice, we should also not limit our understanding of what compassion requires to what we can feel intensely. Our perception that some victims do not deserve their suffering merges, in ways that are intellectually unclear but emotionally very powerful, with our perception that we ourselves might have to endure this kind of suffering. If compassion often leads us into imprudence by moving us to waste resources on those who cannot use them or do not deserve them, it can also lead us into injustice by obscuring the true character of suffering when that suffering just happens to be very unlike any that we are apt to experience.

This problem becomes more acute in a complex society like our own, which is pervasively segregated along lines of race and class. In a simpler day which we at least like to imagine, compassion might lead us to relieve the needs of the poor family down the block or on the other side of the tracks, because we could easily see their difficulty, imagine what they felt, and even conceive how we might some day be in similar need.

But in our own day, the poor live in circumstances far removed from our own. Especially in the larger cities, poverty exists in neighborhoods that are separated from ours by distance, race, and culture. We can scarcely imagine the life of the poor, and—at least for a white middle-class population—we find it almost inconceivable that we ourselves should end up in similar circumstances. When empathy and imagination fail, disgust or hatred may replace pity and compassion. Instead of worrying that justice and prudence may check the impulse to help, we should perhaps worry that alienation will stifle compassion long before we begin to worry about tempering compassion with justice and prudence.

Similar problems grow out of the triumph of scientific medicine, which Professor Kass rightly identifies as the source of many of our attitudes toward need and suffering. Probably, we are less likely than our ancestors to accept a certain amount of human suffering as simply inevitable, but I doubt that our primary response to this changed perception has been to make society accept responsibility for "the continuing presence of personal misery and misfortune," as Kass has it. We will, just as likely, resent the sufferers, regarding their continuing presence as a perverse affront to our utopian expectations or as evidence of their unresponsiveness to our scientifically proven remedies. The relative success of our modern strategies for preserving health and wealth increases the perceived distance between those who are momentarily healthy and wealthy and those who are poor or ill. Imagining a failure of our security systems that might land us in their situation is increasingly difficult, and that diminishes our ability to feel pity or compassion.

There are limits to compassion as a guide to philanthropic action. We must set compassion in a normative context that includes justice and prudence, as well as concern for human suffering. Philanthropy must aim at personal responsibility and the common good, as well as at the relief of suffering. Our collective resources are too small and the magnitude of need is too great to allow us to justify giving on the basis of pity alone. Under the social conditions that we have created in modern America, however, our compassion will reveal its limitations as well in not caring enough about certain kinds of suffering as in caring unwisely.

A more adequate compassion would be informed by benevolence, in the eighteenth-century sense, as well as by pity for suffering that is undeserved. The concern for others that motivates us to care for their needs must include a general satisfaction in their well-being and happiness, quite apart from their particular merits or failings. Before we can appropriately evaluate their needs and claims, we must genuinely want good lives for them. We must take pleasure in their flourishing before we can trust the guidance of the very mixed feelings that may be aroused in us by the sight of their suffering.

Perhaps the best reason to adopt this habit of benevolence is the conviction, which most of the early eighteenth-century writers took for granted, that this is how God regards our lives, as well as the lives of all our neighbors. Because we are not God, benevolence is a virtue we must acquire, rather than a defining characteristic of our being. Because we are not God, our resources to enact benevolence are not infinite, and we must sometimes choose those whom we will in fact assist, on the basis of prudence, or justice, or even mere preference. But unless our choices begin with a sincere wish for the well-being of all persons, we cannot trust the rightness of the contributions we make to the well-being of any of them.

NOTES

1. John Rawls's theory of justice, based on a "difference principle" which measures distributive justice from the perspective of the "least advantaged," is a classic effort to resolve these questions. After twenty-five years, it is more apparent than it was at first how profoundly Rawls's theory was shaped by the issues of social justice that dominated public life in the United States in the decade before its publication. See John Rawls, *A Theory of Justice* (Cambridge, Mass.: Harvard University Press, 1971), 75–78.

2. See, for example, Richard Epstein, *Takings* (Cambridge, Mass.: Harvard University Press, 1985), 306–29.

3. As Leon Kass points out in his essay, "Am I My Foolish Brother's Keeper? Justice, Compassion, and the Mission of Philanthropy," the terms "charity" and "philanthropy" have etymological roots in a feeling, often religiously inspired, for those in need, which motivates the decision to give aid. For present purposes, however, I will use the terms in their more contemporary, institutional sense, such that "charity" refers to individual gifts and donations meant to relieve the needs of others, while "philanthropy" refers to charity on a larger scale, often institutionalized in ways that create agencies to provide continuing services and/or continuing opportunities for others to give charity.

4. Jonathan Edwards, "The Nature of True Virtue," in Paul Ramsey, ed., *Jonathan Edwards: Ethical Writings*, vol. 8 of *The Works of Jonathan Edwards* (New Haven, Conn.: Yale University Press, 1989), 542.

5. Ibid.

6. Ibid. See also Samuel Clarke, "A Discourse of Natural Religion," in D. D. Raphael, ed., *British Moralists, 1650–1800* (Oxford: Clarendon Press, 1969), I: 192.

7. Francis Hutcheson, "An Inquiry Concerning Moral Good and Evil," in Raphael, *British Moralists,* I: 278–79.

8. Jeremy Bentham, "An Introduction to the Principles of Morals and Legislation," in Raphael, *British Moralists,* II: 313–22. This classic articulation of the utilitarian principle, with Bentham's sweeping rejection of other moral considerations, was first published in 1789.

The Nature of Philanthropy

A Response to Kass

Charles E. Curran

Professor Kass raises three important questions of utmost significance for the theory and practice of philanthropy. My twofold response will deal first with his second question and then (my major response) with his overall understanding of philanthropy, especially toward those in need.

First, I want to clarify further an aspect found in Kass's discussion of his second question about how we properly love those we seek to benefit. The essay briefly mentions that institutional philanthropists can often nurture dependency in the recipients of their beneficence, perhaps because these philanthropists too are needy creatures. Proper giving, as Kass quotes C. S. Lewis, should aim to put the recipient in a state in which the recipient no longer needs our gift.

Such a goal logically calls for philanthropy to help poor people form their own community organizations to achieve their goals and opportunities. Philanthropy must not only supply the services and goods that the poor need, but above all it must help them organize themselves to work for their own betterment. Such a goal also incorporates Professor Kass's demand for personal responsibility.

However, one must realistically recognize that many philanthropists find it difficult to support such independence. In supporting independence, the givers lose control over what the recipients do with their gifts. Community organizations also challenge the status quo and attempt to change social structures. Such changes often arouse anxiety and upset those who wield money and power. Still, proper philanthropic giving should support such organizations.

My major response deals with the understanding of philanthropy and its moral basis. As I understand Professor Kass's position, he strongly opposes foolish compassion, the welfare state, and Utopian medicalization of all life. He discusses philanthropy in relation to charity, compassion, benevolence, and beneficence. His essay heavily emphasizes personal responsibility and advocates a justice which would distribute aid according to the perceived worthiness of the needy. However, Kass recognizes that while the principles of strict personal responsibility and help based on one's just deserts form the starting point for the consideration of philanthropy, they do not constitute the whole story. Professor Kass goes on to recognize that we all, the just and the unjust, suffer the unpredictable changes of life, moral weaknesses, the need for some risk-taking, differences in genetic gifts and endowments, and especially inborn differences in intelligence. He thus recognizes that a decent community will try not only to care for the deserving poor who are worse off than others through no fault of their own, but even to bear some of the costs of helping the more or less undeserving poor.

One caveat is in order. I am interpreting Professor Kass's essay as representing the full picture of his understanding of philanthropy, but perhaps he merely emphasizes certain points to support his position on foolish compassion.

I will analyze Kass's position from the perspective of my discipline of Christian ethics. Such an analysis highlights the qualifications that Professor Kass makes to his primary assumptions rather than his emphasis on principles of responsibility and justice which require that philanthropists mete out help strictly according to the presumed merit of the poor.

My understanding of Christian ethics suggests that Kass's presentation depends too much on individualism and fails to recognize social reality.

Professor Kass only once refers to the common good. Common and individual goods do not of course relate as an either/or dichotomy. The fundamental importance of the rights as well as duties of the individual includes the recognition that this individual always lives in multiple relationships with God, neighbor, world, and self. As a result the moral obligation of philanthropy to the poor and the needy goes beyond benevolence and beneficence and includes aspects of distributive justice. I will point out five different aspects or areas in which more attention should be given to the social dimension of reality.

1. At times, need arises from structural sins and not just from the behavior of individuals. Some theologians today heavily emphasize social sin. Indeed, the structures of any society at times incarnate sin. Not all the problems arise from unjust structures: many arise from personal irresponsibility. But we cannot forget the structural aspects. For example, in our society today, we must treat the problem of unemployment as a structural problem and not primarily a problem of individual personal responsibility. Many qualified and responsible people who are trying to work have found themselves unemployed because of downsizing or the relocating of companies.

2. In the Judeo-Christian tradition the goods of creation exist to serve the needs of all. The Judeo-Christian tradition recognizes God as the creator of all persons and all things. God has made the world and all the things in it to serve the basic needs of all humankind. This universal destiny of the goods of creation to serve the needs of all in no way denies the possibility of private property. However, it refuses to make private property an ultimate value. We who have received the goods of creation from a gracious God have the responsibility to make sure that we use them to serve the basic needs of all humankind.

3. Kass's essay seems to assume justice primarily involves relationships between and among individuals, thus stressing commutative or one-on-one justice—to each according to one's deserts. Kass occasionally recognizes other aspects such as the common good but does not relate the common good to justice or rights.

From a more social perspective one recognizes three different types of justice. Commutative justice, or one-on-one justice, analyzes the relationship between one individual and another individual. Of course, this "individual" might be a moral fiction such as a corporation. Commutative justice governs contracts between two parties. The second type of justice, distributive justice, governs the relationship between society and the individual person. Distributive justice deals with how society should distribute its goods and burdens among the members. The third type of justice (legal, social, or contributive justice) governs the relationship of the individual members of society to the society as a whole.

Distributive justice (how society, an entity broader than the state but including the state, distributes its burdens and goods to individuals) forms the basis for positing human rights to food, clothing, and shelter, and also a right to health care. Distributive justice accords to every human being a right to a minimally decent human existence.

Distributive justice by no means implies total material equality; it recognizes and validates differences above and beyond this minimally decent level. Further, of course, advocates of the minimally decent level must recognize that at times one can drag the horse to water but cannot force the horse to drink. Nonetheless, distributive justice forms a part of justice and deals with the obligations of society to its members. The theological understanding of the destiny of the goods of creation to serve the needs of all buttresses this understanding of distributive justice.

The vast majority of Roman Catholic moral theologians before Vatican Council II (1962–65) claimed that the obligation to give alms to the poor from one's superfluous goods comes from charity and not justice.[1] However, many contemporary theologians recognize an obligation in justice to help the poor.[2]

An even more fascinating change occurred in the Middle Ages. Peter Lombard, whose *Sentences* served as the textbook of theology in the Middle Ages, defined justice as coming to the assistance of the poor.[3] When the *Summa* of Thomas Aquinas became the textbook a few centuries later, a new position emerged. Grounding his analysis in Aristotelian categories, Thomas Aquinas based almsgiving on charity and not justice in the strict sense.[4] However, a few theologians still argued that Aquinas related almsgiving to a broader concept of justice as well as to charity.[5]

4. Many theological ethicists have emphasized the need for a preferential option for the poor. Liberation theology first developed the option for the poor, but other theological schools have more or less accepted this understanding. Even a perceived critic of liberation theology such as Pope John Paul II has included the concept of a preferential option for the poor in his own teaching documents.[6]

The preferential option for the poor employs the word "preferential" precisely to avoid any kind of exclusive option for the poor. God's love embraces all persons, but the preferential option emphasizes that God has a special concern for the poor and that people in the Judeo-Christian tradition should have that same concern. The Hebrew and Christian Scriptures clearly indicate God's preferential option for the poor. The Bible often pictures God as the defender and protector of the poor against oppressors.

The preferential option for the poor must influence our approach to different problems. For example, the preferential option for the poor means that we should first, but by no means exclusively, question how proposed laws and public policy will affect the poor. Unfortunately, in our society many political groups and other interested parties try to shape legislation for their own narrow self-interest. Very few try to shape public policy from the perspective of the poor. The preferential option for the poor should also serve as the foundation for philanthropy.

5. Professor Kass strongly opposes the welfare and the bureaucratic state. Determining precisely what is meant by these terms always poses problems. However, recognizing a social dimension to human beings implies that the state is a limited good, a part of our humanity, and a necessity for human existence in this world. Without the state we would find life nasty, brutish, and short. However, what is the proper role of the state? We need to face that question since society includes not only the national government but state

and local governments and a host of institutions between the individual and the government. These varying institutions include families, neighborhoods, communities, voluntary associations, churches, labor unions, the chamber of commerce, the American Medical Association, and philanthropic groups. The progress from the individual through families, neighborhoods, associations, and voluntary groups to levels of government requires a principle of subsidiarity, which maintains that the higher institutional levels should help the lower levels to achieve all they can and only do those things which the lower levels cannot accomplish on their own. According to this principle, the state fills a role, as needed, of strengthening, supporting, and supplementing the mediating structures of society. The principle of subsidiarity thus serves to avoid two extremes: a collectivism which does not give importance to the individual and the local; and an individualism which does not give importance to community and to the varying degrees and kinds of institutional responsibility.

The complex interconnectedness of contemporary life means that the state will at times have to intervene because the lower levels cannot adequately deal with a particular problem. Government must play an important role in helping the poor and the needy because philanthropy and voluntary associations alone cannot adequately address the problem of poverty. However, the different levels of local, state, and federal government should help and encourage voluntary associations to do all they can to help the poor, thus serving as mediating structures and institutions in our society.

We must discuss the whole question of philanthropy within a broader social context which recognizes our multiple relationships with God, neighbor, world, and self and thus sees the obligations to the poor in terms not only of beneficence and benevolence but also of distributive justice.

NOTES

1. Marcellinus Zalba, *Theologia moralis summa*, vol. 1, *Theologia moralis fundamentalis* (Madrid: Bibloteca de Autores Cristianos, 1953), 866–67.

2. Werner Levi, *From Alms to Liberation: The Catholic Church, the Theologians, Poverty, and Politics* (New York: Praeger, 1989).

3. Petrus Lombardus, *Sententiarum libri IV* (Lyons: J. Sacon, 1515), lib. 3, dist. 33, cap. 1. See also Hermenegildus Lio, *Estne obligatio justitiae subvenire miseris?* (Rome: Desclée, 1957).

4. Thomas Aquinas, *Summa theologiae* (Rome: Marietti, 1952), II-II, q. 32, a. 1. See also Odon Lottin, "La nature du devoir de l'aumône chez les prédécesseurs de Saint Thomas d' Aquin," *Psychologie et morale au XIIe et XIIIe siècles* (Louvain: Abbaye du Mont César, 1949), III-1, 299–313.

5. L. Bouvier, *Le précepte del'aumône chez saint Thomas d'Aquin* (Montreal: Immaculata Conceptio, 1935).

6. Donal Dorr, *Option for the Poor: A Hundred Years of Vatican Social Teaching*, rev. ed. (Dublin: Gill and Macmillan, 1992).

A Response
to Curran, Lovin, and Sverdlik

LEON R. KASS

efore addressing the thoughtful comments of my three respondents,
I would like to clarify the intentions of my essay. I intended to open
questions about the limits of compassion as the guiding principle for
philanthropic activity, both in its everyday practice and in the large humanitarian project of modernity. As one test of the adequacy of the principle of
compassion, I chose to explore whether and why we should come to the aid
of those whose troubles result, largely, from their own foolishness or vice. I
argued that they cannot, in justice, claim our help, and, further, that compassion will not oppose this conclusion when compassion operates as properly
experienced sentiment. Nevertheless, I suggested that considerations of the
common good—not of justice or compassion—ought to lead us to care also
for those who have brought their troubles on themselves. The practice of philanthropy even toward the undeserving—of generosity beyond what is
owed—expresses and promotes civic virtue; in this way, it serves the community even beyond its contributions to its direct beneficiaries.

The main weakness of the ideology of compassion as it operates in contemporary philanthropy is its imprudence: it takes too narrow a view of necessary help. Concentrating on material wants and bodily ills, while ignoring
moral and spiritual deficiencies, well-meaning compassionate beneficence

often undermines the worthier goal of enabling recipients to outgrow the need for such charity. In contrast, philanthropy governed by "tough-loving" prudence, while not refusing to help, would have a richer and more truly beneficent idea of what help really means.

Turning from individual philanthropic deeds to the larger humanitarian scene, I argued that the hegemony of compassion may paradoxically endanger and enfeeble human life, precisely as people become increasingly dependent for their well-being on outside powers only unreliably or unwisely responsive to their needs. Compassionate humanitarianism may even make life less human, insofar as the high is always sacrificed to the urgent. Philanthropy needs to care also for excellence, dignity, and virtue—public and private—if it would truly serve human good. Compassion alone is a poor principle for philanthropy.

Charles Curran faults my approach, first, for being "too individualistic" and for failing "to recognize the important social aspects of reality." Second, he argues that justice must be the guide of philanthropy. His first complaint is, I believe, unwarranted. What may look like an "individualistic" bias simply results from my focus on those cases in which people suffer precisely as a result of *their own* shortcomings; however, if believing that people are indeed sometimes personally responsible, through folly or vice, for their own troubles is "too individualistic," I plead guilty. Moreover, though I treat it, admittedly, much too briefly, I make concern for the common good *the* reason why we should care for those who suffer as a result of their own folly. Indeed, it is largely because I care deeply about the state of society that I care about personal responsibility: personal self-command and its absence directly and profoundly affect the well-being not only of individuals but also of their families, neighborhoods, and communities. In addition, far from ignoring "important social aspects of reality," I explicitly call on philanthropies to support religious and other voluntary associations capable of renewing our moral and spiritual capital. (I remind Curran that numerous "community organizations" deserving of philanthropic assistance are not hostile to the status quo and existing social structures.) Finally, I do not oppose governmental assistance to the poor or needy. If I object to many of the social programs hatched in recent decades by the *federal* government, it is because, being remote, bureaucratic, imperious, and ineffective, they tend to enfeeble rather than strengthen local community associations, thus impoverishing real social life and threatening the common good.

Curran and I do disagree about the nature of distributive justice and especially its importance for philanthropy. I agree that distributive justice requires that we distribute the goods and burdens of society fairly among its members. But *which* are the goods that belong *to society* and thus can be so distributed? The rights of citizenship, the protection of the laws, and public honors and offices are communal goods; food, clothing, and shelter are not, especially in liberal, noncollectivist societies. Curran first confuses what he calls the Judeo-Christian (hence, universal and, hence, non- or trans-political) "responsibility to make sure that [the goods of creation] are used to serve the basic needs of all humankind" with the political obligation to distribute the goods of a particular society (which will care only for its own), and he then conflates the goods of creation with the goods of society. Only by blurring these sensible distinctions does there arise a *political* obligation of distributive justice regarding the goods of creation. Curran further aggravates confusion by wrapping his Christian message in the rights language of individualistic liberalism: "every human being has a *right* to a minimally decent human existence" (emphasis added). But the American polity—the society whose goods he and I want to distribute fairly—does not recognize such a right; the Declaration of Independence did not cite it as one of the equal rights with which men have been endowed by their Creator and which governments are instituted to secure.

Let me not be misunderstood. I think that everyone *should* have a minimally decent human existence, and I believe that those who have more than enough should help those who don't. But I do not regard such help as a matter of distributive justice, or even of justice altogether. None of us has a rightful claim against the universe or against society to provide us with any of our wants. It is good when we receive them, sad when we do not, but it is not, in my view, either way just or unjust. In addition, while we can admire philanthropies that address basic human needs, and while various religious charities do so as a duty, I doubt that one can turn this into a matter of justice for philanthropy as such. I would even go so far as to suggest that true philanthropy must spring from generous impulse, not from compulsory obligation. What justice requires is obligatory; what is philanthropic is free and grace-ful.

I have no real quarrel with what Curran calls providing "a preferential option for the poor," and nothing in my essay suggests otherwise. But by speaking indiscriminately about the poor, Curran appears to reject out-of-hand the nineteenth-century distinction between the "deserving poor" and the "undeserving poor"—between, say, a man in dire straits because his employer has downsized or moved his company and a man in dire straits because he refuses to seek employment or gambles away his earnings at the casinos. And why should material poverty, rather than spiritual and moral poverty, get the right of preferential option? Don't victims of ignorance, weakness of will, and bad character equally deserve charitable assistance? Does scriptural religion place lack of money first among the human evils?

With the major points in Robin Lovin's response I find myself in considerable agreement. I welcome his making explicit the valuable distinction between compassion (or benevolence) as *feeling* and compassion (or benevolence) as *norm*, as well as his insistence that we cannot trust feelings alone to do the moral work of guiding right conduct. Also, just as he agrees with me that we must sometimes restrain and discipline compassion by considerations of justice and prudence, so I readily agree with him that we sometimes need to expand compassion by overcoming our indifference to the needs of people whose lives differ widely from our own. Caring too little is often as big a problem as caring unwisely.

Nonetheless, we can usefully explore issues that emerge along the path of Lovin's argument. First, the distinction between feeling and norm, albeit useful, leaves important difficulties unexamined. Even an obviously "good" feeling, such as compassion or benevolence, cannot be turned into a virtue or norm by being made unqualifiedly obligatory—in Lovin's words, "how we *should* feel" (emphasis added). Rather, as we learn from Aristotle about how virtue stands to feeling, one sympathizes virtuously not by sympathizing always but by sympathizing rightly: virtue disposes or habituates one to feel compassion as one ought, toward those one ought, when one ought, for the reason one ought, to the extent one ought, in the way one ought, etc.[1] All of these right-making "as one ought's" require a discerning eye and mind no less than a loving heart. Hence the need for prudence or practical wisdom—not merely to calculate means to ends or to use resources efficiently (as Lovin suggests), but especially to identify accurately and see clearly the just-right-thing-to-feel-and-do, here and now.

The distinction between feeling and doing reminds us that, in philanthropy as in the rest of practical affairs, goodwill (benevolence) will not suffice. "How we should feel," though important, matters less than choosing and acting well (on the basis of that feeling). The road to folly, so I argue, is often paved with the best of intentions and feelings. This surely describes deeds motivated by compassion; it may also describe deeds motivated by benevolence.

As Lovin presents it, the eighteenth-century notion of benevolence—the disposition "to want the best for everyone"—seems to me to be the most trustworthy spring and motive for all philanthropic activity. For benevolence includes much more than compassion, with which we today often conflate it (as does Lovin himself occasionally in his response). Caring for and delighting in someone's well-being and happiness go far beyond caring that they not suffer—unless we shrink well-being to mean the mere absence of suffering. "Wishing well" (*benevolentia*) is a capacious sentiment, fully worthy of serving as a synonym for "loving other human beings" (*philanthropia*). Still, "to want the best for everyone," while desirable, is not sufficient. One needs also to *know* the best, especially if one wants to *do* the best. And benevolence, like compassion, is not by itself an adequate guide to knowing what is best or even what is good.

Lovin might object that when confronting, say, poverty or disease or extreme suffering, it is obvious what benevolence should wish for; one need not know "the best" or even "the good" to recognize certain evils as evil, and to act accordingly to combat them. Fair enough—but only up to a point. For one can pursue an obvious though partial good (e.g., relieving poverty) in ways that (unintentionally) do much harm, for example, by simultaneously undermining other, perhaps more important, goods (e.g., freedom, dignity, or self-respect). Once again, benevolence has need of prudence—not as a competing and correcting principle (as Lovin apparently sees it) but as an integral guide—if benevolence is to constitute a virtuous norm.

Through his analysis of Aristotle's treatment of pity, Lovin incisively shows how compassion may supply too constricted a motive for philanthropy, insofar as it may fail to move us to care for those whose sufferings we believe (rightly or wrongly) that we and our loved ones will escape.[2] He rightly describes how, in modern urban society, with increasing segregation of groups by class and race (and, some would add, cognitive ability) the well-off may grow indifferent to the plight of those whose lives seem alien to theirs. Far from eliciting compassion, the ill-favored may even arouse resentment and contempt. But this callousness may spring not so much from the constrictedness of compassion as experienced sentiment[3] as from the (seemingly paradoxical but in fact predictable) divisiveness of a liberal ideology that exploits compassion as a political principle, especially when it merges with thinking about society not in terms of individuals, families, and real communities but in terms of "identity" groups and pseudo-"communities"—racial, ethnic, socioeconomic, and gendered. Compassion as ideology generally requires practicing condescension toward those it seeks to help (not least by defining them into these stereotypical groups, and also by insisting that the benefactors know better than the recipients what help is needed and how it is to be delivered). Compassion also, to succeed politically and rhetorically, must foment indignation against the more fortunate members of the society, as if their superior fortune were precisely the cause of the ill fortune of the miserable. Advocates of compassion vent envy, anger, and resentment against the very majority that they at the same time are summoning to act on the demands of compassion. Even those whom the imputations of guilt do not repel will have trouble responding when such demands become chronic and unremitting; as Clifford Orwin has astutely noted, "compassion resembles love; to demand it is a good way to kill it."[4] For all these reasons, compassion elevated to political principle will fail to promote the common good: by identifying its objects (and their enemies) in terms of race, class, and gender, it encourages "tribalist" thinking that denies commonality and magnifies difference (hence weakening, not strengthening, the chances of pitying "the other" among one's fellow citizens); and by drying up the reservoir of goodwill that flowed naturally before the politics of compassion demanded it constantly and for all and sundry. This ironic dialectic between compassion and callousness reveals yet another reason why compassion ought not supply the ideological standard for human philanthropy.

Steven Sverdlik's response, though limited to considering some possible policy implications of my argument, I find the most challenging. Sverdlik makes clear how difficult it would be in practice to assess and establish "liability responsibility" if one wanted, after the fact, to deny charitable help to individuals who culpably caused their own troubles. He properly points to the dangers and burdens of adversarial procedures that determining liability would require; he rightfully worries about such "legalizing" of medical and social services. And he suggests that, in deciding about whether to provide liver transplants to alcoholics or bank loans to compulsive gamblers, "prudent compassion" might properly wish to distinguish between those who have and those who have not "reformed themselves" from their irresponsible behavior; yet the willingness thus to disregard past culpability in the presence of reform, Sverdlik shrewdly observes, would require its own "legalization" of services in order to verify genuine reformation. I accept all these objections and acknowledge all these difficulties.

Still, some answer can be made and some practical suggestions may be offered. As I say explicitly in my essay, I am *not* in favor of simply denying help to the undeservingly needy. Neither am I interested in seeing that they suffer as they deserve; I want to encourage wise philanthropy, not to insure retribution.[5] I also have no desire to "legalize" access to (ordinary) medical services[6] and many social services, and I would oppose most efforts to do so. Rather, I am simply trying to defend what I take to be the wisest and most philanthropic principle in these cases: help aimed at undoing the harms caused by past foolishness should be *accompanied by help aimed at making future foolishness less likely.*

True enough, this general principle still faces difficulties in application. We cannot always follow it; and, even when help with reform is offered, it may be refused and it may prove ineffective. But by focusing on past behavior not for deciding *whether* to alleviate present harms but *in order to address their deeper causes,* this principle expresses the higher meaning of philanthropy: to care for the whole person, not just for his misfortunes, with a view to enabling him better to secure his future improvement and well-being.

Concretely, what might this mean? Consider a few examples. This principle would oblige a grossly obese man needing hip replacement or cardiac bypass surgery, as a condition of receiving the treatment, to enter postoperatively into carefully regulated diet and exercise programs aimed at changing his habits of overeating and inactivity. It would urge an unwed pregnant teenager, whether seeking an abortion or carrying to term, to accept the post-pregnancy use of long-acting contraceptive agents or, better, educational and moral/spiritual counseling aimed at correcting her sexual irresponsibility. It would require welfare recipients, in accepting benefits, to accept job training and offered employment—a practice now increasingly part of the welfare reform movement. These programs of personal reform and rehabilitation will not always succeed. But if we are to have any real hope of altering habits and conduct, such programs must be integral to our charitable efforts, and they must be genuine and vigorous, not merely cosmetic and halfhearted efforts.

Real reeducation, of course, requires much more than providing information. Character and conduct derive primarily from habituation, from shaping up one's loves and hates by means of reward and punishment, praise and blame. Getting the facts, however desirable, by itself never cures bad habits; indeed, presented inappropriately and away from salutary influences that shape behavior, mere information may even prove dangerous. Has the massive effort these past few decades to provide sex education in the public schools limited promiscuity, reduced the incidence of sexually transmitted diseases, or lowered the rates of abortion and illegitimacy? Could the value-free presentation of sex information, away from the moral contexts of praise and blame, reward and punishment, itself have contributed to the increases in irresponsible behavior?

Beyond providing or withholding help, and beyond efforts at direct moral reeducation, philanthropy should attend to the highly important matters of fostering cultural norms and creating incentives for improved behavior. Under this heading I can respond to Sverdlik's comments on the dilemma of trying to curb illegitimacy (not only among teenagers) without penalizing the resulting (or already existing) children. Consider, for example, recent data that suggest linkages between welfare and out-of-wedlock births. Welfare reform over the past decade (first in the states, more recently in the federal government) has been followed by sharp drops in teenage illegitimacy rates.[7] Such reductions, predicted by the proponents of welfare reform, are just what one might expect, and not because, under the old welfare system, teenagers were choosing to have children simply in order to get a welfare check. Rather, people are likely to behave more responsibly when they have no viable (irresponsible) economic alternatives and when governments stop sending messages that out-of-wedlock birth is a socially acceptable practice. Sverdlik might point out, rightly, that the changes in welfare policy harm some innocent children. But only by reversing the harmful incentives and the immoral messages of the previous policies can we spare future generations of children the tragic fate now visited upon so many of them by their progenitors' irresponsibility. If successful, the new "tough-loving" policy will prove more philanthropic than its putatively more compassionate predecessor.

But if we mean truly to promote decent behavior and self-command among those who lack it, we need to do more than discontinue offering wrong economic incentives and sending immoral messages. We need *positive* incentives and moral support for the growth of personal responsibility. To some extent, we know how to offer such support. In Boston and other cities, neighborhood religious leaders are succeeding in efforts to reform youth gang members through programs of spiritual guidance and demanding moral practices. Urban parochial schools, practicing discipline and demanding high standards in behavior and performance, outdo their public school neighbors in dropout and truancy prevention, rate of graduation, and academic accomplishment. Alcoholics Anonymous, Weight Watchers, and Promise Keepers enjoy many triumphs at fostering self-command. Yet we need to know a lot more about how to get people to do what is good for them. And we need especially to learn how to educate those young people who lack proper families and who are now beyond the reach of religious institutions or other local organizations that can help them acquire personal and moral responsibility. The support of research that might yield such knowledge should become part of the mission of contemporary philanthropic activity. Only with the aid of such knowledge will philanthropy be able to practice wise benevolence and the proper love of humankind.

NOTES

1. Interestingly, Aristotle in his *Nicomachean Ethics* does not mention any virtue regarding pity, though one may have been expected. Pity appears in the list of passions mentioned in Book II, Chapter 5, where Aristotle is working his way to the conclusion that the ethical virtues are not the passions themselves but our dispositions (*hexeis*) toward them. And all the ethical virtues he does discuss dispose us well toward one or another of the passions: courage, gentleness, moderation, greatness of soul, and (partial) justice are virtues toward, respectively, fear, anger, and the love of pleasure, honor, and gain. The omission of a virtue that disposes us to pity properly is perhaps intelligible once we observe that all the ethical virtues are said to aim at nobility (in the

agent): there appears to be nothing beautiful or noble (*kalon*) in pitying, even in pitying well. Here an important window opens on the difference between Greek and biblical ethics.

2. Lovin is, however, mistaken in claiming, on this basis, that Aristotle sees pity as tainted by self-interest. Aristotle is not here suggesting that we pity *because* we are self-regarding, that we sympathize only out of or because of projected self-concern. When he says that one feels pity for evils "which one might expect oneself or someone of one's own to suffer," he is not giving the motive or cause of pity but merely describing the psychic limitation of pity's scope. It is simply a psychological fact that we have difficulty feeling pity for beings very remote from ourselves or for those whose troubles we cannot imagine suffering ourselves. This, not self-interest, explains why the immortal Olympian gods, generally speaking, simply cannot pity mortal men. (A notorious exception is described in Book XXIV of the *Iliad*, where the deathless gods are explicitly said to pity the corpse of Hector as it is being dragged around the city walls by the hypervengeful Achilles. The poet uses divine pity here to underscore the enormity of Achilles' deed and the depth of Hector's degradation.)

3. Lovin errs when he says that "Kass emphasizes that compassion as sentiment leads us to want to relieve suffering indiscriminately." It is not, I argue, compassion as naturally experienced sentiment but compassion distorted by its use as political principle that is guilty of not making distinctions. Compassion as natural sentiment does distinguish between deserved and undeserved suffering.

4. Clifford Orwin, "Compassion," *The American Scholar* 49 (summer 1980): 331. Orwin's superb discussion illuminates many of the issues we are here discussing. See also his more recent "Moist Eyes from Rousseau to Clinton," *The Public Interest* 128 (summer 1997).

5. For this reason, Sverdlik's correct observation that vice may sometimes be its own punishment is irrelevant to my argument. I discuss the relation between justice and compassion not to endorse retribution for the foolish and vicious but only to show, first, that those whose misfortunes are not unde-

served have no claim in justice to our help and, second, that compassion—if uncorrupted—is not opposed to this judgment.

6. The question of eligibility for optional or heroic service, e.g., organ transplantation, is, as Sverdlik notes, more complicated, at least on grounds of prudence.

7. The National Center for Health Statistics reports that out-of-wedlock births for black teenagers fell by 21 percent from 1991 to 1996, for Hispanics, by 10 percent, for non-Hispanic whites, 4 percent.

PART II

Foundations

Help or Respect

Priorities for Nonprofit Boards

DAVID H. SMITH

D espite great national prosperity, many Americans still need help. That people need help no thoughtful observer will deny; we must ask what—if anything—others can do to help them. Many who think of themselves as potential helpers find themselves in trouble in one way or another. It is not as easy as we might suppose to draw a line between those who need help and those who can give it. I want to identify and comment on four issues: (1) the good life and the obligation to care for others, (2) organized giving and the issue of private vs. public provision of aid, (3) the fidelity principle, and (4) the demands of justice. In the first half of my essay, I will attempt to make the case for philanthropy; in the second half, I will offer some suggestions about the conduct of philanthropy.

I.

In the November 1996 issue of *Worth*, Richard Todd reported on his conversations with some of America's wealthiest citizens.[1] Some give generously; unfortunately, the vast majority do not. On the whole, big *old* money gives more than big *new* money, and Todd points out what a huge impact could be made if more persons with great wealth gave on even half or a quarter of the scale of Walter Annenberg, whose giving as a percentage of total wealth he estimates at 27 percent.

These facts raise the first issue I wish to address: Why should we recommend giving as a way of life? Why should I give at all? Why bother? I won't presume to speak for Mr. Annenberg, but I want to address the question of why his use of his resources is better, in my view, than that of some of his peers whose giving as a percentage of total wealth is much less.

A first rationale for giving appeals to self-interest and self-protection. Give to keep the poor from becoming so envious and angry at inequality that they attack my current position of affluence. Social stability almost guarantees privilege. When significant numbers of persons cannot lead safe and decent lives, they may rock the boat, and there's no telling who may be thrown overboard. Thoughtful investments in amelioration can keep things quiet and assure that I can continue to enjoy the privileged life to which I have become accustomed.

This argument is not crazy, but it is of limited power. It will not motivate me if someone else is taking care of social problems—whether that someone else be business, or government, or even large philanthropic organizations. Furthermore, the self-protection argument has little effect on persons who think they could ride out any social turmoil or leave town to avoid it. Someone with an income of "only" a hundred thousand a year is not a likely target of social or political chaos or revolution. But philanthropy is an affair of the middle class as well as the rich, and fortune is fickle.

Furthermore, this self-preservation motive is singularly unimpressive as a moral argument. The very nature of what it means to be a human being seems to include some fundamental concern for the welfare of others. The most basic question, of course, is why be moral at all. I will assume that the reader at least pays lip service to what William Frankena once called the "moral institution of life,"[2] by which he meant a recognition that the fate of others should matter to me. Because most of us do acknowledge that the fate of others matters, a purely self-interested argument seems inadequate, and we look for ways of explaining why it benefits others for us *not* to help them. Thus we may be tempted to persuade ourselves that we show respect for the poor when we don't help them. At best, we might argue, we should help them learn to help themselves.

This stress on respect, when not cynically offered as a cover for selfishness, serves as a corrective to naïve "do-goodism." C. S. Lewis once claimed to have found a gravestone inscribed:

Erected by her sorrowing brothers,
In memory of Martha Clay.
Here lies one who lived for others.
Now she has peace.
And so have they!

And the issue is not only jocular. It is better to empower people to lead their own lives to the full than to stoop to help—better for the person helped, and better for the helper who is forced to learn the reciprocity that comes with mutual respect. We must acknowledge there are good reasons to review the forms of helping and to consider reforming philanthropic or welfare policies, and changing the structures of charity. But the appeal to respect hardly provides one with categorical grounds for withholding aid.

I do not want to imply that all arguments against paternalistic social policies are arguments made in bad faith. But some are. Others than skeptics or cynics can view calls for welfare reform suspiciously when yoked to demands for reduction in the tax rates. Many people genuinely believe in reform for the sake of respect, but for too many of us this coincidence of self-interest and reform rhetoric is all too convenient. In any case, it is the appeal to the claim that less generous policies will benefit the poor that interests us, for making this altruistic argument at all shows the pressure everyone feels to justify their actions with reference to the interests of others. A decision to give that springs from exclusive reference to the giver's self-interests repels everyone. There must be some more fundamental reason for giving.

Religions urge giving. Judaism, Islam, and Christianity demand care for the poor or needy as a fundamental part of what it means to be human. Active care for others is not an optional decoration, as if I first took care of my soul and then, as a second step, chose to care for the poor. Rather, the traditional *zakat* or *chesed*, alms or hospitality, characterizes what it means to be members of the community of the Abrahamic peoples. These traditions entail a distinctive way of looking at the moral world. A Jew or Muslim or Christian sees the world in a characteristic way. The traditions force someone who takes them seriously to see the world through a distinctive pair of glasses; they provide corrective vision.[3] The central aspect of this Abrahamic way of seeing the world is that God, not the self, is sovereign. People have the derivative status of being made in God's image. The fundamental moral fact about a person is whether she or he responds loyally to God.

We may not see God's goodness, which is neither simple nor obvious. We can clearly see the power of fate, of forces beyond human control. The observant Christian, Jew, or Muslim believes that this power is one and that it somehow works for our good. In the monotheistic traditions of the West, God is the moral hub of the world. This viewpoint may be difficult to sustain, but it also seems to be irrepressible. Sometimes, some people can lead lives based on trust. The effect is that they are freed from defensiveness because a fundamental question about the self's worth and security has been answered. The sovereignty of a God bound to humankind consoles and comforts us, and frees us to think of our lives as gifts or territory over which we should act as stewards.

This self-understanding has powerful implications for the way we relate to each other: as beings who share a common problem and hope we all find ourselves in the same boat. We are siblings. The bond that holds us together is not mutual attraction or liking, but awe before and gratitude to God, the source of our being. There is nothing sentimental about this conclusion. I may learn to care for my friend's obnoxious dog out of love for her. Out of love for God, I must come to care for other persons, even as I see them in their fallibility and brokenness. For, of course, I see myself in that way.

This sense of human sisterhood or brotherhood does not reject private property and appreciation of the joys of wealth; it does not require vows of poverty, but it has two implications that the Abrahamic traditions have always noted. First, it smashes any idolatrous focus on possessions. Allowing one's life to revolve entirely around the accumulation of wealth or power or money contradicts the confession of the sovereignty of God. We can relish the power money brings, or fine clothes, homes, and possessions. We cannot safely lose perspective and treat these things as the end for which we live. For the well-ordered soul, possession is always instrumental, and a little dangerous, even when it refreshes us and nurtures larger life.

Second, citizenship in the community that God rules pushes us to share: to nurture concern for the poor, to despise tolerance of economic injustice, to recognize the interdependence and mutual neediness that bind humans into a community.

Christian tradition puts the issue starkly: God gives; those who identify themselves with God's cause must also give. Authentic religious worship supports persons in their allegiance to this giving God and enables them to give of themselves, albeit imperfectly and in limited ways. With faith and trust in God, Christians turn to the other, "the neighbor," as best they can. How to give, what to give, to whom to give remain hard questions. *Whether* to give does not.

Many people do not share these religious convictions; one of the joys of pluralist democracy is that identities are formed in different traditions, religious and secular. And even those of us who do hold these convictions may believe that others can find good reasons for the same conclusions. In fact, a philosophical tradition going back to Aristotle holds as ideal the magnanimous life—the life of the great-souled person. Aristotle did not praise poverty; he valued lovely possessions and a good party. But he did not think that one could live the good life by simply looking out for oneself. Rather, he thought, the good life required using one's resources to benefit one's community and, by that very process, oneself. Because I draw my identity in part from my community, I benefit when it benefits. That larger, communal, self with which I identify offers me more possible dimensions of joy or tragedy than does solitary self-satisfaction. The communally identified self is more vulnerable than the isolated monad, but the greater risk entails the possibility of greater gains. Aristotle began by assuming that the self *is* social, that humans cannot live except in community. He then argued that the good life must itself *be* social. Without real giving, the good life *is* impossible.

Such arguments for giving may not persuade someone not already predisposed to listen; perhaps, like Scrooge, most persons need a powerful personal experience to show them what they miss if they look out only for themselves or the members of their immediate family. Reasoning can only carry us so far in morals; at some point we must fall back on example, on the lessons learned in the bitter experiences and joys of a life, on suffering and the miracle of love. In my own life, the demands of family, and especially of parenting, pulled me out of myself and made me glimpse the ways in which losing the self can bring joy. And I often work with a kind of implicit principle of exchange formulated in the writings of the Anglican writer Charles Williams: I treat older people as I hope someone will treat my mother, students and employees as I hope faculty and bosses will treat my children. I don't believe in magic; no moral karma works to balance gifts. But some aspects of the lives of those I love, I want to help with, but cannot. My mother needs some help that I cannot give. Providing that kind of help to another woman, to whom I can give it, helps establish a balance. And if everyone contributed to that balance, my loved ones would be okay.

Unfortunately, the experience of many mature persons in the United States today seems to teach a different lesson. Many of my most conscientious peers have suffered a "giving burnout." We entered adulthood idealistic, acting to make the world a better place. We have done some things we ought to have done, but we have left lots undone. As a result we have spent decades overloaded with guilt[4] and have become cynical about the possibility of actually helping others. We think we have cast, and seen others cast, pearls before swine. We know what giving without reciprocation, receiving only recrimination in return, means; we have learned the intractability of social problems. We feel we have given too many checks at the office.

I intentionally cast this lament in the first person, for I can identify with these desperate arguments. But we cannot accept these as the final arguments. They warn only against foolish giving, unrealistic expectations, and naïve optimism. I won't plead for foolish charity, make no case for trying to do more than we can, dream of no rapid end to poverty or illness or suffering. Bill May once taught me, "Once burned, their fault; twice burned, my fault." Foolish idealism erodes all idealism. But while we can sensibly argue that we should rethink a given set of policies or personal actions *in order to make them more respectful and effective*, we cannot thereby suggest that our caring engagements with our fellows are optional, nor vainly imagine that we can live with ourselves if we become callous. In fact, those of us fortunate enough to enjoy discretionary income or time owe major responsibilities. More thoughtful giving—you bet; give up on giving—never, because that option can cost us our souls.

II.

Given the necessity of giving, how should we organize such giving? Every society must develop a structure for communal provision. In premodern or more traditional societies, the religious community and the political authorities, church and state, often hammered out a kind of teamwork. The government assumed responsibility for defense, while the church was expected to manage education, and care for the poor and the sick. The fact that people looked to the church for assistance helped make the church a powerful competitor for popular allegiance. When Henry VIII dissolved the monasteries he not only got his hands on the church's treasure, he also eliminated a competitor for the allegiance of his people. His daughter Elizabeth, taking his point, enacted a historically important set of poor laws.

Despite these conflicts, the colonists brought to this continent a more or less coherent set of institutions for meeting public needs. Indeed, through the nineteenth and well into the twentieth century the sharp distinction our political rhetoric makes between governmental and private or philanthropic provision did not attract attention or analysis. Part of this inattention to the question of who should help whom may have arisen from the fact that most Americans lived in the country or in small towns. In a small town when people are in trouble through natural disaster or disease or invasion, their neighbors care less about who does it than that someone do something. At times of crisis or communal suffering, everyone expects to help out.

Over time, we have become cities of strangers; our visions of the world differ; one person's offer of help has become another's gratuitous insult. The disestablishment of the churches, far from excusing them from their charities, increased their obligation. But their resources were limited, and none appeared as *the* church for everyone.

Pluralism of values and great unmet need conditioned the soil from which modern philanthropy as we Americans understand the term grew. The middle class does some giving, through, for example, the United Way, the Red Cross, and many local and regional community service organizations. Other, more visible giving came from big money that established foundations. Carnegie, Ford, and Rockefeller, however mixed their motives may have been, ended up doing things that were meant to benefit other Americans. In an earlier era people with a comparable concentration of resources might have endowed a monastery dedicated to care for the sick or to education. Now, in the United States, they acted on their own. And their immense resources have proved invaluable in the support of scientific research, medical and educational progress, environmental concern, and Third World assistance.

We have worked out a polity in which human need is met partly through governmental action and partly through the work of nonprofit organizations. How well does our complex system of meeting human needs work? We should be clear about the limits of dependence on voluntary giving, which is unsystematic and ad hoc. Those lucky enough to live in a community that benefits from a local and generous foundation or other benefactor attentive to its own backyard will enjoy benefits that someone living across the state line lacks. Further, the system allows free riders. Taking care of need entirely through philanthropy would mean that the generous help and the selfish don't. At some point, this disparity is likely to become galling to the givers. Insofar as communal provision is nonvoluntary, paid for by tax money, we have a way to try to ensure that all citizens pay an equitable price and that resources can be used equitably.

Obviously, the basis for nonvoluntary provision is taxation; nonvoluntary provision is not a gift as we ordinarily use that term. None of us likes to pay taxes, but taxation and compulsory helping do take seriously the pronoun "we" in the phrase "we the people." It symbolizes recognition of mutual indebtedness and weakness and thus makes it easier for some of us to accept tangible forms of help.

We should not treat public provision and philanthropic provision as alternatives, which we can easily substitute for each other. In fact, as a series of studies by Salamon and associates have shown,[5] the nonprofit world so deeply depends on government support that we could not really disentangle them if we tried. We should continue to use taxation to prevent free riders and as a symbol of our communal interdependence, but we should pair it with renewed and extended voluntary contributions, initiatives, and actions.

Independent philanthropy has many advantages, some more apparent than real. Some people say that governmental provision is slow, unimaginative, and bureaucratic, while independent philanthropy can be innovative. Although true in principle, this contrast is not always true in fact. Private foundations develop their own comfort zones and inertia; government programs can provide seed money for many novel ideas.[6]

Private philanthropy has two great advantages. The first comes from the side of the donor(s): Private philanthropy allows a kind of identification with a particular cause or set of causes. It gives an individual a power to shape the community in an enduring way, to purchase a kind of social immortality. No totalitarian state could acknowledge this extraordinary kind of liberty, for the power to give and to help carries the power to influence and to generate affection and loyalty. Private philanthropy gives people a chance to make a difference. In defending private philanthropy, we say that people should have the right to the kind of immortality that comes from "making a statement." One can give other, perhaps better, gifts than a gift of resources, but the gift of resources often entails a donation of self that we should celebrate. The desire to enjoy public recognition of our generosity is not the best reason to give, but it is honorable nevertheless.

Private philanthropy also matters in the modern world because it can embody pluralism of values. Private foundations can embody values ranging from conservative through liberal, religious, secular, Christian, Arab, or Jewish, and forward their visions of the good life. The modern state must be neutral among these many specific and detailed conceptions of the good life. Of course the state can act for the sake of the common good; it need not be neutral "all the way down." But this neutrality does mean that persons or groups may perceive as genuine needs programs that the state cannot consider basic. They are real needs but needs the state cannot meet or that it would be imprudent to meet by taxing citizens. Religious education and some forms of health care are good examples. I don't deny that drawing lines will be difficult, but still, pluralism of values and a plurality of centers of initiative for doing good must go together.

III.

Giving benefits individuals, and democracy should encourage private giving. I have conceded, if that is the right word, that there is such a thing as naïve generosity, that givers need to be wise and savvy and not just well intentioned. Thus some moral constraints should regulate organized nonprofit giving.

The trustees of nonprofit organizations almost always control major philanthropic action in this country. The rationale for this arrangement recognizes that while the benefactor's life is short, the need—health or education or the arts—is unlimited. A board takes responsibility for directing resources toward the need(s) the benefactors identified. This connection between the founding purpose of an organization and its ongoing choices provides not just a description, but a key moral charge. The connection sets a *fiduciary constraint* on the board. The benefactors or donors specify a cause or set of causes, and thus oblige the board to be faithful to that charge.

That is easily said; not so easily done. The original cause may become dated; it may come to seem perverse; it may be hopelessly vague. The benefactor may have identified a complex of causes, and setting priorities among them may pose an insurmountable task. Without these problems, we could omit the board and simply work with a pool of money and a staff. But these problems inevitably develop, and they call for judgment, not just action.

A great professor once said that he thought of hell as surviving in posterity through the notes of a B-minus student. He meant, of course, surviving through the record of someone who got the words right but who basically missed the point. The student would think he was speaking in the teacher's name, but would have lost the priorities among ideas or the context. Great comedy and tragedy occurs when someone follows directions overly literally. Indeed, doing literally what someone suggests can be an act of betrayal rather than fidelity. When a parent or other loved one fails or dies, we suspect that, in following the letter of exactly what they said, we violate their spirit.

To one degree or another conflict between the letter and spirit always confronts trustees. I think it's helpful to think of these conflicts as problems of interpretation—of translating the core intentions of the benefactor(s) into policies and priorities for the present. I have already mentioned one form of going wrong in this task: *literalism*, in which one keys on the exact words, rather than the overall objectives shaped and formulated in a specific context. But trustees can make a polar error: *forgetting* the cause, casting loose from the specificity of the gift, and rethinking from the ground up. That forgetting amounts to an improvisation of the trust.

The fact that the board's main task is interpretive has major implications for the question of who should serve on the board. At the outset it may imply that the best board members are family members or others who knew the benefactors best, but people are not always best understood by their families or closest associates, and, in any event, that generation won't be around forever. Boards need to develop processes of recruitment that will identify persons who are likely to be able both to grasp the core objectives of founders and to contemplate fundamental social or technological forces that may require changes—perhaps very fundamental changes—in policy. In my opinion, too many boards are constituted with an eye on social position or some kind of demographic representation, rather than through seeking out trustees who combine relevant expertise with the ability to listen and learn.

IV.

Considering interpretation as the key task of trustees brings up the question of good intentions. As the quotation from C. S. Lewis suggests, good intentions and helping out, active concern for others, are not always appreciated. People want the freedom to live their own lives, and make their own mistakes. Paternalism—doing people a favor that they don't want—constantly threatens to trap philanthropy. Every parent knows this dilemma: walking the line between helping out and meddling, between respect for a child's own choices and indifference to his difficulties. The parent wants both to do good and to respect the child's need to take responsibility for herself. Thus, a commitment to active giving raises the issue of help or respect.

For parents, the line between helping and meddling takes one form with young children, another with teenagers, and yet another with adult children. The problem of identifying this line never goes away, but the priority shifts in the direction of respect as the child matures. The model of the adult child offers the best paradigm to philanthropy because even if the beneficiaries of our assistance are children, they are children who have come from somewhere, from a family or culture with a distinct set of values. Perhaps philanthropy should override those values sometimes, but first we must make sure that our help respects the recipient, takes the recipient seriously as a responsible being with a set of values, commitments, and hopes. I want to stress two implications of treating recipients with respect.

First, it means one may have expectations of recipients—usually appropriate use of the assistance, and accountability. Marcel Maus in his highly influential book, *The Gift*, argues that gifts impose obligations on the recipients: obligations, first, of gratitude and then of reciprocal giving. The colloquial "tyranny of the gift" recognizes that gifts inevitably impose obligations. Givers cannot eliminate this psychological dynamic, but they can give with a sensitivity that makes it possible to discharge the reciprocal obligations with dignity. Any ways in which a benefactor or beneficent institution can acknowledge its own neediness and accept help and advice from the recipient offer first steps to such sensitivity.

Second, however, giving with respect means that the philanthropist can legitimately offer limits. To explain, let me go back to my parental analogy. I am professor of religious studies, and a particular form of Christianity is important in my life. Suppose I tell my adult children that I will pay for their flights home at Easter so that we can go to church together. That may sound inoffensive, but suppose one child has become a Buddhist. My offer may impose my view on all of them, but to the Buddhist it would add to the imposition an insulting failure to respect who he is.

Just so, respectful philanthropy should be constrained by values that the recipient can be presumed to hold. If philanthropy amounts to a call for religious conversion, it becomes a sort of spiritual bribe. Sometimes, of course, we can respectfully hope that recipients of philanthropy will change their lives or even their basic values. Benefactions for education and health care rightly support such changes. Still, encouraging changes in directions antithetical to recipients' most basic values precludes respect. We should also avoid tailoring help to an imagined needy abstraction, but rather focus on the concrete needs of specific people, perhaps specific populations.

I think it helpful to think of these considerations bearing on justice as a *common good constraint*,[7] for they suggest that philanthropy must observe limits beyond those built into the fidelity principle. In addition to keeping an eye on the past and the cause they serve, trustees who set policy must ask about how to serve with respect, about what they can reasonably expect from beneficiaries, and about what those intended beneficiaries themselves think they need. Respect for beneficiaries requires knowing a good deal about the worlds in which they live, and that knowledge will rule out some things that a philanthropy might like to do that are, in themselves, consistent with the basic mission of the philanthropy. Thus, a board must constantly reconcile the fidelity and common good principles.

Reconciliation of giving and respect is difficult, and no set formula will resolve the difficulties. A thoughtful and responsible board will constantly find itself in doubt and perplexed about how to reconcile giving and respect. It should show courage and admit as much to itself. It must also develop a board culture that fosters these admissions and serious discussion. Of course, we should not model board meetings on inconclusive graduate seminars; boards need leadership from a CEO, board members, or staff. Good boards will bring intellectual vitality and concern with moral issues to discussions of need, respect, care, and steadfastness. The fact that these moral qualities pose difficult issues to talk about does not excuse a board from considering them.

Moreover, the board must see that the organization subordinates itself as means to an end—the end named in the cause to which the board pledges faith and specified through a process of interpretation and reflection on the common good. Educational, health care, and philanthropic organizations should serve human purposes, not seek institutional immortality. Thus, trustees should ponder the question of whether the organization is necessary to serve its purpose and thus the common good. I was very proud to vote for the closing of a hospice I had helped to start fifteen years earlier—proud not because I had changed my mind on hospice care but because our organization had served as a catalyst for provision of hospice services by the local hospital and had therefore made itself redundant as a separate organization. May more charities suffer such a fate! And may more boards be attuned to the issue and be sufficiently committed to cause and common good that they will recognize institutional death or redundancy when they see it.

We find fulfillment in giving. Institutionalized voluntary giving complements collective caring by honoring our liberty and respecting our diversity.

Boards should serve as custodians of purpose and shape purpose to serve the common good. Board membership is a kind of unsung and insufficiently analyzed form of public service in the United States today. It is one important form of giving oneself, and giving of oneself is what life is all about.

NOTES

1. Richard Todd, "Looking for Andrew Carnegie," *Worth* (November 1996), 69–82; the reference to Annenberg is on page 80.

2. William K. Frankena, *Ethics* (Englewood Cliffs, N.J.: Prentice-Hall, Inc., 1973), 6.

3. William F. May, *The Physician's Covenant* (Philadelphia: The Westminster Press, 1983), 13.

4. A wise Catholic friend of mine describes guilt as "the gift that keeps on giving."

5. See, for example, Lester Salamon, "Partners in Public Service: The Scope and Theory of Government-Nonprofit Relations" in *The Nonprofit Sector: A Research Handbook,* ed. Walter W. Powell (New Haven, Conn.: Yale University Press, 1987).

6. See James Douglas, "Political Theories of Nonprofit Organization" in *The Nonprofit Sector.*

7. I use the terms "fiduciary constraint" and "common good constraint" in my book *Entrusted: The Moral Responsibilities of Trusteeship* (Bloomington: Indiana University Press, 1995), where the argument of these last paragraphs is expanded and developed.

The American Spirit in Philanthropy

CURTIS W. MEADOWS, JR.

Our philanthropic spirit grows from roots in our nation's unique history and continues to unfold into our time.

Our philanthropic legacy interweaves the stories of wealth and poverty, of dreams and frustrations, of good intentions and arrogance, of the head and the heart.

When we talk about the origins and philosophical underpinnings of what Jim Joseph, former President of the Council on Foundations, calls the "charitable impulse," we must emphasize that this impulse has roots, and flowers into different expressions, in almost all cultures. In *The Charitable Impulse,* he notes that "the charitable impulse is triggered whenever people see themselves as part of a community, whether it be the family, the neighborhood, or the nation. As the sense of community expands, so does the scope of philanthropy."[1]

The ancient Greeks coined the word *philanthropos* to mean love of humankind. The early Christians used the Greek word *agape* to represent a blending of love and charity, not just liking, but unconditional acceptance. The words reminded the congregation that the neighbor it enjoined them to love was everybody and that they must *care* about the welfare of the neighbor helped as well as assist that neighbor.

Joseph analyzes the moral imperatives of religion that influence actions to help others, citing the Jewish tradition that charity requires not only a self-less act but a concern for the oppressed and a search for justice. The giver must give humbly, thoughtfully, reflectively, respecting the receiver. In the Jewish teachings, how you give matters as much as what you give.[2]

Islam challenges Moslems "to practice the virtues of benevolence and justice in order to retain a relative state of purity."[3] Confucius taught that benevolence characterized the person who had matured toward true humanity.[4]

As religious believers respond to God's benevolent gift of life, they should extend benevolence to other human beings.

Most cultures, as well as religions, enjoin charity and giving. Wealthy Armenians honored a tradition that they should give as much as nine-tenths of their money to charity. Some Native American tribes believed that they acquired status by distributing, rather than accumulating, wealth. They gave away everything they had accumulated at death.[5]

The Japanese normally directed their charity to an individual, family, or institution with whom the donor had close personal ties. Early Hispanic and African charitable traditions directed charity to the family and then the extended group. In this country, minority and ethnic groups used churches and benevolent societies to help other members of their group and extend charitable assistance to others.[6]

As early immigrants came to America, they brought with them a deep suspicion of government, strong religious faith, and fierce independence. They fought for and obtained a constitutional bill of rights that limited governmental authority over their lives. In so doing, they claimed substantial responsibility for their own welfare and, indirectly, for their neighbor's as well.

In a country so vast, new settlers often arrived in an area long before a local government. They learned to depend upon themselves; and, drawing on their various philanthropic traditions, they formed associations with their neighbors to resolve common problems.

Associating with others to address social problems rather than appealing to the government became a characteristic of our new democracy. Our forefathers felt so strongly about the expressed rights of assembly, freedom of speech, and petition of government for redress of grievances that they guaranteed them in the First Amendment of our Constitution. The American voluntary sector rose from these freedoms. No similar voluntary enterprise of such vast size, scope, and variety of activities has arisen elsewhere in the world.

More than a million and a half American nonprofit organizations, churches, and associations exist today. A recent Gallup poll reported that close to 70 percent of all American households contribute to charitable organizations. More than 100 million people volunteer about 20 billion hours of unpaid service every year. Studies have consistently shown that most Americans, of whatever race, religion, or creed, join in voluntarily helping other people.[7]

And we give out of our private and personal resources an estimated $174 billion, 77 percent of which comes from millions and millions of individuals,[8] most of whom financially benefit only from a small tax break.

The givers decide to give, one at a time, and most don't expect, nor do they seek, recognition for their selfless acts of love and personal choice.

Answering a survey that asked them to list the words that describe American philanthropy, the respondents replied:

- Love, service, compassion, caring;
- Hope, idealism, common good, community;
- Freedom, independence, liberty, responsibility;
- Equality, dignity, diversity;
- Truth, integrity, trust;
- Prudence, wisdom;
- Justice, fairness, equity;
- Valor, courage, fortitude, risk-taking;
- Temperance, and humility.

These words express values and principles because the American nonprofit system appeals to passion, belief, idealism, generosity, and hope. The system

---

depends on feeling and emotion as well as rational thought. It focuses us on others, not on ourselves.

Joseph thinks that people who believe they share humanity with others build community. Thus a civil society that wants peace and harmony among its people must continue seeking to widen each citizen's sense of significant connectedness to an ever expanding group of others.

In America, organizations in the voluntary action sector contribute to this effort by teaching and involving millions of American citizens in our religious, cultural, educational, and other nonprofit institutions.

Despite its size and many contributions to our nation, the voluntary action sector rests on a very fragile base of *trust:*

- Trust between the donor and donee;
- Trust between the client and service-providing agency;
- Trust between volunteers and a nonprofit's staff;
- Trust between the public and an agency's Board of Trustees;
- Trust between government and all those responsible for the institution and its actions.

Fittingly, then, we call the governing bodies of nonprofit organizations "trustees." We trust them to act ethically when they carry out their duties and responsibilities. Their duties and responsibilities demand undivided loyalty to the enterprise and the commitment to avoid conflicts of interest. If they fail to act ethically they lose our trust. Once they lose our trust, they will find it very hard to reestablish or replace. It is precisely because this sector calls on our values and principles that its failures hurt us more when we discover malfeasance or abuse. But such failures or breaches of trust rise not so much from a failure of the American spirit as from a failure of individual will and personal responsibility.

Around the world, countries that are opening their societies and permitting more freedom for their people are approaching the United States for assistance in expanding or establishing voluntary self-help systems independent of government or business.

Such voluntary self-help systems require the freedom to associate—they not only help preserve liberty, develop a sense of community, and protect the interests of minority groups, but they cannot survive in a totalitarian society. They allow people to challenge the status quo and to act independently from governmental solutions and programs.

The caregivers among us bless our society and do God's work in this world. You find them wherever they can fulfill need. They are changing lives by their selfless service. Whether they are teaching, healing, comforting, feeding, or encouraging, they nurture and keep alive hope in America.

Some come to such service answering a call to lifetime vocation, others seeing the opportunity for voluntary action. They most often work under difficult conditions, and for very little recognition or reward. Their faith, their humanity, or their sense of fairness draws them into the lives of the impoverished, suffering, or neglected. Encouraging the gifted and talented actualizes their aspirations for a world filled with human achievement and creative expression.

Whether demonstrating what Millard Fuller, the founder of Habitat for Humanity, calls the "theology of the hammer," what de Tocqueville defined as "habits of the heart," or what Thomas Jefferson urged as "the principle of citizen participation," these individuals in voluntary service to others are answering, in their own way, fundamental questions about the meaning and purpose of life and our relationship to our fellow inhabitants of this planet.

They are also exercising their fundamental American freedoms of association, speech, and individual choice as they answer. And because they act independently, they introduce an extraordinary richness and diversity of response to the concerns of our times. I believe that this vast array of nonprofit voluntary action groups supplies a fundamental unifying strength to America. These volunteers weave a tapestry of liberty, conviction, and humanity.

Our citizens of conscience and persuasion have created, out of different perceived realities and visions, the organizations, foundations, and programs that they believe we need to form a better society. The voluntary societies forge the connecting links between diverse philanthropic interests and the human requirements and aspirations they address.

The volunteers make up the frontline troops in the battle against poverty, disease, injustice, and abuse. They nurture, teach, comfort, and assist. They inspire, shame, and challenge us to do more, to do better, and to feel. Their commitment and passion amaze us. They move us to join them on a crusade to that higher hill where hope endures.

For the last eighteen years at the Meadows Foundation, I have listened to their dreams, read their appeals, and seen their work. They have changed my understanding of the realities of the world. I am a different person because of what they have taught me.

All of us can give something to others, no matter how meager our resources. Whether we give our time, our talents, or our money, in helping others we make our beliefs and principles real. When we give without hypocrisy, honoring those we serve and sharing in their struggles, we break down boundaries of distrust and division in our society. That process changes us.

Those supported and enabled find and achieve dignity in the accomplishment. Those serving gain humility and appreciation by experiencing the journey. In that journey, more often than not, the donor becomes the real beneficiary of the partnership.

Mahatma Gandhi once said, "I cannot imagine anything nobler than that for . . . one hour in the day, we should all do the labour that the poor must do, and thus identify ourselves with them and through them with all mankind. I cannot imagine better worship of God than that in His name I should labour for the poor even as they do."[9]

I have been blessed in my work to have seen many examples of this spirit of giving, but the immense need calls for equally immense growth in the spirit of others. Every religion teaches caring for others, yet those who profess religions often neglect to act on the teaching. In many cases, people feel the impulse to become involved, but they cannot find a connection. The nonprofit organization offers the donor or volunteer this essential connection. It identifies a place of service and provides the opportunity to act.

This last Christmas, volunteers on the staff of the Meadows Foundation helped build a home for a family of six. Most of us worked on a

Habitat for Humanity house for the first time and it was fun as well as rewarding. We joined with other community volunteers and inmates from the Hutchins state prison who volunteered their services to participate in the project.

At the dedication of the house, all of us stood together holding hands, singing, praying, and celebrating. The prisoners presented a Bible to the family that now lives in the house; their guards brought a Christmas tree. Other participants brought housewarming gifts, and all of us pointed with pride to the places where we painted or hammered to complete the house. By giving each of us a tangible way to personally help someone else, Habitat provided the opportunity for each of us to express our human and religious values in service to others.

Robert Bellah wrote: "Our problems today are not just political. They are moral and have to do with the meaning of life. . . . We are beginning to understand that our common life requires more than an exclusive concern for material accumulation. Perhaps life is not a race whose goal is being foremost. . . . Perhaps there are practices of life, good in themselves, that are inherently fulfilling. Perhaps enduring commitment to those we love and civic friendship toward our fellow citizens are preferable to restless competition and anxious self-defense."[10]

The theologian Francis Schaeffer poses a question that each of us must ultimately answer: "How then shall we live?"

We learn our morals and values from our families, from our religious institutions, and from our schools. The world in which we live tests and influences these lessons. As we create opportunities to learn from experiencing the joy and purpose of giving to others, we reinforce those lessons of faith and humanity.

We cannot hope to solve the difficult issues of our time without some sense of connection to others outside of our own circle. We must build community and fulfill civic responsibility to sustain a just and fair, as well as a peaceful and orderly, society.

Studies predict that in the next twenty years as much as ten trillion dollars will pass from one generation to the next. Whatever the actual amount, it will be the largest transfer of wealth in history. Imagine what a difference such funds could make if we dedicated them to bettering the conditions endured by humanity.

Our nation needs the nonprofit societies, with all their diversity of choice of service, and we must tell their millions of success stories as often as we can to inspire hope and encourage greater participation.

We must also vigilantly and quickly correct abuses of the system, but we must not let such abuses deter or discourage us when so many have accomplished so much good.

The American spirit in philanthropy constantly evolves through its varied expressions by our citizens. Enabled by freedom, shaped by religious conviction, blended with cultural teachings, molded by historical experience, people of passion and compassion throughout our nation *daily* demonstrate, in millions and millions of individual acts of kindness, enlightenment, and generosity, that "two vital principles abound in this land: the need to do good for one another and the need to love and respect each other."

Martin Luther King articulated the spiritual challenge so many Americans are answering:

Every man must decide whether he will walk in the light of creative altruism or the darkness of destructive selfishness. This is the judgment. Life's most persistent and urgent question is: "What are you doing for others?"[11]

NOTES

1. James A. Joseph, *The Charitable Impulse* (The Foundations Center, 1989).
2. Ibid., 19–20.
3. Ibid., 19.

4. Robert Lee, "The Confucian Spirit," *Foundation News* (May/June 1990).

5. Clara Sue Kidwell, "True Indian Giving," *Foundation News* (May/June 1990).

6. Jennifer Leonard, "A New Age for Mutual Aid," *Foundation News* (May/June 1990).

7. Virginia Ann Hodgkinson and Murray S. Weitzman, *Dimensions of the Independent Sector, A Statistical Profile* (Independent Sector).

8. American Association of Fund-Raising Counsel, *Giving USA* (1999).

9. Mahatma Gandhi, *All Men Are Brothers* (The Continuum Publishing Co., 1995), 121.

10. Robert Bellah, *Habits of the Heart* (New York: Harper & Row, 1985), 295.

11. Coretta Scott King, *The Words of Martin Luther King, Jr.* (Newmarket Press, 1987), 3.

The "Natural History" of Philanthropic Management

STEVEN C. WHEATLEY

M y title pays tribute to the generation which brought the philanthropic foundation into being. Most of the nineteenth century
treated "natural history" as one of the major elements of science,
and the modern general purpose foundation represents the most enduring
product of the movement which called itself "scientific philanthropy." That
phrase conveyed the hope, indeed the expectation, that through the power of
science the new philanthropy would overcome the problems of poverty, illness, and ignorance which traditional charity previously had addressed but
never vanquished. We may now snigger at this hope and reluctantly but, we
think, "realistically" accept the idea that certain problems may not admit of
solutions. Our skepticism marks not only our historical distance from the
ideas of that earlier age, but also our moral distance from its zeal. It is hard to
know if we are the better off for our wisdom.

Webster's dictionary contains several definitions of natural history,
among them the following: "1: a treatise on any aspect of natural history but
esp. on ecology . . . 2: a chronicle of the natural development of something
over a period of time, usu. presenting an assemblage of principal facts and
characteristics . . . 3 a: a former branch of knowledge embracing the study,
description, and classification of natural objects."

Webster's definition of natural history includes ecology, and my analysis of foundation management emphasizes the importance of the ecology of the foundations, both the ecology within the foundations and their role in the political and organizational ecology of modern America. A brief essay like this can only suggest the dynamics in these ecologies, but I hope it spotlights the intersections.

Philanthropic management developed as a distinct role in American society in response to political tension, which has been a principle element of the ecology of foundations. A double bind has constricted foundations throughout their history. Foundations developed because Americans distrusted state power. But, once developed, foundations themselves attracted that same suspicion.

Americans invented the general purpose foundation because they needed it. A deep suspicion of state power has characterized American political culture and political history. At the beginning of the twentieth century, the American state (the sum of federal and state governments) was astonishingly weak in its institutional development and administrative capacities—just the way Americans wanted it. Foundations provided what that weak government could not: the vision and the means to manage the social, educational, and scientific apparatus of an advanced industrial nation.[1]

But the American suspicion of state power springs from a larger suspicion, from distrust and resentment of all power, public as well as private; of social power, economic power, and cultural power. The democratic revolutions of the eighteenth century not only overthrew monarchical government, but also assaulted aristocratic pretension.[2] These antimonarchical and democratic impulses have persisted in American political culture, and give us even today handy critiques of power in any form. Both the political right and the political left have used these critiques to attack and constrain foundations. This tension between programmatic opportunities and political limits, as mediated through the immediate social and institutional ecology surrounding the foundations, has conditioned the evolution of foundation management. The "mature" pattern of philanthropic management reflects not so much the original intention of the philanthropists as the accommodation of the foundation form to that ecology.

I draw evidence for all this generalization from highly specific cases. I use the terms "philanthropy" and "foundations" interchangeably in this essay. I certainly recognize that some philanthropies are not foundations and some foundations are not philanthropies. Further, I primarily speak of the Rockefeller and Carnegie boards, two clusters of foundations established between 1902 and 1914. While undeniably the two most important groups of foundations in the period I am considering (the period before World War II), they are not of course the only ones. While contemporary foundations need not wrestle with the problems of institutional invention that confronted turn-of-the-century philanthropists, many of the issues which emerge from the early history of foundations—issues of trustee selection, the role of donors, institutional networks, and presidential leadership—confront foundation leaders today. Moreover, the developmental pattern of the Rockefeller and Carnegie boards is likely to be repeated as other foundations respond to the same ecology. To use, or perhaps abuse, another scientific metaphor, in philanthropy as in biology, ontogeny recapitulates phylogeny.

We know the entire apparatus of philanthropic management so well today that we must avoid assuming the inevitability of the general phenomenon of a professional foundation staff operating on the basis of policies targeting selected problems. While the legal instruments of each institution's founding clearly mandated the outward form of foundation leadership (a corporation governed by trustees who presumably oversee executive agents), the founders did not anticipate the inner dynamic by which the present managerial arrangements evolved. The need to adjust politically the institutional ecology of twentieth-century America supplied that shaping dynamic.

The creators of these first foundations paid great attention to the problem of selecting trustees and almost none to the question of selecting staff. The original constitution, if you will, of the Carnegie Corporation of New York offers a telling example. The Corporation was the last endowment Andrew Carnegie created, and he clearly intended it to be the most broad-gauged of all his benefactions. His earlier donations all had had more or less specific objects: the Carnegie Foundation for the Advancement of Teaching, the Carnegie Endowment for International Peace, the Carnegie Institute of Washington, the Carnegie Institute of Pittsburgh, the Carnegie Hero Fund. The charter of the new Carnegie Corporation, however, dedicated it to nothing more specific than "the advancement and diffusion of knowledge and understanding." But in designing the management of this grand effort, Carnegie did a curious thing: he committed the management of the general to the representatives of the specific. The presidents of his other endowments, ex officii, made up the board of the new benefaction. While we may argue with this approach and foresee the difficulties ahead (it did, as you might expect, turn out to be a disaster), we must recognize the attraction of this arrangement to Carnegie. As he wrote to John D. Rockefeller, by adhering to this scheme, he would set up a "perpetual executive of men of character & ability," as "all the heads of these Institutions [are] bound to be A1 men."[3] To Carnegie, if you had solved the question of trustees, you had solved the question of executive management.

Similarly, the Rockefellers, in their vain attempt to win a congressional charter for the Rockefeller Foundation, proposed, as a major concession, that various public officials and university presidents would appoint a number of the foundation's trustees. This proposal could not have been inconsequential since Rockefeller and his advisers did not include this or a similar provision in the charter which they eventually obtained from New York state. Compared to the importance attached to the selection of trustees, the role of foundation staff and the foundation presidency ranked as a second-order consideration.

Yet the offer by the Rockefellers to allow outside nominations to their foundation's board illustrates another point, the constant political tension which has surrounded the foundations since their early beginnings. That tension has bubbled up repeatedly in the history of the foundations. The hearings of the Commission on Industrial Relations following the Ludlow massacre in 1913, the McCarthyist Reece Committee investigations of the

1950s, the Tax Reform Act of 1969, and the current congressional initiatives to limit the political role of nonprofits are all just the peaks in a continuous ridge of political tension thrust up by the collision of the philanthropic project with American political culture.[4]

The philanthropic project was a bold effort indeed. The rhetoric which supported the development of the philanthropic foundation attempted to separate the public arena from the political arena. The identity of these two realms formed a basic axiom of the stream of political thought running through American political culture which historians label as "republican." But, beginning in the 1880s, elements of the nation's cultural and educational elite, frustrated with the state's inactivity and incompetence, sought to redefine the distinction between the public and the governmental arenas. Harvard president Charles Eliot made the point that philanthropic trusts, in the American context, served as public agencies, even if privately administered: "The fact that the property of these public trusts is administered by persons who are not immediately chosen or appointed by the public, obscures to some minds the essential principle that the property is really held and used for the public benefit; but the mode of administration does not alter the uses, or make the property any less property held for the public."[5]

An exchange between John D. Rockefeller, Sr., and his lawyer, Starr J. Murphy, repeated this view of the philanthropist's role—as a public force which paralleled the state. In 1917, Murphy, at the behest of Rockefeller, Jr., appealed to the senior philanthropist for a contribution to the "National Aeroplane Defense Fund," which supported training pilots, a function the government had theretofore neglected which became obviously important with U.S. intervention in World War I nigh. At first, Rockefeller testily replied, "We are already paying into the Federal Treasury very large amounts of money each year for taxation to maintain the Government, including the War Fund, and we have in prospect the doubling of these contributions in the early future, and we have a temper shown on the part of legislators to exact much more in the future. . . . does it not seem that we should not be expected to tax ourselves again to do the same work?" But, after a further exchange of letters, Rockefeller became favorable to the proposition. He was, he said, impressed by Murphy's argument that "in view of my peculiar responsibilities, I should continually appear in endeavors to sustain the Government, as well as to bless and provide for the individual members of society." Note the symmetry this conception assumes: Rockefeller the philanthropist with separate and distinct obligations to government and to society.[6]

Abraham Flexner, Secretary of the Rockefeller-funded General Education Board, put it more concisely: "Democracy marks itself off from aristocracy, not only in governing itself through agents of its own choosing; it goes far outside official lines in self-governance. The successful, responsive, progressive democracy is that in which official and non-official agencies are found in close sympathy and interaction."[7]

This rhetorical formula—that a democracy requires institutional pluralism—found wide acceptance at the turn of the century and still does. It underpins the professional ideology of nonprofit institutions, whose representative association is the "Independent Sector." This formula points to a visible historical lineage. Almost every publication which views private philanthropy favorably includes a quote from Tocqueville about the remarkable tendency of Americans to voluntarily associate to accomplish common purposes.

Nonetheless, this notion that we can separate the public realm from the political sets up a fundamental tension with the equally deeply rooted notion that only the political process can secure the public good. If that second notion seems hazy academic theorizing or European statism, rephrase it as "Democracy is the only fair way of doing things," and you will hear the echoes of high school civics and B-movie moralism. Given that assumption, we need make only a small step to think that democracy is constantly at war with arbitrary power. Foundations pose a special case of this political problem as rich, powerful, and remote organizations which no one elected.

These two notions are in tension, but not mutually exclusive. The rhetorical justification of private philanthropy evolved as foundations created a public or publics which accepted their role. Thus their quest for political survival led them to seek a place in the institutional and social landscape where symbiotic relationships could operate to create a sector which, while independent of government, needed foundations. For without such relationships, without a public which would mobilize in their defense, the foundations would be isolated and, therefore, the target of democratic suspicion. The more acute members of the philanthropic sector understood this keenly. Charles Eliot cautioned John D. Rockefeller, Jr., in 1917 that: "[The] Possibilities of the permanent trusts created by your father seem to me to be greater than those of any other of the large trusts created by men of his generation; but they are, and will be, exposed to the criticism of a jealous public which believes, and is likely to believe, that money-power can be used not only to defeat popular impulses or purposes, but to build up institutions which are undemocratic in their tendency, or, to use the modern word, unsocial in their effects."[8]

Almost twenty years later, Abraham Flexner used almost the same words to warn the incoming president of the Rockefeller Foundation, Raymond B. Fosdick, that "A democracy is a jealous type of society. It tends to be envious of large fortunes and of large privately directed enterprises. There are, therefore, limits to what a foundation may wisely attempt."[9]

The first regime of philanthropic leadership, the direct donor-managers, painfully learned these lessons. Originally the donors set up the foundations as fairly closely held corporations with boards containing immediate associates and selected college and university presidents who, in the nature of the case, were likely to be tractable. The donors themselves held the direct management of the foundations in their hands. In the Carnegie case, while independent heads ran the subsidiary foundations, Andrew Carnegie himself headed the Carnegie Corporation of New York, which was the central treasury of the other underendowed benefactions. Under Carnegie's leadership, from 1911 to 1919, the Corporation never could set a steady course. After the outbreak of World War I in 1914, a severe depression brought on by destruction of his dreams of international peace compounded Carnegie's unpredictability. His trusted advisers barely preserved the institutional integrity of the Corporation until a permanent president, psychologist James Angell, was selected in 1920. Angell departed two years later to become president of Yale.

The Rockefeller Foundation found direct donor management equally uninspiring. John D. Rockefeller, Jr., served as first head of the Rockefeller Foundation from the incorporation of the Foundation in 1914 until 1917. His relatively brief tenure was the only formal position he ever held. It discouraged him from any further efforts in direct management. Young Rockefeller seems never to have found his footing on the path from serving as a private to serving as a public actor. Fascinating correspondence between Charles W. Eliot, a Rockefeller Foundation board member, and the oil heir illuminates Jr.'s travail. Eliot repeatedly urged Rockefeller to seek a knowledgeable staff and not simply rely on the advice of a longtime associate who "seems to be only your attorney employed to devise legal ways of accomplishing what he understands to be your wishes." Moreover, he suggested that all Rockefeller, Jr.'s obligations were miring him in an "unwholesome mode of life." "You work hard and long," he wrote, "often without enjoyment in your work, and you experience constant anxiety, not only about the success of your undertakings, but about your family." (Presumably not their finances.) He concluded by suggesting, "It is wholly unnecessary that you continue to be the real manager of these trusts—much less that you should be made by a constitution and by-laws the real responsible manager."[10]

The Rockefeller Foundation did eventually engage a capable secretary Eliot recommended: Jerome D. Greene, formerly secretary of the Harvard Corporation. Yet the Foundation never gave Greene a real job to do and he continually chafed under the restraints of Rockefeller, Jr.'s leadership.

This entire arrangement came to grief in the wake of the Ludlow massacre. The close identification of young Rockefeller with the Rockefeller Foundation's research program in industrial relations became particularly problematic as the labor troubles of the family industries exploded into newspaper headlines. The Foundation could not publicly sustain the distinction between the industrial Rockefeller and the philanthropic Rockefeller. As Rockefeller, Jr., testified to a hostile Commission on Industrial Relations: "Our office staff is a sort of family affair. We talk over all kinds of matters of our common interest. We have not drawn sharp lines between business and philanthropic interests."[11] After the hearings, the trustees reorganized the Rockefeller Foundation. When George Vincent was selected as president, Jerome Greene departed, and Rockefeller, Jr., took leave of daily managerial responsibilities.

Direct management of the philanthropic foundations by the donors failed in part due to personal incapacities, such as young Rockefeller's insecurity and Carnegie's eventual senility. But foundations faced problems larger than flawed personalities. These early philanthropic leaders failed to find, or to define, a public which would accept their role. President William Howard Taft had opposed granting a congressional charter to the Rockefeller Foundation on the ground that such a step would be equal to "the incorporation of John D. Rockefeller."[12] In undertaking to address public policy issues of its own choosing and through its own agency, the Rockefeller family's management of the Rockefeller Foundation inadvertently lent support to that fear. Rockefeller, Jr., could not articulate any justification for the Foundation other than as a systematization of his father's private charitable goals. He answered the question concerning what safeguards might protect the public interest against potential menace from the foundations by suggesting that the government could repeal the charter of the offending foundation. This reply encapsulated his dilemma: How could a public realm exist apart from the political if the only public safeguards came from political action?

When this period of direct management passed, a second regime of philanthropic leadership came to the fore. In this new pattern, the initiative lay not so much with the foundation presidents as with the second tier of managers, generally what we would today call program officers and program directors, whose titles varied in relation to the organizational configuration of the various philanthropic boards. Essentially institutional entrepreneurs, they came to the foundations with their own reputations and their own particular publics and clienteles or with commitments to developing them. Indeed, that was their very method.

These new managers took advantage of the opportunities offered them by the failure of early leadership to design policies geared to working through adjacent organizations. The new managers set out to do so, even creating new organizations when necessary. This approach succeeded originally because it drew power from the great enthusiasms of the early twentieth century: institution-building and networking. Organizational experimentation, the consolidation of professions, the emergence of new fields, and the construction of national systems of influence marked the teens and twenties. Philanthropic resources both fueled and shaped the outcomes of this experimentation. Operating from the large foundations, these new institutional entrepreneurs became the arbiters of the organizational form of their selected fields: Abraham Flexner in medical education, Nicholas Murray Butler in international affairs, F. F. Russell in public health, and Beardsley Ruml in the social sciences.

These entrepreneurs did what the donors had neglected to do: they defined a public relevant to their activities. Not surprisingly, they defined that public in institutional terms. Abraham Flexner described his work this way: "Education broadly conceived necessarily involves organizations, systems, institutions, as well as individuals: hence, if you are going to deal broadly with education, you must have contacts with, knowledge of, and influence over, institutions and systems." He rejected the notion that "foundations dole out money to deserving organizations or institutions without attempting leadership," and felt that foundation philanthropy should place "at the disposal of persons dealing with local problems a broader experience and wider outlook than they usually possess or can acquire."[13]

This entrepreneurial approach to philanthropic management flourished initially. It multiplied linkages to adjacent organizations and thus helped the foundations fit into the emerging institutional ecology of the U.S. Universities, research institutes, hospitals, and social service organizations all came to view foundations as valuable resources, even if these organizations saw the foundations as perhaps insufficiently generous. But this new pattern of management also resulted in two problems. First, as the entrepreneurial activity of program officers became more elaborate, it threatened the organizational integrity of the foundations. Cumulatively, the existence of all these petty empires within larger philanthropic boards resulted in overcommitment to a large number of disparate programs and institutions. Frederick P. Keppel, president of the Carnegie Corporation during the 1920s and '30s, decried the fact the foundations were no longer their own masters, but had become "milk cows" for other institutions around the nation and the world.

Moreover, this "institutionalized leadership" approach to philanthropic management also eventually presented a political problem. As the philanthropic entrepreneurs continued to build, rearrange, and decide about the relative merit of a variety of institutions, their publics began to see their relationships as more predatory than symbiotic. The very institutions which benefited from foundation largesse questioned whether New York foundation officers should umpire their development, picking winners and losers in the competition for prestige and resources. These beneficiary institutions expressed their dissatisfactions in a political vocabulary. Critics denounced "the abuses of philanthropic power by an invisible government of . . . a self-perpetuating body of gentlemen who, by the very force of the established relations, cannot help extending their influence over all important centres of American education."[14]

In a series of reorganizations of policies, personnel, and institutional structures, the Rockefeller and Carnegie boards addressed these intertwined problems of institutional fragmentation and threatened political legitimacy. These reorganizations took place in the late 1920s and early 1930s and resulted in a new regime of philanthropic management which carried with it a new means of defining relevant publics.

The foundations reconceptualized and reconstructed their purposes. The general mission—"the well-being of mankind throughout the world" or some other broad aim stated in their charters—remained the same, but the method changed. Foundations would no longer develop institutions and networks of institutions; they would work through developed institutions. This new policy represented a turn away from the earlier pattern of organization-building and broad institutional support and a turn toward the support of research along selected lines through targeted smaller grants. At a stroke, this method lowered the level of institutional entanglements into which the foundations entered. It also permitted foundations to spread bounty more widely overall, if in smaller amounts to individual recipients. But most importantly, it achieved what Rockefeller Foundation president George Vincent hoped it would do: "give the president a real job." As the presidents of the Rockefeller and Carnegie endowments won control of the foundation mechanism, the modern foundation presidency took shape. The president not only supervised the development and management of philanthropic policies and programs, he did so while continually acknowledging the various publics that legitimately, if quite variably, influenced the development of foundation programs: foundation staff, recipient institutions, political elites, trustees, donors, and the general public. The flexibility of these programs of managed research allowed the foundation to reconstruct its relationships with those various publics as needed.[15]

While this approach successfully met the political and organizational exigencies of the foundation's situation, it provoked criticism. Not surprisingly, the institutional entrepreneurs strongly objected to the notion that small grants would produce large outcomes. Nicholas Murray Butler wrote to Frederick Keppel that most grants for academic research wasted resources since most such scholarship was "merely mechanical rearrangements of the obvious."[16] Abraham Flexner, writing to Raymond Fosdick, made a typically categorical statement: "There is no such thing as 'managed research.' Foundation management, running into such details . . . can mean only one thing: that the Foundation is doing temporary, specific tasks through inferior men, while it should be giving universities funds that would enable them to hunt out and favor the unusual man."[17] But even philanthropic managers who matured under this regime came to doubt it. Alan Gregg, Director of Medical Sciences of the Rockefeller Foundation, and eventually its Vice President, regretfully noted, "We are really in many cases, a University playing hide and seek in other universities' buildings."[18]

But that discretion was precisely the point. This less obtrusive approach to philanthropic management has endured precisely because it has allowed the philanthropic foundations to blend into America's institutional ecology in the most politically unobtrusive manner possible. Hiding occasionally was not such a bad idea. When facing political challenges and controversies, foundations have been able to mobilize a wide variety of defenders who understand their role.

An interesting irony has developed. Foundations began on the assumption that "scientific philanthropy" would differ from charity. It would attack the root causes of problems with bold policy prescriptions. Political realities have obliged foundations to choose more nuanced, less bold approaches, and in so doing they have identified more closely with the general set of charitable and nonprofit institutions. I would just note in passing that this identification may not offer a safe harbor for long. Many observers predict—and I think we see indications they are correct—that the nonprofit sector is losing much of its political legitimacy as it becomes more commercialized, professionalized, and dependent on government funds.

Am I suggesting that in adjusting to the American political culture philanthropic wealth made a disreputable bargain? Not at all. The debate over the relationship of the public and political realms is an important one. Even if the philanthropic project of asserting the disjunction between the two realms did not completely succeed, provoking that debate was both a public and political service. I only wish that the debate continued with equal vigor today. Any inquiry into the ethics of philanthropy must, I feel, address that question of the relation of the public and political realms of our civic life.

NOTES

1. Stephen Skowonek, *Building the New American State: The Expansion of National Administrative Capacities, 1877–1920* (New York: Cambridge University Press, 1982); Barry D. Karl, *The Uneasy State: The United States from 1918 to 1945* (Chicago: University of Chicago Press, 1983).

2. Gordon S. Wood, *The Creation of the American Republic, 1776–1782* (New York: W. W. Norton, 1965).

3. Andrew Carnegie to John D. Rockefeller, Jr., May 7, 1914, Rockefeller Boards Collection, Rockefeller Family Archives, Rockefeller Archive Center, Pocantico Hills, N.Y.

4. U.S. Commission on Industrial Relations, *Final Report,* 64th Cong., 1st sess., S. Doc. 415; House Select Committee to Investigate Foundations and Other Organizations, *Final Report,* 82nd Cong., 2nd sess., H. Rept. 2524. Investigations; William H. Smith and Carolyn P. Ciechi, *Private Foundations before and after the Tax Reform Act of 1969* (Washington, D.C.: American Enterprise Institute, 1974).

5. Charles W. Eliot, "The Exemption from Taxation of Church Property and the Property of Educational and Charitable Institutions," in *Exemption from Taxation* (Boston: privately printed, 1910), 42.

6. Starr J. Murphy to John D. Rockefeller, Sr., August 1, 1916; Rockefeller to Murphy, August 4 and 17, 1917; Papers of John D. Rockefeller, Jr., Box 14, Folder 173.3, Rockefeller Family Archives, Rockefeller Archive Center, Pocantico Hills, N.Y.

7. Abraham Flexner, "Aristocratic and Democratic Education," *The Atlantic Monthly* 108 (1911): 304–5.

8. Charles W. Eliot to John D. Rockefeller, Jr., February 10, 1917, Eliot Papers, 416, Pusey Library, Harvard University.

9. Abraham Flexner to Raymond B. Fosdick, July 17, 1936, Fosdick Papers, Mudd Library, Princeton University.

10. Eliot to Rockefeller, Jr., February 10, 1917.

11. Testimony of John D Rockefeller, Jr., U.S. Commission on Industrial Relations, *Final Report and Testimony,* 64th Cong., 1st sess., S. Doc. 415.

12. Quoted in Raymond B. Fosdick, *The Story of the Rockefeller Foundation* (New York: Harper and Brothers, 1952), 6.

13. Abraham Flexner to Charles Howland, April 12, 1927, Rockefeller Foundation Archives, Record Group 3, Series 900, Box 17, Folder 123, Rockefeller Archive Center; Abraham Flexner to Simon Flexner, January 5, 1928, Simon Flexner Papers (microfilm copy), Rockefeller Archive Center.

14. Hans Zinsser, "The Perils of Magnanimity: A Problem in American Education," *The Atlantic Monthly* 159 (1927): 248.

15. R. M. Pierce to R. B. Fosdick, April 1, 1926, Rockefeller Archives, Record Group 3, Series 900, Box 17, Folder 121, Rockefeller Archive Center.

16. Butler to Keppel, October 18, 1937, Carnegie Corporation Archives, New York, N.Y.

17. Flexner to Fosdick, July 17, 1936.

18. Alan Gregg, memo, "Limitations and Size of Projects," March 5, 1937, Box 9, Alan Gregg Papers, National Library of Medicine.

The Ethics of Philanthropy and Trusteeship

The Carnegie Foundation: A Case Study

WALDEMAR A. NIELSEN

I want to illustrate the ethical possibilities of philanthropy and trusteeship by analyzing a specific and very instructive case, namely, the large and respectable foundation—one of the best in the U.S. today—created by Andrew Carnegie. Very large foundations such as Carnegie's (some two hundred hold assets ranging from $100 million to several billions of dollars) control a large portion of the total assets of all the nearly thirty thousand grant-making foundations in the country. This control makes their influence and visibility disproportionately great.

Because of the scale of their assets, and because of their professional and technical capabilities, they can work in fields of advanced science and on complex problems of national and even international scope. They can influence whole categories of cultural, social, and scientific institutions, and they can influence the policies of governments.

They wield money and, consequently, power. Because of this money and power, once the original donor has departed from the scene, competition (polite or rowdy) for control of that power frequently emerges.

The troubling question then arises: Who, over the longer term, will tend

This essay is an excerpt from Mr. Nielsen's book *The Big Foundations*.

to acquire control over such institutions? Who will keep faith with the donor's vision and intentions after he or she is gone?

In theory, power and control flow from the donor, who sets the general course and character of the institution, to the trustees, who set policies and priorities within that broad guidance, to the chief executive and the professional staff, who formulate and execute programs to accomplish those directives.

In reality, foundations depart from this theoretical pattern so frequently and widely that we should regard it as, if not quite a myth, then at least a great simplification.

To take some obvious examples, such major donors as Henry Ford, Howard Hughes, and John MacArthur left their trustees no real policy or program guidance other than legal boilerplate language. So the donor in such cases made himself virtually a nonfactor from the start. At the other extreme, donors such as Buck Duke, in setting up his Duke Endowment, not only specified its general purpose but also the unalterable list of permitted grantees and the percentage of income it should give to each. In between these extremes, donors have made many shadings, from broad and ambiguous guidance to narrow and precise restrictions.

The powers given the board as "trustees" of the donor after the donor's departure rest on three familiar premises: namely, that they will serve the donor's purposes and intent faithfully; they will act in a disinterested and responsible spirit; and they will bring to bear in their policy-making a broad and informed view of the changing needs and opportunities in the sphere of the foundation's programs.

In this textbook conceptual structure, the trustees decide ultimate policy and the staff and officers, including the president, fulfill this policy as subordinates to them.

So much for the theory. In real cases, not a static hierarchy but dynamic and shifting patterns of influence and control usually direct a foundation. In the very large foundations, if the donor did not impose real guidance from the start, or if donor and family influence greatly dissipates after a generation or two, the board of trustees and the chief executive officer and staff contend with each other for power and control of the institution. The dominance of the one or the other ebbs and flows, with sometimes great and unpredictable effects on the foundation's programs and effectiveness.

Examining one actual and important "best case" offers the most helpful way to gain a sense of the longer-term prospects for the performance of a donor foundation in accordance with the donor's intent.

Andrew Carnegie and the Carnegie Corporation offer a particularly instructive real-life instance. Carnegie, one of the greatest American donors, held an almost unparalleled belief and interest in philanthropy: He had fully developed a philosophy of the charitable responsibilities of the rich, articulated in his famous "Gospel of Wealth" and other writings. Throughout his life he gave generously and by the end he had committed virtually all of his great fortune to philanthropy.

An exceptionally entrepreneurial and experienced donor, he had created a series of outstanding philanthropic institutions during his lifetime, from the Carnegie Institute and the libraries project to his Foundation for the Advancement of Teaching and his Endowment for International Peace. He personally wrote statements of policies and objectives for these creations in prose that offered models of clarity and practicality.

A man of extraordinary breadth of interests in education, science, culture, and international affairs, he also had a remarkably wide acquaintance with outstanding leaders in many fields of American life—from government and business to intellectuals, scholars, and scientists. In the formation of his various philanthropies he brought his own extensive experience in creating and developing new organizations to bear as well as his wide range of acquaintances in nonprofit fields. He assembled as boards of trustees not mere sets of old business cronies but rather groups of distinguished and strong individuals from public life.

His own wealth and prestige enabled him to attract such leaders to his philanthropies, and he trusted them to carry out their responsibilities. He made the classic statement of confidence in the fidelity and capability of foundation trustees: "As in all human institutions, there will be fruitful seasons and slack seasons. But as long as it [the foundation] exists there will come, from time to time, men into its control and management who will have vision and energy and wisdom, and the perpetual foundation will have a new birth of usefulness and service."

Thus this man, his competence and experience as a donor almost unparalleled, should have done as well as a donor could possibly hope in setting up a new major foundation. To his new "Corporation" he bequeathed the huge remainder of his estate at the end of his life.

How in fact did his hopes and plans turn out after his death in 1919?

The story, covering more than seventy years, breaks into some four chapters—the Betrayal; the Slump; the Muddle; and the Renaissance—with the final chapters yet unwritten.

Carnegie named to the board of his Corporation the heads of the five principal philanthropic institutions he had previously created, plus his financial and personal secretaries. Even though advisers told him that the situation of the institutional trustees contained inherent conflicts, since they would both distribute and benefit from the funds, he ignored that advice. (It was not until 1946 that the foundation dropped these ex officio trustees from the board.) He also reserved to himself the right to administer the foundation as long as he lived, which he did from 1911 until 1919. During that period, the board met only once a year merely to ratify decisions he had already made. So despite his protestations of confidence in his trustees, as long as he was alive he behaved egocentrically if not dictatorially.

Almost as soon as he died, these confusions and contradictions produced serious problems. He left a foundation (confusingly called the "Corporation") with almost no qualified staff and with a board dominated by built-in grantees. Within three years they had appropriated nearly $40 million in grants without benefit of long-range planning or serious consideration of the impact of the spending spree on the foundation's future. (Because the charter required that the foundation pay grant commitments only from the foundation's income [then some $6 million a year] and not from capital, this spree restricted its programs for the next fifteen years.) Not surprisingly, the bulk of this money went to institutions represented on the foundation's board.

Was this a betrayal by the board? Did Carnegie provoke it by his own conduct and his questionable choices of eminent but compliant and conflicted trustees? Certainly the trustees made a self-interested grab of money for their own institutions. But since Carnegie himself created these, the trustees did not divert funds to unauthorized purposes. Still, though not unlawful, was it at least greedy?

Soon thereafter, the Corporation's two most influential and ambitious trustees at the time radically redirected the substance, spirit, and general thrust of its programs. Henry Pritchett, head of the Carnegie Foundation for the Advancement of Teaching and former president of the Massachusetts Institute of Technology, and Elihu Root, a prominent attorney, former Secretary of War and of State, and a Nobel Laureate, envisaged the foundation not as a mere dispenser of benefactions but as a private instrument to foster "reforms." Their general approach used the foundation to create powerful nongovernmental agencies of scientists and experts to counter what they regarded as dangerous populist influences threatening "traditional American values" and the power of the established Anglo-Saxon elite.

In carrying out their new grand design for the foundation, they led it to make a series of substantial grants to the National Research Council "to organize Science"; to a National Bureau of Economic Research; and to the American Law Institute. Ostensibly they intended to introduce more "scientific management" into the nation's affairs. Actually, they urgently wished to block what they regarded as the growing threat of immigrants, Negroes, demagogues, laborites, socialists, and others of "inferior heredity, morals, and understanding of business and American-style democracy."

They intended the National Research Council to counter the "pacifistic" tendencies of some scientists, which they felt inhibited the development of new military technology. The National Bureau of Economic Research grew out of mounting industrial tension and violence, and an escalating concern of prominent businessmen to counteract these tendencies by using a private group of "experts."

In the field of economics, Pritchett explicitly planned to develop economic "propaganda" to counter the appeal of "popular agitators." To this end, he at one point even recommended that the Corporation purchase an independent newspaper, the *Washington Post*. (In the end they dropped the idea, not on grounds of impropriety but because Root and others thought it "a bad investment.")

In 1923 the trustees again took the initiative in creating the American Law Institute (ALI). They feared that the intrusion of immigrants and the lower classes into the legal profession constituted a national danger. Trustee Root, in a speech to the New York State Bar Association a few years earlier, had deplored the fact that "50% of the lawyers in this city are either foreign born or are of foreign born parents, and the great mass of them . . . have in their blood necessarily the traditions of the countries from which they came."

In its support for ALI and its other large initiatives in its first years, the Corporation tried to implement an underlying agenda which was not only elitist but racist—not only to help preserve the dominant position of a particular segment of American society but also to preserve its "racial purity." The trustees explicitly worried about "the alien stream flowing into our citizenship," and they made the foundation a leading supporter of eugenics studies at the time, some of which urged policies of selective breeding and forced sterilization of the "unfit."

In these various grants to set up private agencies to influence public policy—forerunners of our contemporary "think tanks"—the original Carnegie trustees not only clearly understood the potential power of private funds to shape public opinion and government policy but they had an obsession to utilize and exploit that power on behalf of the values and interests of their particular social and economic class.

In exploiting that power, they in a sense followed the kind of program Carnegie had in his libraries project and in setting up his Endowment for International Peace, for example. But with a difference: Carnegie had taken initiatives on behalf of such goals as giving opportunities for the average citizen to have access to books for self-development and for the general advancement of science, education, and world peace. He came from a poor family, he himself had immigrated, and he had lifted himself by his own bootstraps. He was descended from old Scottish radicals; he battled against unfair and unequal privilege; and he believed in the unlimited potential of the common man.

He was not saintly and benign in all his business dealings, or clear and consistent in the purposes of his philanthropies. (Indeed, like the other industrialists of his time, he fought the trade unions hard, and in his philanthropy he could give erratically and impulsively—giving pipe organs to churches even though he was not religious, and offering medals for personal acts of heroism.)

Nevertheless, the spirit of his philanthropy was always democratic, hopeful, and constructive. That within five years of his death his Corporation should have turned into a racist and reactionary machine to defend the privileges of the old WASP elite and block the advancement of immigrants and the underprivileged deformed his spirit and intent. And a group of gentlemen of high reputation and the utmost respectability perpetrated this ugly deformation.

What does this say about Carnegie's absolute trust in trustees? Did some fault, some pretentiousness, in the man himself cause him to entrust his great philanthropic creations to a group of individuals whose background and social class biases fundamentally contradicted his own?

These first years after the donor's death form the chapter of Betrayal.

The trustees' outburst of activist and politicized philanthropy lasted until 1923, when the foundation hired a personable young man, Frederick P. Keppel, a certified member of the WASP establishment, as president. He headed the Corporation for the next nineteen years. If the preceding regime had furthered a grandiose and sinister underlying agenda, Keppel chose almost effete goals. After his appointment, the Corporation added seven new trustees and the balance of forces on the board changed significantly. The Corporation then dropped its crusade to save the nation from the newcomers and shifted its emphasis to a program to uplift the cultural level of the general citizenry. Just why Keppel chose this new direction is still difficult to understand. Perhaps the choice sprang from a spirit of resignation: If the great unwashed would be always with us, then the foundation might at least try to wash them. In any case it led to rather peculiar, even quaint actual projects.

The Corporation wanted to attract the multitudes into adult education centers, the art museums, and—in at least one tie to Andrew Carnegie—the libraries. Exposing the ordinary citizenry to classical art and literature, the Corporation believed (and stated), would improve their character, judgment, and tastes—and in addition would promote social stability. In the end and by virtually every measure the effort failed miserably.

Keppel, a warm and likeable person, presided ineffectively and brought a remarkably narrow social outlook to his job as head of a major foundation. The 1920s and 1930s, when he directed the Corporation, brought severe strain and friction to American life and growing international dangers. By the early 1930s a devastating depression had struck, followed by the period of the New Deal, and when he retired World War II was already raging in Europe. Yet his gracefully written annual reports contain hardly a hint of the great issues and problems of the times. In the isolated environment of the Corporation, training for librarians, adult education conferences, and the distribution of art teaching sets continued to preoccupy. During his long tenure, the Corporation indulged in endlessly trivial pursuits.

In Keppel's final years as president, the foundation commissioned what it intended as a study of how cultural projects could address the uplift of Negroes, but by mistake chose a Swedish economist, Gunnar Myrdal, to head it. Myrdal produced a classic and highly controversial report on the general problem of race relations in America, a report that powerfully influenced later progress toward racial integration. However, the report so embarrassed and dismayed the foundation that it did everything but disavow the study it published.

For prospective donors of large foundations, several questions arise: How, in the first twenty-five years after his death, did Carnegie's keystone foundation come to focus on matters that the donor would probably have regarded in the first years as pernicious and in the later years as preposterous? And how did it happen that the Corporation hired a president of inferior capability to head the institution for the next two decades and that the trustees in that long period could not bring themselves to replace him? Where did the trustees keep faith with Carnegie's aims and values? Why did they fail utterly to bring to the foundation's programs and priorities some awareness of the sweeping changes taking place in American society and in the world? This long second chapter of the story we can charitably call the Slump.

After these two initial phases in the foundation's history—the Betrayal and Slump (which some scholars have now euphemistically designated as its periods of "scientific philanthropy" and "cultural philanthropy")—came a thirteen-year period of doldrums, 1942–55, years that brought a crucial time of war and ensuing postwar developments and problems, under three ineffective presidents.

The period of doldrums generated further questions for donors: Does such a span of years provide a reasonable turnaround time for an organization with perfect freedom to change its direction and with only a handful of staff? What about board responsibility to face a foundation's problems and address its own mistakes?

But then, after some thirty-five years, the foundation finally entered a fruitful period—vigorous programs reasonably related to the spirit and concerns of the donor and relevant to the needs of the times.

John Gardner, trained as a psychologist, joined the staff after World War II. By that time the board had ossified and the staff floundered, virtually leaderless. Gardner quickly showed his abilities by designing several promising new program initiatives in research on foreign regions of the world. He thereby became the obvious choice to succeed the ill and incapacitated John Dollard, then president, which he did in 1955.

Almost immediately thereafter the foundation moved forward in a program of "strategic philanthropy" to study and recommend changes in public policies on major national questions, especially education. Carnegie philanthropies had always proposed to use foundation funds to affect the policies and programs of other institutions, especially government. But Gardner mastered the strategy and practice of the technique. He made the goal of "excellence and equality" in American education his mission, and with the help of his able vice president, James Perkins, he pursued that goal simultaneously on a number of fronts. First, he financed a number of important educational research projects and experiments. Then he formed a prestigious commission of both laymen and experts to study the nation's educational problems and to recommend solutions. He timed the publication of their reports carefully to produce maximum impact on policy-makers.

In parallel, Gardner, through his own cogent and elegant essays and books, became important in public advocacy. By 1964, the combined impact of these activities had made Gardner a national force, and in that year President Lyndon Johnson asked him to head a task force on education—the report of which established clearly and finally the responsibility of the federal government in this crucial field. To no one's great surprise, the President called Gardner to Washington the following year to become Secretary of the Department of Health, Education and Welfare. By that point the Carnegie Corporation had finally regained the level of prestige that its founder had enjoyed as a philanthropist a half century earlier.

Another very able man, Alan Pifer, followed Gardner in 1965. Pifer had served under Gardner and quickly took firm control. Pifer ardently advocated social and economic justice and he preached eloquently and incessantly for the federal government to accept its responsibility to help achieve those goals. Unlike Gardner, who simply accepted the rather passive Establishment board he inherited, Pifer took a strong hand in selecting more liberal and more diverse members as resignations and retirements occurred.

Shortly after he took over, the foundation enjoyed a quick triumph by its sponsorship of a Commission on Public Television, which reported its findings in early 1967. Within a month President Johnson recommended passing a Public Broadcasting Act, which the Congress did in November of that same year, bringing into being a public television system supervised by an independent corporation.

As a second major initiative, Pifer created a Carnegie Commission on Higher Education to make a comprehensive study of the future financing problems of colleges and universities, which were then beginning to drown under a huge new influx of students. Ultimately the group, with $12 million of foundation funds, published scores of reports and monographs on every aspect of the problems of the nation's colleges and universities. These significantly influenced the policies of both the government and the schools themselves thereafter.

The foundation also, under Pifer, created the popular educational program *Sesame Street*, and the Children's Television Workshop, which has now become a national, and indeed international, institution.

As the years progressed, and as the nation became more troubled socially and more conservative politically, Pifer became an increasingly ardent and activist proponent of liberal policy positions. In a sense he supported the rights of the poor and disadvantaged in the United States as radically as old Andrew Carnegie attacked the English Establishment and its treatment of the Scots in the nineteenth century. Pifer also focused the grants of the foundation on support for the more promising and influential new advocates for the disadvantaged.

Fortunately for Pifer, the conversion of the board by the late 1970s from a virtually all white, male, Establishment body to a more diverse membership of women, blacks, Hispanics, and Jews protected him as his militantly stated views increasingly diverged from the country's conservative mood under Presidents Nixon and Reagan.

For prospective large donors, the Gardner and Pifer periods raise a number of interesting questions. Both led vigorously and effectively and took the foundation in directions that carried on the spirit and style of old Andrew Carnegie. Their accomplishments would surely have given him much pride and satisfaction. But did Gardner's presidency—given his elegance of style as well as the brilliance of his ideas—simply exemplify trustees passively traveling on a purposeful president's train, as they *had* for years on one going nowhere, namely Keppel's? And did Pifer not, by carefully reshaping the board in a liberal direction in accordance with his views, violate at least the theoretical concept of presidential subservience to the policy authority residing with the board?

Whatever the answers to those questions, the Gardner and Pifer period generated a renaissance in the history of the Carnegie Corporation after several uninspiring decades.

In 1982 Pifer retired. Dr. David Hamburg succeeded him. Hamburg has more quietly pursued policies generally in line with those laid down by Pifer, but focused the Corporation's attention largely on international issues and the problems of children.

So what can the history of the Carnegie Corporation teach those in the coming generation of large donors who determine to set up a general purpose grant-making foundation?

That a foundation's purposes over time will inevitably change and diverge from original intent, and that the donor should realistically understand and accept that fact?

Or that a donor should try to tie down the objectives of his foundation so tightly and specifically that no board or administration can abandon or subvert them, ever?

Or that if the foundation of a donor as wise and experienced as Carnegie can encounter such grave problems for decades at a stretch, then the foundations of donors who are more ordinary mortals face even worse prospects?

Or that time has proven the wisdom of Andrew Carnegie's faith that over the long term, and despite periods of decline, "the perpetual foundation will have a new birth of usefulness and service"?

A Voice from the Metroplex

The following statement is an excerpt from the comments made by Jeverley R. Cook, Vice President, Grants, Communities Foundation of Texas. In his statement, Dr. Cook addresses the changing grantmaking environment which intensifies claims upon foundations to develop standards both as they choose recipients of their funds and as they measure the results of their use. Please note, the views expressed are those of the author and do not necessarily reflect the views of Communities Foundation of Texas.

Boards and Their Priorities

JEVERLEY R. COOK

I n recent years, America's favorite charities—community foundations, museums, congregations, and educational groups—enjoyed an upswing in giving. However, troubles dot the horizon. We are all aware of the government retreat from philanthropic activities and the looming crises in the funding of health, education, and welfare needs. In response to these problems foundations have turned inward to evaluate their grant priorities and charitable missions.

The task of establishing priorities requires that staff and board members devise criteria by which their charitable philanthropic missions can be carried out most effectively. They must establish focus, demark the areas of their program interests, and select the criteria by which they make funding choices among candidates. Making grant decisions according to established priorities requires the existence of certain mission-related values and making consequent and consistent funding decisions based upon them. An ethically centered grant-making program rests upon clearly articulated priorities and sound policies. Trustees and staff of nonprofit philanthropic organizations must balance knowledge, compassion, understanding, and fairness with business insight, common sense, good management, and analytical reserve when developing the policies and priorities that govern their grant-making activities.

In the complex task of reaching priorities and making decisions, foundations must also maintain healthy symbiotic relationships with the recipients of their charity. The health of such relationships will help us address fundamental problems affecting the quality of life and the social welfare of communities throughout the nation. We will do so keenly aware of the seemingly inexhaustible need and the limited resources available to meet it.

THE GRANT-MAKING ENVIRONMENT

Four significant facts affect the development of priorities in today's grant-making environment. First, over the past decade, need has intensified in response to two sometimes directly competing forces: (a) the societal urge to build, to reform crumbling infrastructures, and to enhance the quality of institutional and community life; (b) the compassionate human inclination to improve the welfare of unfortunate individuals.

We live today in a moment of historic generational transition, a time when our nation's comparatively recent wealth busies itself with thoughts of succession and the leaving of lasting footprints. Riding a crest of post–World War II wealth, an entire generation of donors looks to create and endow permanent community institutions. This passing generation's bold plans and consummate generosity will influence the quality of life in our communities for generations. Yet even in the midst of what is claimed to be the largest intergenerational transfer of private wealth in history, and despite a booming national economy, individual need abounds. Individual suffering, poverty, illness, and homelessness emerge as constant subjects in priority discussions among foundation staff and trustees. Issues such as AIDS care, violent-crime prevention, crumbling educational systems, domestic abuse, homelessness, and poverty vie constantly for priority funding consideration, public attention, and societal redress. These needs appear even more alarming because our traditional safeguard systems are weakening. Traditional institutions, social service agencies, and even government itself, the ultimate safety net, no longer guarantee long-term interventions.

The second factor affecting the development of priorities is a redirection of traditional funding patterns related to social service needs. We know this redirection by many names, most commonly by the term "devolution," and most candidly as "passing the buck." In this case, the federal government is literally passing its traditional funding bucks for a safety net back to the states in order to extricate itself from the morass of the modern American welfare state. The impact of this devolution upon local governments, volunteer communities, and private sector funders will be staggering. They will face the choice of paying for ongoing social services or finding alternative ways to provide desired services for a population that is increasingly ill, aged, and destitute. Devolution cannot but have profound impact upon all philanthropic organizations and their funding priorities.

Who will assume the role the government will be abdicating in the course of its downsizing? Purportedly the states will assume a part of the role, but who will carry the burden for local communities? What politicians will advocate increased income taxes or restructured property taxes amid the noisy local debates over smaller government and tax reform? Undoubtedly, the politicians and citizens will look to community volunteerism and private philanthropy to shoulder an increasing burden of funding ongoing programs that address community-based needs such as the funding of educational programs, police departments, fire protection, parks improvements, and emergency response services. Local nonprofit organizations, long the backbone of America's outstanding charitable volunteer communities, will be expected to supply the services required, but without full guarantee of ongoing adequate funding. This devolution could result in problems. The nonprofit research organization Independent Sector estimates that by the year 2002, "charitable organizations will experience a dramatic decline in their capacity to offer services to those in need" as a result of reductions in governmental funding. This future presents a very serious challenge to trustees and staff of recipient and funding organizations who must find ways of addressing growing social needs with limited resources. Their determination of priorities will affect the welfare of millions.

For foundations, the fear and the reality of devolution lead directly to the third factor: increased competition among charitable recipients for available funds. The *Chronicle of Philanthropy* (December 12, 1996) recently identified the emergence of a new trend among grant seekers that involves public institutions—particularly schools, libraries, parks, and hospitals—developing fund-raising foundations and employing professional fund-raisers in order to offset cuts in governmental aid and to take advantage of the present intergenerational transfer of private wealth. Even some state and federal agencies, including the National Forest Service and the National Fish and Wildlife Service, have fund-raising arms. In effect, the pool of potential recipients has increased numerically *and* substantially as large public institutions with enormous ongoing costs approach the private sector for charitable funding relief, as they compete for the first time with thousands of smaller 501(c)(3) tax-exempt organizations. Private sector funders, foundations, corporations, and individuals face an escalating number of proposals from agencies previously funded by taxpayers. This increased competition will test the mettle of trustees and staff who must respond to needs that are unrelenting.

Finally, the government, even as it continues to *reduce* its own traditional funding role, is aggressively *increasing* its regulatory control of charitable organizations. In 1994 the IRS issued regulations pertaining to the deductibility of certain contributions to charitable organizations, effectively placing the burden of tax substantiation upon charitable organizations and drastically reducing the potential for quid pro quo benefits for donors. As a result of legislation passed in 1996, the IRS is now able to apply draconian remedies, called "intermediate sanctions," in proven cases of improper conduct by nonprofit trustees and officers. This regulation will certainly have substantial influence over the future actions of nonprofit trustees and staff in the conduct of their business affairs.

The changing nonprofit environment dictated by increased need, redirected funding patterns, heightened competition, and expanded regulation will place great stress on nonprofit organizations. In order to survive and to meet the challenges ahead, boards will have to refocus their priorities in ways that will move us in the direction of increased cooperation, improved relationships, and better philanthropy in general.

TOWARDS BETTER PHILANTHROPY

Contrary to popular belief, charitable giving and receiving do not create or imply the existence of a pure partnership or a permanent blending of interests between donor and donee. Obviously nonprofit charitable organizations need funders, and funders need charitable groups to receive and to administer their grants. Other than achieving a specific charitable result, however, neither group usually desires a partnership. In fact, most charitable groups and funders rarely seek partnerships in the full meaning of the term. The "myth of partnership" masks a relationship that is rarely one of equality or of matched leverage.[1]

Perhaps we should view the relationship as symbiotic rather than partnered. The relation is a mutual, temporary, purpose-defined interdependence shaped by the ability of both organizations to meet given charitable needs according to their established organizational priorities. At its best, the relationship between donor and recipient organizations reflects a match between independent organizational priorities. Cooperation between mutually independent entities should produce a public good reflecting the missions and the priorities of both organizations. Such a relationship may help avoid the ethical pitfalls in which funders interfere in the operations of grant recipients and recipients feel compelled to tell grantors what they want to hear in order to maximize charitable contributions.

On close examination, trustees and staffs of foundations and nonprofit charities have much in common. Trustees of public charities, both funders and recipients, face similar ethical, legal, and public responsibilities. For example, trustees of community foundations, one of the most dynamic segments of the American foundation community, have special duties to both the general public and to the private individuals who form their donor base. Ethical issues faced by trustees of these organizations include maintaining fidelity to the organizational mission; assuring fiscal integrity and good stewardship over publicly entrusted funds; evaluating community needs; establishing grant policies and priorities; making charitable grants in the spirit of the original donor's intent, and evaluating grant-making for community benefit, balance, and fairness.

Trustees of tax-exempt recipient organizations have similar public responsibilities. They stand responsible for the financial integrity and the good management of the charities they govern. They establish policy and oversee the implementation of mission-related programs by professional staff. These nonprofit trustees provide assurance to the public, including the funding community, of the charity's activities, its financial management, and the relevance of its programs to community needs. Their dutiful supervision of business management and their watchful monitoring of organizational mission give evidence of good management and accountability. To potential funders, a healthy independent voluntary nonprofit board, carefully composed of community representatives to balance talent, influence, wisdom, and clout, signals the viability of any nonprofit organization. Balanced representation of experts, volunteers, community representatives, and clients of the organization's services indicates a nonprofit's stability and potential effectiveness.

SUMMARY

Today many funders have dramatically altered their priorities in giving as they respond to dramatic changes in the funding environment. In meeting their obligations to be trustworthy, foundation boards face intensified needs, changing funding patterns, fierce competition from other institutions and local governmental agencies, and increased public regulation and scrutiny.

Perforce, they are heavily engaged in reviewing their traditional ways of doing business and evaluating the effectiveness of their giving programs.

The retreat of the government from its traditional welfare responsibilities has forced communities to rely more and more upon private philanthropy to determine the ultimate quality of life of their citizens. In the future, the cooperation of foundations with recipient organizations will become the highest priority. We will all have to find new and meaningful ways to cooperate and to enhance healthy symbiotic relationships in response to the significant challenges that lie ahead.

NOTES

1. Michael Josephson, *Ethics in Grantmaking and Grantseeking: Making Philanthropy Better* (Josephson Inst. of Ethics, 1992), 54.

PART III

Voluntary Communities, Churches, and Supply Lines

Congregations and Leaders

Realities about America's Primary Voluntary
Religious Communities

JAMES P. WIND

Once upon a time the place of the local congregation in American community life seemed clear enough. Maps of colonial villages or small antebellum Midwestern towns placed their churches on the green, the commons, or the public square, indicating the churches' central place in the lives of people and communities. Nowadays, our public squares, if we have them, boast huge governmental and business monoliths, corporate and bureaucratic cathedrals, which dwarf all but a few of our religious institutions. Usually congregations have retreated to side streets and subordinate niches in our urban and suburban ecologies, signs that the times, and the roles of these institutions, have changed.

Some fashionable and influential interpreters of American life, especially during the sixties and seventies, read into these changing ecological realities a trend that indicated that more than relocation or loss of place in the modern cityscape was going on. Some, like Peter Berger and others, saw the public role of congregations diminishing. Such analysts, to use an overworked phrase, increasingly saw congregations as institutions of the private sphere, less and less relevant to the larger public realities of our time.[1]

This essay challenges the equation of changing location with loss of public significance. Congregations have been and remain central to the flourishing of American life; they have been and remain leaders in their communities; and they have shaped and continue to shape leaders for all sorts of public roles. They led and shaped leaders in this country from at least the time of the first settlers of New England, New France, and New Spain. They remain pivotal institutions. And they will offer special sources of leadership in the future and help our distinctively American experiment to continue.

Churches, synagogues, mosques, ashrams, and other forms of local religious institutional life which we call congregations[2] weave inextricably through the rich fabric of life which includes the government, business, and not-for-profit sectors of our society. Few of us can trace the connections between pew and boardroom, between vestry meeting and classroom or laboratory, between church choir practice and proposed legislation before a governmental body. But that lack of skill or energy or attention does not mean that the connections are missing. Rather, they are often invisible, or we overlook them when something else attracts our eyes. Yet if we take the time to track the people who migrate among the major sectors of American life, we find that what happens or does not happen in the local congregation shapes all of the organizations we care about and serve, whether arts organization, social service agency, legislature, courtroom, or school.

This point of view entails several corollaries. Congregations and arts groups, social service providers, educators, and the like fundamentally share the huge work of human flourishing. In a time of great change in the institutional infrastructure of our society such as that in which we live, we must increase our skills at nurturing and supporting relationships and partnerships among congregations, arts groups, and social service providers. Further, if we probe deeply enough we will find that congregations have shaped, in fundamental ways, many of our leaders, whether well-knowns like Jimmy Carter, Jesse Jackson, Bill Moyers, Joseph Lieberman, and Mother Teresa or lesser-knowns like many of the readers of this essay. Often they encounter in their home congregations their first lessons about leadership, their earliest exemplars, their first experiments with leading, their first more public successes and failures at mobilizing people to do something. Thus, the serious challenges that beset these important leadership sources demand our fresh energies and renewed attention.

A THOUGHT EXPERIMENT

Rather than continue in this assertive mode, let me appeal to your imagination. Picture your local community (either your current home world or one important to you from another time) without any congregations. What would it look like? Some of our best and worst architecture disappears from the street corners. Great neo-Gothic cathedrals and tacky boilerplate suburban churches leave behind big and little holes. But in countless communities, social and benevolent organizations founded by or primarily supported by these institutions also vanish.[3] Many of our schools, hospitals, nursing homes, orphanages, AIDS clinics, and homeless shelters would go. Many of the social and professional networks that gave rise to our universities, museums, and libraries would go too. So would those that give rise to the new Boy Scout troops, softball leagues, children's choruses, not-for-profit organizations, etc., that continue to come to life in our communities.

Sometimes the legacies of a single congregation defy our imaginations. In graduate student days I discovered a stunning example when preparing a dissertation on the origins of the University of Chicago, one of the great research institutions of the world and at first glance a most unlikely progeny of a congregation. Yet this complex, highly scientific, highly secularized institution of higher learning came to life partly because of conversations between parishioners of Morgan Park Baptist Church, where university founders Thomas Wakefield Goodspeed and William Rainey Harper worshiped and taught Sunday School together.[4]

Continue the thought experiment a bit further. What kind of community life would a now congregation-free habitat nourish? Lacking the First Baptists, the St. Peters and St. Pauls, the Temple Beth Israels, or the Calvary Chapels, what would the community's leadership pool look like? Would families break down more or less often? Would we see more or less child, spouse, or substance abuse? Would small businesses and large corporations act more or less ethically? Minus all the other institutions that congregations spawn and nurture—the choirs, food pantries, counseling ministries, substance abuse programs, day-care centers—how much community would survive at all?

Lest I seem hopelessly Pollyannaish about congregations, I must balance the picture just painted. Those who live in and work with congregations know that they contribute negatives as well as positives to our communities and to our public life. While they can and often do evoke self-sacrifice, moral character, and voluntarism from people, the churches and synagogues of our land can also foster patterns of self-serving and vindictiveness like few other institutions. The same pulpits and altars from which flow words, practices, and rituals about love, forgiveness, and hospitality too often teach lessons of exclusivity, intolerance, and hatred. For better and for worse, these institutions have formed and continue to form our primary stances toward the world, the neighbor, the self, and the Ultimate. Here we develop our convictions, commitments, and many forms of social and spiritual capital for release in the larger environment.

NOT JUST AN AMERICAN PHENOMENON

While this essay focuses largely upon the (North) American experience, we must recognize that congregations make public impacts in other countries also. On January 9, 1997, Mary Kay Magistad filed a report for National Public Radio's *Morning Edition* from Hong Kong. Her story reported that the then imminent transfer of sovereignty from Great Britain to the People's Republic of China raised real questions about the future of religious freedom in the city. Magistad predicted enormous consequences from the loss of that freedom to the overall health of Hong Kong. Then she went on to conduct a Chinese version of the experiment we just conducted. Hong Kong's six million citizens are overwhelmingly not Christian. Yet the more than half a million Christians (roughly 9 percent of the total population) provide "more than 60 percent of the social service agencies all over Hong Kong, about 45 percent of schools and colleges, about 25 percent of hospitals and clinics." To take away the congregations weakens the common good enormously, even in a land that does not claim Christianity as a major heritage.[5]

THE SIZE OF THE CONGREGATIONAL SECTOR OF AMERICAN LIFE

Commonsense thought experiments and news reports from faraway places give some insight into the importance of congregations in the not-for-profit sector. So do more statistically credible evidences. For years the *Yearbook of American and Canadian Churches* has counted the congregations that its reporting denominations tote up. In its 1998 edition the number of American congregations accounted for is 373,985 (25,990 in Canada and 347,995 in the U.S.). That figure, while disputed by some, does not include many congregations that fly below the statisticians' radar screens, the independents, the storefront churches, etc.[6] In 1990 Robert Wuthnow, one of the most respected religion watchers and interpreters of our time, reminded us of the vastness of this group of institutions and of the tremendous resources at their disposal. Based on a more conservative estimate of between 250,000 and 300,000 congregations he estimated one congregation for every one thousand members of our national population. While a few loners may have gone to great lengths to keep their distance, most Americans lived within a few miles of some local church or synagogue. Wuthnow went on to report that between 65 and 71 percent of those Americans told pollsters that they belonged to one of these institutions. Forty-two percent attended on any given Sunday. Fifty-two percent of American households gave some money to congregations, a higher proportion than gave to any other single type of charity (that added up to an astonishing $50 billion given to congregations). An immense labor force served these institutions. Half a million clergy joined with countless other professional and volunteer workers to staff these institutions and carry out their missions. Further, the sector was clearly growing. Wuthnow and his colleagues counted more than $2 billion spent each year on new church construction.[7]

Big and little platoons form this congregational phalanx. The largest denomination in America, the Roman Catholic, currently counts more than twenty-two thousand parishes (remember that those often number their faithful in the thousands of families rather than in the low hundreds of individual members counted by American Protestants). In 1990 Wuthnow reported that these parishes in turn operate more than 7,000 elementary schools, and support at least 239 colleges and universities. The huge structure of Catholic benevolence in America, which includes at least 731 hospitals and the thousands of ministries embraced under the umbrella of Catholic Charities, sits upon this parish foundation. But little denominations, too, such as the Albanian Orthodox Diocese in America, which has two U.S. churches, or the Swedenborgians and the Church of Illumination, which count three churches each, contribute to the public weal and woe. At least two hundred denominational families appear in the *Yearbook*, ranging from Adventists to Wesleyans. But many more with more exotic names such as Vedanta and Wicca do not report. All of them shape people for life in the American experiment.

In, with, and under the religious pluralism that complicates and enriches the congregational part of the not-for-profit sector flow the many ethnic and racial streams. If Protestants, Catholics, and Jews, and now increasingly Muslim and Hindu believers, participate in what Stephen Warner has called our "de facto congregationalism,"[8] so do all the immigrants who have come and continue to come to our country. English Episcopalians, Scottish Presbyterians, German Lutherans, Irish Catholics, Ashkenazic and Sephardic Jews have preceded the Asian and Hispanic newcomers who continue to deepen our pluralism.[9]

This amazingly diverse universe of institutions shapes our common life in an amazingly diverse set of ways. In a separate Independent Sector report published in the same volume with Wuthnow's findings we read that "79 percent of all congregations provide family counseling, 71 percent send relief somewhere abroad directly or indirectly, 56 percent support voluntary care in health institutions such as hospitals and nursing homes, 46 percent claim involvement in some kind of community development effort, 42 percent sponsor activities in culture and the arts, 32 percent list housing or shelter for the homeless among their activities, 31 percent provide day-care services, and 19 percent provide some form of housing or housing assistance for senior citizens." In other words, congregations contribute enormously to the common good, and statistics such as these do not begin to account for the impossible to document "first order" level of care that goes on through personal networks in congregations. When we read that 10.4 million volunteers gave an average of ten hours per month in congregations, we know that such a statistic describes only the countable tip of a much larger volunteer iceberg. In 1986 individuals gave $41.4 billion to congregations, almost half of that for programs and services not specified as "religious."[10]

CHANGING PUBLIC ROLES

Given the size and diversity of the congregational part of the independent or voluntary sector we should expect congregations to take various public stances, and they do. In *Varieties of Religious Presence,* a team of Hartford Seminary professors identified at least four different congregational approaches to the public life of Hartford, Connecticut. Some congregations take *activist* roles in their community, lobbying city hall, marshaling protesters to march, and boldly calling attention to pressing community issues. Others serve the public in *civic* ways, providing space and resources to help citizens prepare for their individual roles in the public arena. Two other public stances arise out of less optimistic readings of the chances to truly transform and improve public life. *Sanctuary* congregations provide a haven from the public world, a place to retreat and rearm for public engagement.

Evangelistic congregations, the fourth type, less optimistic but more aggressive, try to rescue people from the dangerous currents of daily life to change them so that they can pull still others into the lifeboat of a vital congregation.[11]

To complicate matters still further, congregations can perform different public roles at different times in their histories. St. Peter's Catholic Church in San Francisco, for example, provided a very distinct public service in the late nineteenth and early twentieth centuries when it ministered to and organized an Irish enclave in the city's historic Mission District. Under the leadership of powerful priests like Peter Casey and Peter Yorke these parishioners built a "Peterite village," a snug Irish sanctuary for Irish newcomers. Under Father Yorke's leadership, St. Peter's became a full-service parish with elementary and high schools, sodalities, convent, rectory, hall, newspaper, elaborate fundraising apparatus, and grotto. St. Peter's created and bolstered an Irish Catholic world. As its primary public, it concentrated on the Irish community within its parish boundaries. When events down at city hall threatened life within the Mission District, Yorke and his fellow priests acted as religious ward bosses, protecting the interests of their constituency.

St. Peter's, like many other downtown congregations, lost the original world it created to the erosions of modern urban life. The church plant that Yorke built, suffering from the loss of its historic sanctuary to a recent fire, now serves a very different constituency. Beginning in the 1950s and then accelerating in the sixties and seventies, St. Peter's metamorphosed into a congregation of diverse Latino and Asian peoples. As the working-class Irish succeeded and migrated to the suburbs, the needs of non-English-speaking, often undocumented, immigrants changed the public stance of the church. Clergy took on different jobs, as did the parish. For instance, the radical worker-priest Father Jim Hagan contrasted notably to the refined and saintly Yorke. Padre Jaime, as he came to be known, abandoned the traditional clerical collar and made work boots, black jeans, and T-shirts his official garb. A street ministry of fixing cars, washing machines, and other things his parishioners needed but could not afford took priority over maintaining an elaborate parish school system. Hagan helped build *communidades de base* to meet different educational and spiritual needs and on one notable occasion made headlines when he was arrested for leading a ragtag flotilla of rowboats and motorboats to blockade the aircraft carrier USS *Enterprise* at the height of U.S. involvement in the Vietnam War.[12]

Congregational histories such as that of St. Peter's disclose the amazing adaptability and institutional creativity that congregations bring into public life. A recent study of the activity of congregations in south central Los Angeles following the explosive verdict handed down on April 29, 1992, in the Rodney King trial offers a sure sign that such creativity still abounds in the American story. In the wake of the looting, fires, bloodshed, and other acts of violence in and around the Watts community, congregations have innovated in a variety of ways to create what sociologists John B. Orr, Donald E. Miller, Wade Clark Roof, and J. Gordon Melton have called "a new civic infrastructure." In the ashes of the failed efforts of government and philanthropy, local congregations joined hands across lines of race, culture, and class in all sorts of creative coalitions and partnerships. The sociologists found an impressive array of new not-for-profit organizations that came to life to meet the needs of this troubled community. They counted at least twenty interfaith coalitions, such as the Greater Hollywood Health Partnership and the Asian Pacific Law Center, which formed to pray together, to work with gangs, drug addicts, and inmates, and to address deep issues of racism, recidivism, unemployment, and access to health care.[13]

HOW DO THEY DO THIS?

At its deepest level, the stirring and moving of the human spirit to work for the common good presents a mystery beyond our ability to fathom. We do know that this mysterious kind of motion at deep spiritual, psychological, and interpersonal levels occurs in congregations. Through practices, habits, attitudes, rituals, and inculcated values churches and synagogues fill and then tap into deep imaginative reservoirs which directly and indirectly shape commitments. So in the Sunday after Sunday or Saturday after Saturday preaching, ritual, prayer, and sacramental life, a host of powerful metaphors, principles, and mandates come into play that push people to love their neighbor and care for the world. In practices as simple as passing an offering plate people learn about giving and voluntarily choosing to support worthy causes. Even rites of passage which seem focused on individuals can have enormous public significance. William May captures the essence of this public orientation when he describes the Christian rite of Holy Baptism. "The folksy sentiment with which we surround the sacrament obscures its daring as a public rite. . . . The sacrament asks the parents, in presenting their child, to give up their obsessive private hold on their child."[14] Sunday schools teach decorum and respect as well as lessons of religious truth. Congregational meetings hone skills in political process at the same time as they accomplish congregational work and define congregational stances.

Perhaps we can best see how congregations contribute to public life by picking a local church, entering deeply into its world, and looking for the connections. Samuel G. Freedman has done that for us in his moving book *Upon This Rock: The Miracles of a Black Church*.[15] Freedman, both a professor of journalism at Columbia University and an award-winning reporter who has published in the *New York Times* and *Rolling Stone*, takes his readers into the world of St. Paul's Community Baptist Church. This city church thrives in one of the least promising sections of Brooklyn, New York. This African American congregation includes thousands of members, not the small numbers much more typical of Protestant America. As I retrace Freedman's journey into this congregation, the power of this kind of institution, the way its leaders work and are fashioned, and the variety of ways that congregations contribute to the public sector will come into view.

Freedman begins his story in a familiar enough place, listening in on a Christmas Eve sermon in 1990. For almost two millennia preaching has been central to leadership and molding congregational commitments and identity in the Christian church. In Freedman's story the sermons offered in this congregation will draw our attention again and again. The primary preacher, the Rev. Johnny Ray Youngblood, at the time of Freedman's study a forty-one-year-old pastor, during his fifteen years of ministry at St. Paul's brought the sixty-two-year-old congregation from a low of eighty-four members to its current membership of more than five thousand. The congregation's $4 million annual operating budget and its staff of fifty-one can easily obscure the situation which Youngblood faced when he first arrived. Three weeks into his new ministry there, the young pastor had a showdown with his board of elders over money. Seven months later the congregation had adopted a tithing system and had raised $30,000, twice what it had taken in the year before.

This very successful congregation sits in a landscape of tenements, housing projects, vacant lots, and locked and barred bungalows. The parish's neighborhood in East Brooklyn has the unwelcome distinction of having the greatest concentration of violence in all New York City. A chain-link fence topped by razor wire surrounds St. Paul's parking lot to protect its members. The congregation has engaged in a running battle for "Christ Square," the little business district right around the church. Over the years St. Paul's bought several pieces of property to gain control of the neighborhood, then worked to get the police to patrol more regularly, and finally paid for extra security to augment the inadequate police protection. One Palm Sunday Youngblood led fifteen hundred members in a march around Christ Square to reclaim it from the hookers, pimps, dealers, and muggers who had invaded and occupied it.

They call St. Paul's the "Church Unusual." Indeed. This black congregation includes one white member, Tom Approbato, a Roman Catholic who once studied for the priesthood. One Sunday the congregation allowed him to preach a trial sermon to test his fitness for ministry among black Baptists. His sermon recounted fifteen years of personal searching as a stockbroker, divorced man, and father of a son who attempted suicide. Approbato joined St. Paul's when he dated one of its members. The relationship failed and yet he stayed, as "the white minority" of the church. Talk about mystery.

St. Paul's congregation confronts the crisis of black males with a "theological affirmation action" program: its all-male board of elders and its all-male ministry program called Eldad-Medad, which combines Bible study, group therapy, and lodge camaraderie, seek to provide safe places for males in a community where church members are killed, just around the corner, in arguments over parking places.

St. Paul's leads the coalition of East Brooklyn Congregations, an organization of fifty-two churches and one synagogue that has built more than two thousand low-cost single-family homes that cost as little as $39,000—in NYC!—in the now famous Nehemiah Project. The coalition plans to build three thousand more and expects to have to buck city hall every step of the way. Youngblood shapes the congregation's aggressive public stance by calling his parishioners to battle the "principalities and powers" for decent lunches in school, police protection, and economic opportunity. At times this means that St. Paul's has sponsored confrontational public meetings with the police. On several occasions the congregation's leaders went head-to-head with Mayor Koch over real estate politics.

St. Paul's community regularly brings the Scriptures into direct contact with people's lives. In a powerful sermon Youngblood linked the great biblical narrative about the Virgin Birth to the painful situation of two young unwed mothers. At the high point of his sermon the pastor called the two embarrassed young women down to the front of the church and then began to weave a new supportive community of care around them. Instead of exiling them as many members wished and as many congregations in other times and places have done, Youngblood forged a public commitment to support them.

The "Church Unusual" also fosters retrieval of African connections, sending members to Ghana to recover pre-slave origins, supporting a school there, using African garb in its worship. Freedman heard echoes of tribal patterns and processions in the church's liturgical practice. By stressing ancestors—in the local church community (grandparents, aunts, and uncles), but also American heroes such as Marcus Garvey and Martin Luther King, Jr., and those back in Africa—St. Paul's builds strong identities for people who often hear messages calling them nobodies. The preaching here—and the pastoral care and social outreach—gives people the resources to find a story, a plot, for their lives. Youngblood says bluntly that such an identity sets people "on a collision course with society as we know it."[16]

As one of its primary tasks, this congregation encourages congregants to make a rich exploration of their lives. Rev. Youngblood exemplifies this exploration, talking about his New Orleans roots, his spiritualist mentor Mother Jordan, and his experience in a Catholic grade school. As a "system outside the system," St. Paul's offers a safe place where the pastor first preaches publicly about his abandoned son, Jernell, and then brings that son to New York for a public moment—in worship—of reconciliation. Following Youngblood's lead, St. Paul's has become a middle ground for healing the relations between fathers and sons. And so it brings members' lives into view and into healing. People with cocaine in their pasts, prison records at Sing Sing, or guilt over failures which ended up in other people's deaths now share their stories of breakdown and healing publicly with the congregation—in public worship but also in many of the support ministries of the congregation.

St. Paul's also celebrates its people's accomplishments, empowering them to work harder, set higher goals, become leaders. The congregation recognizes each child's success on a report card or entrance into college on Sunday morning—with cheers and standing ovations. To open horizons and lift expectations the congregation sends high school kids on tours of colleges and then provides scholarships to help them reach their new goals. Its York Fellows in Excellence program provides help with SATs, tutoring, etc.

In countless ways the congregation restores its members and people in the community to wholeness. Sometimes this restoration comes through innovative efforts such as the congregation's Wounded Healers program for drug and alcohol abusers—created and led by Robert Sharper, a former drug addict. In transformations such as these, Youngblood points to "a resurrection going on." At other times a combination of pastoral care and congregational support can help an individual survive a tragedy. Freedman tells a powerful account of how first Youngblood and then a whole congregation accompanied Annie Nesbitt through her ordeal of having watched her husband bleed to death from a gunshot in front of her apartment. They came to her in the time of shock and grief. Then they spent more than a year seeking justice through the dilatory criminal justice system: the congregation sent 446 letters to the judge on Nesbitt's behalf. In addition, St. Paul's operates a retreat center, day camp, adult evening school, drama troupe, church dance company, numerous choirs—all places in which people can put their lives back together.

In, with, and under all of these amazing actions the congregation deals with America's greatest public problem—racism. Here people come to terms with the larger historic background of slavery, reconstruction, the great migration northward, the loss of black self-confidence in the early twentieth century, and its powerful reassertion after Rosa Parks refused to give up her bus seat in 1955. Currents of black theology and elements of Saul Alinsky's community organizing strategy mix to shape the congregation's public commitments.

Even in the congregation's moments of deepest ethical confusion and pain, it forges public commitments. Perhaps the most painful account in Freedman's narrative recounts the filing of a sexual abuse charge against one of the church elders, Carter Naulls. Freedman describes a process of reconciliation between an outraged parent and the accused elder after a church board listens to the charges and returns a not guilty finding. Never have I read an account of the Lord's Supper as moving and as troubling as Freedman's account of the sacrament at the end of the meeting between that mother and that elder. This work at the most morally ambiguous and painful crisis points in human relationship has enormous public significance. The congregation's ongoing programs of marital and other types of counseling heal people and relationships so that life may go on.

Freedman, although not a professional anthropologist, tells a story that comes from his fifteen months of participant-observation experience in the congregation's life. It reveals that Rev. Youngblood and his congregation are building a local culture quite distinct from that of the larger American environment. Youngblood spoke of it as the work of building a caring village of his people. The worship services with their blend of African vestments, Gospel music, emotional heat, real-life drama, and the Christian Gospel fuel that local culture-building process. So do the ecologies of care, the educational programs, the civic activism, and the personal relationships. All of these culture-building strategies have consequences in the larger public ecology of New York. Workplaces, schools, street corners, police departments, court systems, construction industries, city hall, and a wider circle of institutions around the world all feel the shaping influence of the leaders and members of St. Paul's Community Baptist Church.

CHALLENGES FACING CONGREGATIONS AND THEIR LEADERS

Not every congregation has a story as exciting to tell as the "Church Unusual." Many, smaller, have much lower profiles in their community. A sizable but unknown number of congregations face possible extinction as their members and financial resources dwindle. Yet, many more congregations serve as powerful public benefactors, like St. Paul's, than we usually acknowledge. And a still larger cohort of congregations makes less dramatic but very important contributions to our public life.

Whether high-profile and successful or unnoticed and struggling, all congregations in America face a set of changing realities which, if ignored or unmet, will threaten their existence and diminish their impact. All of these institutions combine a strange mix of strengths and fragilities. Denominational leaders tell countless stories about congregations that should die, given economic, leadership, and demographic realities, but refuse to. They tell painful stories about congregations that seemed to have everything going for them, that suddenly stumbled into paralysis or terminal illness in the face of a tragedy, a leadership failure, a dramatic change in the environment, or a destructive conflict. While the specter of the congregation-less city—or landscape—does not immediately threaten us, we must marshal great creativity and new resources to give these existing institutions—and the new ones coming to life every day—a chance at an ongoing place in our public life.

Among the challenges reshaping congregational life are:

1. The explosion of new knowledge and technical power. Computers, media, universities, think tanks, and many other sources create new knowledge at an incredibly fast rate. Some of that new knowledge, for example, many of the genetic breakthroughs in medicine, poses direct challenges to religious traditions. Other forms, such as the expertise of the Honda mechanic or the wizardry of the software consultant, leave people with paradoxical senses of new power and new dependence at every encounter with a new technology. Our understandings of the world's origins, our amazing powers to intervene in the natural order derived from these new technologies, manifest themselves in the personal decisions of congregation members.

2. Ecological destruction. Increasingly the viability of our planet is becoming a central concern in congregations. Congregations respond by shunning Styrofoam cups at coffee hours and teaching responsible consumerism. They also minister to victims of ecological crises and try to foster lives that care for the creation. Such ministries will increasingly form the central concerns of congregations. Sometimes, as we see in certain rural areas, technically influenced decisions about agribusiness and mining practices form life-and-death problems for local congregations.

3. The mixing of peoples. America's experiment with pluralism and multiculturalism is intensifying. Each congregation is finding newcomers at the door from very different cultural worlds. Sometimes one ethnic group simply replaces another. But mobility patterns, the media, and the unending wave of immigrants to this continent also produce intermarriage, denominational switching, church shopping, and other fluid patterns. Increasingly congregations must constantly fashion their identities anew rather than assume them or take them for granted. As a result, these congregations endure a kind of endemic uncertainty about "who we are" and "what we stand for."

4. Restructuring. Currently congregations must engage in intense institutional reconfiguration. We are downsizing government, reengineering

corporations, and transforming education by distance learning and other new technologies. Each of these massive waves of change causes personal consequences in congregations. Congregants lose jobs and move to find new ones. The very nature of work is changing for many, if not all, Americans. Members come and go from congregations more rapidly than before. Their economic lives feel more precarious. The old patterns and practices of congregational life must do their work of shaping public commitments in less time.

Within the religious world restructuring occurs in several ways. The denomination, once the principle method of organizing religion in America, is becoming less of a factor in local congregational and personal religious life. Increasingly congregation members do not share a similar denominational history. The gap between the agendas of national headquarters and local concerns widens. Congregations pick and choose among a growing set of entrepreneurial resource and service providers.

Further, society is redrawing old lines between societal sectors. Where people once assumed a high wall of separation of church from state, they see, increasingly, a thin, blurred line. Amazing partnerships stretch across sector lines. Public-private partnerships of all sorts are coming to life. People from religious communities which once had little in common come together around common causes, sometimes to wage culture wars over divisive issues such as abortion, other times to build houses for the poor.

5. Thinking electronically. Most American religious communities are peoples of the Book. They cherish a set of sacred Scriptures as a central religious treasure; their central practices revolve around reading, interpreting, and applying texts. Suddenly, the print-oriented world of congregations has met the new electronic world of TV and Internet. This collision of old and new ways of thinking roils congregational attempts to educate children most vigorously. Martin Luther's *Small Catechism* has to come to terms with MTV. These powerful new media bring different values into the living rooms and Sunday school classes of congregation members. Traditional understandings of sexuality collide with powerful images from films and advertising. Congregations find themselves in the center of a huge technology-driven

debate about how to define a beautiful, good, successful person—often with
very few resources in comparison to Disney or Calvin Klein.

6. A changing leadership ecology. Congregations follow time-tested and
timeworn traditions of leadership. They bring those traditions into a time of
great leadership flux in the world. Everywhere we turn, old patterns of leadership are being challenged and reformed. Often, as in the dramatic Velvet
Revolution that brought Communism to its knees, people topple them. The
feminist movement, the results of greater access to higher education, and the
ongoing spirit of democracy have combined to challenge "great men" models
of leadership. Increasingly, congregations demote clergy from their pedestals
as experts on everything, including their supposed specialty, religious topics.
Lay and clergy alike are trying to make sense of powerful changes which have
affirmed the "priesthood of all believers" and encouraged people to see themselves as partners in ministry rather than as supporters of religious specialists
who did the "real ministry."

7. The triumph of the dollar. In an era which elects a president on the
platform of "It's the economy, stupid," this triumph appears obvious. But it is
very challenging for congregations in several ways. As people respond to the
commodification of life which appraises everything—including one's self—in
terms of cash value, as they take responsibility for their personal destinies
through various personal retirement investing plans, as they watch the stock
market climb to dizzying heights, and as they watch the world's economic
systems genuflect before American capitalism, congregations face huge challenges at helping people find an alternative sense of worth and purpose.
Moreover, congregations must accept huge justice and compassion responsibilities as they try to call overextended people to care for the growing numbers of the poor on the other side of the ever widening chasm between the
rich and the poor.

Institutionally, congregations face a growing list of economic challenges
as well. Many find themselves slipping off the threshold of economic survival.
Others don't know how to invest and make use of the windfall bequests that
make them "endowed parishes." Few know how to apply for and administer

grants, and all too many are shocked to discover that their funds have been misappropriated or frittered away. Raising and using money for church purposes in a consumerist culture poses problems about integrity for religious leaders and religious communities.

8. Confusion about our treasure. Given the kinds of challenges just described—and there are indeed others—it should come as no surprise to learn that congregations suffer increasing confusion in trying to identify their treasure. This confusion, which lies at the source of the streams of wisdom, morality, and commitment that have fed the public commitments of congregations and their leaders for centuries, means that most congregations face the daunting challenge of reconstructing their interior lives at the same time that they face the external challenges posed by a rapidly changing world. In this era of spiritual searching, even the Barnes & Noble bookstores find that their spirituality shelves do a very brisk business. Clergy and lay leaders know that there is widespread theological illiteracy in the land and in their pews. Most preachers do not assume anymore that if they refer to Elijah or Moses or Sarah or Ruth in a sermon that a majority of listeners will recognize that person. The suburban Lutheran congregation, whose members come from Mormon, Episcopalian, Jewish, Roman Catholic, Evangelical, and None of the Above backgrounds, treads water in a conflict of interpretations and traditions. The Sacred Scriptures and the central liturgical traditions of most mainline religious communities have had so many experts question so many dimensions of these sacred texts and traditions that certainty is difficult to achieve.

WHAT CAN WE EXPECT?

History suggests, and I think it is one of the best guides available to us, that we face mixed prospects. Some congregations will not rise to the challenges they face. They will lose their public voice and role; they may wither and die. That has always happened in religious traditions. But we have abundant evidence, both in the rich histories of the faith traditions and in our present circumstances, that congregations will rise to these challenges, as St. Paul's has done, and lead in new and powerful ways. America has generated a wealth of examples of congregational inventiveness and experimentation. As the American experiment unfolded, some congregations powerfully influenced and shaped the national response to major issues such as slavery and racism, to poverty, homelessness, and hunger, to each set of new challenges that arose. This history teaches us that congregations provide indispensable sources of public leadership and service—and that we must care for these institutions so that they can continue to nourish and heal our communal lives.

NOTES

1. Peter L. Berger, *The Noise of the Solemn Assemblies* (Garden City, N.Y.: Doubleday, 1961) and Gibson Winter, *The Suburban Captivity of the Churches* (Garden City, N.Y.: Doubleday, 1961) are two of the best-known examples of this literature.

2. I have defined congregation as "people who regularly gather to worship at a particular place" first in James P. Wind, *Places of Worship: Exploring Their History* (Nashville: American Association for State and Local History, 1990), xvii, and James P. Wind and James W. Lewis, editors, *American Congregations: Volume One: Portraits of Twelve Religious Communities* (Chicago: The University of Chicago Press, 1994), 1.

3. Partners for Sacred Places, a Philadelphia-based not-for-profit organization dedicated to saving historic church buildings, has recently published a study of the unrecognized contributions that churches and synagogues make to their communities through their buildings. After studying historic congregations in Chicago, Indianapolis, Mobile, New York, Philadelphia, and San Francisco, the investigators concluded that on average each congregation contributes a subsidy of between $100,000 and $140,000 of donated space for various community service programs (average per con-

gregation is four distinct programs) per year. See Diane Cohen and A. Robert Jaeger, *Sacred Places at Risk: New Evidence on How Endangered Older Churches and Synagogues Serve Communities* (Philadelphia: Partners for Sacred Places, 1998).

4. See James P. Wind, *The Bible and the University: The Messianic Vision of William Rainey Harper* (Atlanta: Scholars Press, 1987) for a description of the shaping of the founding vision for the University of Chicago.

5. Mary Kay Magistad, "Hong Kong Christians Wary," *Morning Edition* (Washington, D.C.: National Public Radio, January 9, 1997), 5–8.

6. Eileen W. Lindner, editor, *Yearbook of American and Canadian Churches 1998* (Nashville: Abingdon Press, 1998), 298–317.

7. Robert Wuthnow, "Religion and the Voluntary Spirit in the United States: Mapping the Terrain," in *Faith and Philanthropy in America*, Robert Wuthnow, Virginia A. Hodgkinson and Associates (San Francisco: Jossey-Bass, 1990), 4–5.

8. Stephen Warner, "The Place of the Congregation in the Contemporary American Religious Configuration," in Wind and Lewis, *American Congregations: Volume 2: New Perspectives in the Study of Congregations* (Chicago: University of Chicago Press, 1994), 54–99.

9. For a fascinating introduction to the new immigrant congregations rising up in America see Stephen R. Warner and Judith G. Wittner, editors, *Gatherings in Diaspora: Religious Communities and the New Immigration* (Philadelphia: Temple University Press, 1998).

10. Virginia A. Hodgkinson, Murray S. Weitzman, and Arthur D. Kirsch, "From Commitment to Action: How Religious Involvement Affects Giving and Volunteering," in *Faith and Philanthropy*, 96–97.

11. David A. Roozen, William McKinney, and Jackson W. Carroll, *Varieties of Religious Presence: Mission in Public Life* (New York: Pilgrim Press, 1984).

12. St. Peter's story is beautifully told in Jeffrey M. Burns, "¿Qué es esto? The Transformation of St. Peter's Parish, San Francisco, 1913–1990," in *American Congregations: Volume 1*, 396–463.

13. John B. Orr, Donald E. Miller, Wade Clark Roof, and J. Gordon Melton, *Politics of the Spirit: Religion and Multiethnicity in Los Angeles* (Los Angeles: Center for Religion and Civic Culture, University of Southern California, 1994).

14. William F. May, "Images That Shape the Public Obligations of the Minister," in James P. Wind, Russell Burck, Paul F. Camenisch, and Dennis P. McCann, editors, *Clergy Ethics in a Changing Society: Mapping The Terrain* (Louisville: Westminster/John Knox Press, 1991), 61.

15. Samuel G. Freedman, *Upon This Rock: The Miracles of a Black Church* (New York: Harper Collins, 1993).

16. Ibid., 37.

What Time, Money, and a "Calling" Produced

A Comment on Women, Volunteering, and
the Process of Social Reform

SUSAN M. YOHN

very year the *New York Times* runs its "Neediest Cases" campaign.
For weeks (and the period seems to grow longer each year, shading
from the winter holidays into the summer "Fresh Air Fund") the
Times tells its readers stories of personal hardship and redemption and
encourages and moves them to send their donations. The *Times* informs them
that it will pass these donations on to six local organizations providing social
services and cash assistance to the poor and those in need. The paper also tells
readers that this *Times* tradition began at the turn of the century. The editors
intend to put the reader (presumably affluent, comfortable, and secure) "in
touch" with the poor and the disadvantaged, to make palpable their hardships. They encourage us to "reach out" by digging deeper into our pockets
and contributing to a potpourri of secular and religious social service agencies.
Certainly these stories move us, but they also daily remind us of the structure
of the system of social welfare that has emerged in this country in the twentieth century, a patchwork of services provided by public and private agencies
(religious and secular) and supported by our mandatory taxes and voluntary
donations.[1] Rooted in a larger national history of charitable appeals and voluntarism going back to the beginnings of this country, the "Neediest Cases"
appeal exemplifies how our system of charity has evolved over the years.

Seemingly the general public (which associates "welfare," for example, primarily with AFDC, food stamps, and housing vouchers) does not know what those who work in the area of social services know well—that public and private agencies work in partnership. Cutbacks in public expenditures shift the burden to private agencies. Even as Americans continue to increase their charitable contributions, leaders of the private social service agencies have been quite clear in saying that these larger donations cannot substitute for lost public monies. Yet public officials have persisted in their cutbacks. As debate about welfare reform ensued, Bill Clinton reportedly said that churches could reduce welfare rolls substantially if only each church in America would hire an adult currently on welfare.[2] Those who support dismantling the welfare state argue that the state should return social services to private agencies (supposing that government agencies have somehow "taken them away"). These demolition experts advocate harnessing a vast untapped pool of voluntary resources to deliver services more efficiently and effectively. In this spirit, Colin Powell and Bill Clinton called their much ballyhooed "President's Summit for America's Future," a three-day meeting held in Philadelphia in April of 1997, intended to inspire greater voluntary effort on the part of the American public. Sidestepping criticism of the event as "hoopla and propaganda," Powell reportedly said, "This is not the time to say, Are you substituting for Government? This is a time for each and every one of us to look into our own heart, to look into our own community, find someone who is in need, find someone who is wanting."[3]

Can more people giving more of their time and money address contemporary social problems? Can we solve them simply by having social service organizations manage their resources more carefully and efficiently, or individuals recommit themselves morally and spiritually to do good for our communities? Or can we make the poor, or the "needy," take more responsibility for managing their lives? The current debate disheartens many historians of the welfare state.[4] Comments like those of President Clinton and Colin Powell mentioned above imply that we can correct such problems by a return to old-fashioned voluntarism. However, the constellation of social forces which gave rise to our current system of social welfare during what historians have termed the "age of reform" at the turn of the nineteenth and twentieth centuries no longer prevails. To pretend that it does, or that we can reconstitute it, is not only simpleminded and frankly unethical, but also distorts the history of the current system.

Our current system of social welfare grew out of a half century of activism by female reformers on behalf of the American working class, whose material conditions worsened with the rise of the industrial economy in the nineteenth century.[5] One example of female reform activities—and one which suggests answers to the questions posed above—is the Protestant women's mission movement. This movement skillfully and brilliantly brought together women's voluntary labor and money with the goal of transforming the United States (and, they hoped, the world). We live with the fruits of their labors, and today we are reevaluating the system they helped to construct. To do so responsibly, however, we must know both the strengths and weaknesses of the voluntary community which helped to build this system, and to understand why female reformers felt "called" to this work. What did they envision as their goals? What would come of their work? And why, over the long term, did they press for expanded government involvement in issues of social welfare?

With the mandate that they "go everywhere and do everything" the Protestant women's mission movement that emerged in the late nineteenth century touched the lives of millions. This movement attracted and enlisted some 3 million followers at its peak in 1915—the majority white and middle class.[6] By my calculation this reform movement included about 8 percent of American women (or almost one in ten). Contrast this total to the woman's suffrage movement, which claimed 1 million members in 1920, and the General Federation of Women's Clubs, which counted roughly 1 million by World War I. The women's mission movement formed a truly interdenominational movement.[7] To cite just one example, in 1924 (before being gobbled up in a contentious takeover by the male-dominated Board of Home Missions) the Presbyterian Woman's Board of Home Missions counted

421,656 members in its women's missionary societies and young people's organizations. It employed 451 missionaries, and helped send them to Alaska, the Asians on the Pacific Coast, the Spanish-speaking in the Southwest, American Indians, the Mormons of Utah, poor whites in the Southern mountains, Southern and Eastern European immigrants in the cities, as well as stations in Puerto Rico, Cuba, and the Dominican Republic. It budgeted $1,120,000 for the 1923–24 year with which it administered twenty-four boarding schools and twenty-one day schools, serving four thousand pupils, twenty-eight community stations from which workers made eighteen thousand visits to private homes, as well as eight medical centers which treated forty-nine thousand patients. The women who worked in New Mexico, the approximately 230 women assigned to work among Hispanic Catholics between 1870 and 1924, formed only one part of a much broader movement.[8] By 1920, Protestant women had built a veritable social service empire.

The Presbyterian Woman's Board of Home Missions, like the other Protestant women's organizations, began in the 1870's as a response to the desire by women to expand their role in the mission enterprise. These organizations ended up serving a dual purpose. They strengthened the position of women in the Church, broadening the range of responsibilities open to women.[9] Even more importantly they gave women a vehicle by which to enter the debate about national identity. They could join with their male counterparts to fight the variety of "isms" thought to be eating away at the soul of the nation.[10] Though these women refrained from partisan political activity, they formed a quintessentially political movement. Women took as their "charge" proselytizing among those they thought "foreign" or "exceptional" populations, believing that these people could not become "good" citizens without first undergoing a religious conversion. Initially they believed, and they would come (to their credit) to realize the naïveté of this idea, that conversion could also cure the pervasive poverty that afflicted so many. Poverty, they contended early on, resulted from immorality, or misguided religious beliefs and commitments. At the outset of the enterprise, these women preferred not to see poverty as the result of industrial capitalism and an economic expansion which rewarded the rich with fabulous wealth, insured the comfort of the middle class, and left those at the bottom of the social ladder working longer hours for less pay. Their original purpose: To recruit single or widowed women as missionaries, to open schools (because schools proved a more effective tool of evangelization than building churches), and to solicit donations from the female membership of the Church to support this part of the mission enterprise.

How did the Board implement these ideas, and what did mission work look like? In New Mexico, the subject of my research, missions focused on education. Women missionaries opened schools for Hispanic Catholics in small villages that lacked public education or endured poor-quality education. Missionaries trained to teach staffed mission schools that offered more amenities, more equipment, and better supplies than public schools and kept classes seven to nine months a year. Mission teachers became patrons, of sorts. They taught their neighbors English; they translated and interpreted legal and other official documents written in English. They sponsored the best of their students for admission into mission boarding schools—offering the opportunity of an otherwise unavailable secondary education. They offered the possibility of social mobility. Anthropologist Suzanne Forrest, writing of the Hispanic population in northern New Mexico, has argued that mission schools attracted Hispanos who had "upwardly mobile ambitions." These schools produced an elite corps of teachers, lawyers, politicians, and businessmen who "formed the nucleus of a new professional Hispanic middle class."[11] In the 1910s mission schools began to close. Protestants did not want to compete with improved public schools in the villages nor undermine the efforts of their own graduates who worked as teachers in these schools.

The career of Alice Blake supplies an example of the evolving work of missionaries as they more broadly served human needs. In 1889, Alice Blake, a Presbyterian missionary who described herself as from a "traditional New England home," took up a new assignment as schoolteacher in Rociada, New Mexico (a village made up of Hispanic Catholics in the mountains northeast of Santa Fe). Blake spent the next forty years of her life working as a missionary in northern New Mexico. She began her career as a schoolteacher, opening and maintaining mission schools, stressing the importance of literacy, of learning the English language as she emphasized the "Word" or the reading of the Bible. With the support of the Woman's Board of Home Missions she soon branched out. The increasing poverty and hardship faced by her clients forced her to take a more practical approach and to address other issues. She used her school as a base, turning it into a community center. She procured smallpox vaccine and inoculated her neighbors during epidemics. She took on issues of sanitation and hygiene, raising money to build a community well. Thirty years into her career she took a brief sabbatical to earn a certificate in Public Health, after which she worked with New Mexico's fledgling Department of Public Health weighing and measuring children (with money provided to states from the federal Sheppard-Towner Act), before she returned to mission work. As a missionary, Alice Blake realized a kind of power and influence (albeit limited in scope) that few other forms of work gave women of her generation. She aimed, like the mission enterprise generally, to generate social, if not financial, capital—to increase a community's "wealth," in skills, services, interdependence, and goodwill.

Missionaries did not see themselves as substitutes for the state—indeed they believed themselves to be building an infrastructure for expanded state services. They formed a partnership with the state. Hence they opened schools in areas that lacked public education; seeing former students running public schools proved their enterprise's success. When in New Mexico, for example, the public school system grew stronger, the missions shifted into health care. They wanted, they contended, to see client populations grow more independent. They had believed at the outset of the enterprise that conversion to Protestantism would, ipso facto, create this independence. As they familiarized themselves with the lives of their clients, they came to a deeper appreciation of impoverished material conditions over which their clients had very little control.

Blake's career trajectory from mission teacher to social worker reflects the transition that the women's home mission enterprise in general made. What started as a movement intended to save the Protestant and democratic character (and it assumed these two to be coupled) of the United States, by the 1920s addressed issues of social justice, arguing against policies which resulted from racist or xenophobic attitudes, and for programs they designed to improve the material conditions of the poor. These women embraced the social gospel, modeled themselves after settlement house leaders like Jane Addams, and in the 1930s supported and advocated New Deal programs. Those missions that remained opened their doors to the programs of the Great Society—housing and supporting, for example, Head Start nursery schools. The services women missionaries provided at the turn of the century laid an important part of the foundation on which the government built the welfare state. And insofar as they sought out government aid and public money to broaden the reach of their programs, they forged a partnership with government to deliver social services. If we apply political labels, they exemplify what we have come to think of as twentieth-century welfare liberals.

A cautionary note: This movement embodied a deeply pervasive paternalism. (The term "paternalism" more accurately conveys the nature of the relationship that they established with their clients than "racist" or "classist.") Women missionaries at the turn of the century had limited ideas about social equality, or democracy. They accepted as natural that certain groups of people would remain dependent and largely subject. They themselves underwent a conversion of sorts as they struggled to bring services to groups that upper classes had largely written out of the American experience. They came to appreciate and grew more sympathetic to the idea of cultural pluralism, but they stopped short of becoming cultural pluralists. Missionaries sought to incorporate their clients into the state by representing them to the larger society. Alice Blake exemplifies this conversion. At the outset she condemned those Hispanics whom she served, writing that she had entered "Sodom and Gomorrah." She called her neighbors "so corrupt in their moral nature that they would scorch the soul of an angel." When she retired from mission work forty years later, she sounded a different tune. In defense of New Mexico and its people, Blake warned of "how many people there are who are wont to bolster up a prejudice with any passing impression that would seem to justify it."

She took issue with those who believed Hispanics "worthless" and New Mexico "nothing but a great desert." Instead Blake pointed to the "beautiful and wonderful everywhere." As for her neighbors and clients she said that "a casual visitor might easily note only what seems to him uncouth and unpromising; where one who had had the opportunity of knowing them intimately will have discovered many beauties of character and admirable attributes."[12] Like Blake, many women missionaries became vocal advocates of those with whom they worked. They became leaders in defending the interests of the poor and politically disenfranchised. In the process they enhanced their own social positions. However, they found sharing power with their "clients," and relinquishing authority, more difficult.

As the earlier reference to the numbers of Protestant women involved suggests, women's mission organizations proved tremendously successful. Membership in a national network of mission societies grew, women pledged millions of dollars, and increasing numbers of women expressed interest in "going to the front." Not only did Anglo women welcome the enterprise, but client populations welcomed the services missionaries provided. In New Mexico, for example, mission teachers attracted many students; their schools were extremely popular, even if their students did not convert. They provided much needed education and social services at a time when the material conditions of the Hispanic population were changing dramatically. The imposition of a new legal system when the territory passed from Mexico to the United States, the demand that title to land be documented on paper, and the imposition of cash taxes left Hispanics vulnerable to land speculators. Hispanic subsistence farmers had lost 80 percent of their land by the turn of the century. Stripped of their former means of production, Hispanic New Mexicans turned from agriculture to wage labor. Growing numbers of New Mexico's villagers left home for extended periods, migrating seasonally in search of wage labor. Today the villages to which Protestant missionaries went remain the poorest in the state of New Mexico, with 32 percent of residents living on incomes below the poverty line. People survive by combining small-scale agriculture, out-migration, and seasonal employment with welfare benefits. Indeed, northern New Mexico (one of the most scenic parts of the state) suffers from tremendous speculation—as Anglo developers move in to buy land on which to build condos with hot tubs for the second home and ski tourist trade.[13]

The Protestant, and largely middle-class, women who supported the mission movement did so as Christians and as Americans. Their ethnocentric impulse, to bring "backward" and "uncivilized" people to God, makes many of us squirm today. And their paternalism had important implications. But the issue of their "calling" deserves consideration. Why do people give money or time? What motivates them to do so? What constitutes a legitimate "call" on a person's resources or time? The Alice Blakes of the Protestant mission movement responded to multiple motivations. Women, who otherwise had few opportunities, could do respectable work, sanctioned by God, in which they had the support of women (and also men) across the nation. In other words, they did not work entirely selflessly. Those women who went into the field as missionaries came to understand that their effectiveness depended directly on how their clients received them, and they subsequently grew more open to the needs of clients (needs not solely spiritual). They modified their views and work as a result of their experience.

This movement reminded more affluent Americans regularly of their social obligations—as Christians and as citizens. Missionary reports served the same purpose that the *New York Times* appeals do today—they made real the difficulties poor populations endured. They reminded more affluent and privileged Americans of people in need. Mission organizations structured, rationalized, and systematized the philanthropic impulses of middle-class women. They acted as a collection agency, a depository for small donations, which they could efficiently apportion to the places with the greatest need. They helped set a pattern of giving that the Community Chest first secularized. Similarly, they may have prepared people for a system of taxation in which some portion of income taxes went for the extension of public welfare services. Growth also brought drawbacks. As the movement grew bigger and more successful, it also grew more bureaucratic. These organizations came to privilege expertise and special training over service born out of voluntary impulse. In the early days, the movement made few distinctions between leaders, employees, and volunteer/members. These categories became more rigid as the movement matured. By the 1930s the movement limited the kind of work that volunteers could perform if they wished to serve—it valued members for their monetary donations. Belonging to this movement offered nothing distinctive or special. Giving to the local Community Chest drive probably offered more satisfaction. The predecessor to the United Way, the Community Chest let you actually see the fruits of your donations, which went to support local public services. This bureaucratization and rationalization, however, lost the national focus that had been one of the strong points of the mission enterprise. A regular reading of mission literature had informed members of conditions across the country (indeed, around the world) and had, in the heyday of the enterprise, reminded members that they should, could, and did make a difference in areas thousands of miles removed from their homes. Members supported the mission movement as a patriotic act, the duty of one both Christian and American.

The national (and international, if one includes foreign missions) outlook of this movement made it a compelling and powerful movement. It may seem ironic to focus on this issue in an age which bombards us with information via radio, television, computers, etc., when we supposedly can easily know about what is happening across the country and around the world. But does a New Yorker today know any more about the conditions of the poor in Texas than did our grandmothers' generation? The women who created the mission organizations engaged in a national project, they were building a national enterprise, they had a vision of social capital that they intended to encompass and benefit the whole of the nation.

While the women reformers of the early part of the twentieth century deserve applause for their strong sense of calling, for their belief that their work would strengthen the nation, and for their broad national outlook, the leaders of these organizations ultimately chose professionalization over politicization. They grew increasingly preoccupied with the internal workings of their organizations and turned their attention to improving the delivery of services. In the process they failed to connect their work adequately with larger political movements. Indeed, the Protestant women's reform movement refused to champion one party over another, or to take partisan positions (even though they stated their positions on some issues explicitly and their leaders participated in Progressive and later New Deal initiatives). Though they never stated such a fear, women may have feared that partisanship would alienate donors.

This glorious "age of reform" left a legacy of a more extensive and far better system of social welfare than the laissez-faire policies which preceded it. Certainly the "poor" and needy fare better today than in the 1890s. The reforms also produced a cadre of professional social service providers who more efficiently and expeditiously, and perhaps more fairly, deliver services than their counterparts in the 1910s. Finally, our society still relies on volunteers because in the press for expanded governmental support, reform leaders did not let go of their commitment to the importance of voluntary action. In fact, whether or not our system of social welfare survives seems increasingly to depend on the motivation and support of the "volunteer."

We must remember that middle-class white Protestant women in the late nineteenth century undertook to build their social service empire in part to compensate for their disenfranchisement and because few had respectable economic options open to them. For much of the history of the United States women gained access to the public arena through their voluntary work, and the work they did as volunteers informed their political sensibility. Over the last thirty years especially, women's opportunities have expanded tremendously—women can achieve power and influence by other means than producing social capital.[14] Today we can sit in the boardrooms of corporate America. My great-grandmother, grandmother, and to a lesser extent my mother volunteered their time: my generation writes checks. We continue to volunteer, but we usually focus our activities on organizations and institutions in which we have a vested interest, such as our children's schools (an extension of what we see as our community).[15] We make our connections to the poor, to those in need, largely by reading the newspaper or by direct mail appeal. The political repercussions of this alienation: we do not see a connection between our interests and those of the poor or the marginal in this society. We do not participate in activities which force us to recognize our relative privilege, to see what we have that others do not.

Many voluntary efforts may actually exacerbate class differences. For example, the willingness of affluent parents to step in and fill the gaps created by budget cutbacks in their own children's schools makes attempts at equalizing educational resources across school districts, so that children from different classes may have similar opportunities, more difficult.[16] Under these circumstances, we should not simply implore Americans to volunteer, we must also tackle the larger, and far more complicated, issue of social stratification and address how we distribute voluntary resources and who benefits from this expenditure of social capital. Rather than pine for the "good old days" when middle-class women acted as "friendly visitors," dispensing alms to the needy, let us do what social reformers at the beginning of the twentieth century did, realistically assess what volunteers can do. A volunteer may tutor children, but counseling mentally ill people may require a level of training that most volunteers do not have. Looking to volunteers to provide specific social services previously provided by professionals because taxpayers do not want to pay for those services may prove more expensive in the long run if it means continuing social stratification.

As one observer has noted about volunteers, they contribute most significantly by "building . . . political will," rather than by the specific tasks they perform. This is the real lesson we learn when examining the history of women and voluntarism. Moved by the nature of their work, their inability to adequately address the social problems they encountered, the women's mission movement—and the women's social reform movement more generally—called for a more activist government. Rather than distort this history by engaging in nostalgia about women's voluntary roles (particularly that their labor cost nothing), we should remember that these women viewed their voluntarism as the foundation of their citizenship. By our standards today their largely uncritical celebration of the superiority of Protestant Christianity was further flawed by their ethnocentric sense of national identity. They did, however, champion a definition of citizenship which recognized that different classes and groups had responsibilities and obligations to one another that extended beyond each one's own neighborhood. Their lesson reminds us that voluntary communities do not replace, but rather complement, the government, and that they moderate discussions about the practice of democracy.

Analysts have said, and continue to say, much (in a constant refrain these days) about making the poor more responsible, more independent. Paternalism formed a major flaw in the women's mission movement. At the point where the missions might have prepared students and clients to take over the institutions and services of the enterprise itself, the enterprise declined as the government took over its programs. These developments largely precluded confrontations within this voluntary community about issues of governance and how to redistribute power.

Recently a conference on foundations raised questions about the very process which sets priorities and makes grants. The participants voiced much concern about whether or not the process included democratic decision-making. Did recipients (clients) participate in making decisions? One foundation was moving towards a more inclusive process—the Haymarket Fund of Boston, in which former grantees help develop and review proposals and choose recipients in subsequent years.[17] The discussion which followed did not suggest that other foundations will follow the example of Haymarket, nor does recent history suggest that the privileged in this society will volunteer to share power with the disenfranchised. Over the last twenty years we have seen a growing clamor against taxation and any suggestion that Americans should redistribute their wealth. Interestingly, this clamor comes at a moment in our history when a larger number of people can participate politically and when we see an increasing number of women and minorities represented in government, and in a position to make policy. William May has raised important questions about the relationship between benefactors and beneficiaries, suggesting that an "assumption of asymmetry" has dominated private giving, leading us to overlook the benefits that accrue to the more affluent. Benefactors can control and demand but they can also give expecting nothing in return. These attitudes demean the recipient because they do not allow the recipient a voice in the process. The recipient remains on the sidelines, *in* society but not *of* it.[18]

Philanthropy and voluntary action should act politically to create a society which shares power across communities, and across the differences of class, race, and gender. As Ernesto Cortes states the motto of the Industrial Areas Foundation (at the center of a national network of broad-based, multiethnic, interfaith organizations in primarily poor and moderate-income communities): "Never do for others what they can do for themselves." He notes that the Industrial Areas Foundation works to "establish a public space in which ordinary people can learn and develop the skills of public life, and create the institutions of a new democratic politics."[19] The women's mission movement attempted, in precisely this way, to increase the political skills of and opportunities for the millions of women who joined its ranks, and who then used this experience to lobby for a greater share of political power. Unfortunately history offers many instances of groups who, having succeeded in expanding their own power and gaining a degree of self-sufficiency, then pulled up the ladder, making it difficult for those left behind to follow.

We can find the best contemporary illustration of our halfhearted commitment to making all Americans self-sufficient in the way that Cortes envisions in the current debate about welfare mothers. No work better illustrates this society's recalcitrance against sharing power than the studies of Annelise Orleck, a historian at Dartmouth College, who is currently writing the story of a group of black women on welfare who built the Operation Life Community Development Corporation in Nevada in the 1970s. Her work illustrates just how our society has accepted deeply entrenched paternalistic stereotypes of poor women as "financially irresponsible" and in need of supervision and control.[20]

Working with many of the same assumptions that Cortes makes and believing that they knew best what their community needed, this group of

women marshaled grants from a variety of state and federal programs and
foundations to undertake an ambitious program of community development
which provided desperately needed services and jobs. At the height of their
activities in 1980 they brought millions of dollars to the Westside of Las
Vegas. Their capacity to raise and manage such funds was constantly questioned. Early on, welfare officials expressed concern that welfare mothers
could not manage a local WIC program. When the women produced their
accounts, officials found that they had developed an averaging method based
on local consumption patterns. When they audited the books, these same
officials found that Operation Life used a far more efficient method of
accounting than welfare officials had heretofore employed. The Operation
Life method had allowed a cash discrepancy, for seventeen hundred transactions totaling more than $200,000, of only seven cents. Federal auditors
adopted the OL system.[21]

However, the critics persisted. From within the community, local male
activists suggested that men rightfully owned economic development. The
local prosecutor charged fraudulent practices and dragged Operation Life
leaders to court, where they were eventually exonerated (though the process
cost the organization energy and resources). In the 1980s, Reagan administration officials found excuses to withdraw funds, and slowly shut the organization down. In 1989 the one remaining Operation Life clinic closed, its
contract from the Public Health Service transferred to another group. Said
one former state legislator, local officials "could not accept the idea of poor
women administering anything, much less multi-million dollar programs."[22]
Orleck argues that "it is revealing of how hard . . . stereotypes die, even when
poor women learn to navigate the capitalist welfare state and demonstrate
highly refined capacities for planning and money management."[23]

The middle-class women who built the mission organizations labored
under similar stereotypes in their time. Male critics questioned whether
women should run organizations as vast and complex as those they had created. However, the fact that they lived, as wives, daughters, and sisters, with
those men who doubted their capabilities tempered the criticism these

women faced. Men had to consider that they might possibly impair familial relations if they objected too strenuously to the actions of their female relatives.[24] Unfortunately, today's welfare mothers, essentially alone, lack male patrons to shield them. They do not have the social, political, or familial connections of the earlier generation of women reformers. The men in their lives wield no political power; they cannot offer protection or patronage. Women on welfare have depended on a political consensus which deemed it socially beneficial to extend support to women raising children alone, but this consensus is now fraying and society labels these benefits regressive. Ironically, welfare mothers offer many of the most forceful criticisms of the current system. If we listen to their demands we hear that they do not ask for more money per se (or for charity), but for the opportunity to become self-sufficient, to work at jobs that pay them a wage with which they can support their children. In light of this irony, the service (or more to the point, the indentured servitude) required by current workfare schemes seems needlessly cruel.

If we want to make those whom we persist in defining as "dependent" responsible, we must include them in the process of governance. We must recognize their achievements as, not personal milestones, but important social contributions and applaud rather than suspect their successes. We must allow that they too can generate social capital and deserve tangible rewards for their work. This redefinition requires a commitment from those of us with means to contribute more than our time and extra dollars voluntarily. By all means continue sending checks to appeals like those of *The New York Times*. Recognize, however, that these checks may serve to ameliorate whatever guilt or uneasiness we may feel about the misfortunes of others, but they do not generate the broad-based political dialogue that we must begin if we hope to reshape social policies to best suit the needs of the twenty-first century.

NOTES

1. Charities are supported by public and private monies. A report by the group Independent Sector found that payments from dues and the like accounted for 43.5 percent of charitable revenues, followed by government money (29.4 percent), private contributions (17.7 percent), and other (9.4 percent). See "Who Supports Charity," *U.S. News and World Report,* January 16, 1995.

2. Remarks reported on *All Things Considered,* National Public Radio, January 6, 1997. See also "Clinton Seeks Help for the Nation's Spirit," *New York Times,* January 7, 1997, sec. A, p. 12.

3. "At Volunteerism Rally, Leaders Paint Walls and a Picture of Need," *New York Times,* April 28, 1997, 1.

4. Prominent among these are women's historians. In the last few years we have seen the publication of many historical works which seek to explain how welfare policy developed and how it was gendered in such a way that men were seen as entitled to certain benefits from the State while women remained largely objects of charity. See, for instance, Linda Gordon, *Pitied But Not Entitled: Single Mothers and the History of Welfare* (Cambridge, Mass.: Harvard University Press, 1994); Gwendolyn Mink, *The Wages of Motherhood: Inequality in the Welfare State, 1917–1942* (Ithaca, N.Y.: Cornell University Press, 1995); Molly Ladd-Taylor, *Mother-work: Women, Child Welfare, and the State, 1890–1930* (Urbana: University of Illinois Press, 1994).

5. The literature on the female reform movement of the nineteenth century is voluminous. Among the principle works are Lori Ginzberg, *Women and the Work of Benevolence: Morality, Politics, and Class in the Nineteenth-Century United States* (New Haven, Conn.: Yale University Press, 1990); Robyn Muncy, *Creating a Female Dominion in American Reform, 1890–1935* (New York: Oxford University Press, 1991); Ellen Fitzpatrick, *Endless Crusade: Women Social Scientists and Progressive Reform* (New York: Oxford University Press, 1990); Kathryn Sklar, "Hull House in the 1890's: A Community of Women Reformers," *Signs* 10 (Summer 1985): 658–77; Ruth

Bordin, *Women and Temperance: The Quest for Power and Liberty, 1873–1900* (Philadelphia: Temple University Press, 1981).

6. If we include the membership of the Woman's Christian Temperance Union (WCTU) and the Young Women's Christian Association (YWCA)—the two other leading religious women's groups at the time (which also coupled religious inspiration with social reform)—the number would be closer to 4 million.

7. When the Council of Women for Home Missions was formed in 1908 it included, among others, representatives from the Boards of the Baptist, Christian, Congregational, Evangelical Lutheran, Methodist Episcopal, Methodist Episcopal South, Presbyterian, and United Presbyterian denominations.

8. For more information on the Presbyterian women's home mission movement see Susan M. Yohn, *A Contest of Faiths: Missionary Women and Pluralism in the American Southwest* (Ithaca, N.Y.: Cornell University Press, 1995). The specific incidents and people discussed in this essay are taken from this larger work. For more information on Protestant women's missions (home missions specifically) see Peggy Pascoe, *Relations of Rescue: The Search for Female Moral Authority in the American West, 1874–1939* (New York: Oxford University Press, 1990); Ronald Butchart, "Recruits to the 'Army of Civilization': Gender, Race, Class and the Freedmen's Teachers, 1861–1875," *Journal of Education* 172 (1990): 76–87; John P. McDowell, *The Social Gospel in the South: The Woman's Home Mission Movement in the Methodist Episcopal Church, South, 1886–1939* (Baton Rouge: Louisiana State University Press, 1982); Ruth Crocker, *Social Work and Social Order: The Settlement Movement in Two Industrial Cities, 1889–1930* (Urbana: University of Illinois Press, 1992).

9. In most of the Protestant denominations women could not be ordained, in many they could not even serve as elders or deacons, and there was even debate in some congregations as to whether women should be allowed to speak from the pulpit.

10. The list included Mormonism, nihilism, communism, atheism, Romanism (meaning Catholicism), and, though not an "ism," infidelity.

11. Suzanne Forrest, *Preservation of the Village: New Mexico's Hispanics and the New Deal* (Albuquerque: University of New Mexico Press, 1989), 29.

12. For a more extensive discussion of Alice Blake, especially as she exemplifies the kinds of experiences women had while participating in the mission enterprise, see Chapter 4, "I Am Part of All I Have Met: Women Home Missionaries in Hispano New Mexico," in Yohn, *A Contest of Faiths.*

13. For a more lengthy discussion of why Hispanics sought out Protestant services see Yohn, *A Contest of Faiths,* Chaps. 2 and 5. For a discussion of survival strategies developed by Hispanics, see Sarah Deutsch, *No Separate Refuge: Culture, Class and Gender on an Anglo-Hispanic Frontier in the American Southwest, 1880–1940* (New York: Oxford University Press, 1987), and Forrest, *Preservation of the Village.*

14. This is true especially for younger women. Voluntarism remains a principle mode of power and influence for women who are older and have been out of the labor market for many years. For more information about this group of women see Arlene Kaplan Daniels, *Invisible Careers: Women Civic Leaders from the Volunteer World* (Chicago: University of Chicago Press, 1988).

15. Even though the number of women in the labor force has grown over the century—and now a majority of women work full-time—women are still more philanthropic than are men. Various reports find that 61 percent of donors are women, as are 55.8 percent of all volunteers. The largest number of donations and volunteer hours go to religious organizations (49.2 percent), followed by human services agencies (26.7 percent), health organizations (25.7 percent), and educational causes (17.5 percent). See "Women Are More Philanthropic than Men," *About Women and Marketing* 9 (March 1996): 11–12.

16. This issue has been particularly vexing to policy-makers as they have tried to equalize educational programs across states. For a discussion of the impact of this problem in New Jersey see "Advantage Hard to Duplicate: Parent Volunteers Help Affluent Schools Fill Needs," *New York Times,* May 7, 1997, sec. B, pp. 1, 14.

17. The conference was the "Philanthropic Foundations in History: Needs and Opportunities for Study," sponsored by the Center for the Study

of American Culture & Education, New York University, School of Education, November 1996. The information on the Haymarket Fund comes from the presentation made by Susan Ostrander, of Tufts University, in her paper "Philanthropy, Democracy, Accountability, and Social Relations between Grantors and Grantees."

18. See William F. May's Introduction to this volume.

19. Ernesto Cortes, Jr., "Reweaving the Social Fabric," *Boston Review* (June–September 1994): 14.

20. Annelise Orleck, "'I Got to Dreamin'": Welfare Mothers and Community Economic Development, 1969–1990" (paper presented at the Berkshire Conference of Women Historians, University of North Carolina at Chapel Hill, June 1996). See also Orleck, "If It Wasn't for You I'd Have Shoes for My Children: The Political Education of Las Vegas Welfare Mothers," in *The Politics of Motherhood*, ed. Annelise Orleck, Alexis Jetter, and Diana Taylor (Hanover, N.H.: University Press of New England, 1997).

21. Orleck, "'I Got to Dreamin,'" 12.

22. Ibid., 18.

23. Ibid., 3.

24. The men who were in favor of merging the men's and women's mission boards were very careful to express their deep admiration for the work done by women even as they sought to take over women's work. They did not intend for their actions to become as contentious as they did and were surprised by how vehemently women (in many cases female family members) defended their separate organizations. For a more complete discussion of the controversy generated by proposals to merge men and women's mission work see my article, "Let Christian Women Set the Example in Their Own Gifts: The 'Business' of Protestant Women's Organizations," in a collection edited by Virginia Brereton and Margaret Bendroth (Urbana: University of Illinois Press, in press).

Mediating Structures

Social Empowerment through the Church

CARL C. TROVALL

*Nothing, in my opinion, is more deserving of our attention
than the intellectual and moral associations of America.*
ALEXIS DE TOCQUEVILLE

I. INTRODUCTION

The church, whether as a local congregation or as a church social agency, forms an integral part of American history and life. Churches have benefited from their engagement with society, as society has benefited enormously from this "voluntary" institution we call the church, despite its imperfections. This essay does not focus on the church's own understanding of its social mission (however much its motivation and the integrity of the church's witness to a loving God depends on that self-understanding). Rather, it will examine the church's role as it actually works itself out in seeking the common good, especially for the neediest and most uncommon, whom the greater society has marginalized. I call them "uncommon" deliberately, reflecting the truth uttered by David Heim, that "the poor are not people related to us—they seem to lie in another country, or at least in some other city or in a part of town we don't drive through. Their habits are strange, their culture alien. . . . The notion that our fate is somehow inter-twined with that of our poor neighbors has lost rhetorical credibility."[1] A good society will always need places that remind people of the uncommon people in our midst. The church serves as just this sort of place.

Most Christians would agree that private charities perform critical serv-ices in delivering care to broken and hurting lives in our society. Furthermore, most Christians would agree that the government must not impede or under-mine these private efforts, but rather support them, for governments cannot substitute for these mediating structures of family, church, private social care agencies, and other social service groups. Partly as a result of these convic-tions, some Christians have increased political pressure to turn numerous governmental services back to private charitable organizations, including churches. This current process of devolution in social responsibility poses a cluster of questions: How much does our common life need private, volun-tary organizations, particularly churches and ecclesiastical charities? What can we as a society realistically expect, or not expect, of them? How does the church mediate in society? How do church-sponsored agencies empower the people they serve? What ethical function does the church fulfill? And what justifies the church and its service agencies as a mediator in society?

A. MEDIATING STRUCTURES

With the publication of *To Empower People* in 1977, Peter Berger and Richard John Neuhaus renewed the debate about the role of Tocqueville's voluntary associations (Edmund Burke's "little platoons") in American society.[2] Said Tocqueville, "Feelings and opinions are recruited, the heart enlarged, and the human mind is developed only by the reciprocal influence of men upon one another. I have shown that these influences are almost null in democratic countries; they must therefore be artificially created, and this can only be accomplished by associations."[3]

Berger and Neuhaus have noted two contradictory tendencies in current American life: (1) an ongoing and increasing desire for the myriad services offered by the modern welfare state; and (2) a deep skepticism about largeness, especially the governmental and bureaucratic sort.[4] Thus American society must decide not *whether* to provide services but *in what way* and *to what extent* to expand or diminish them. The 1996 welfare reform has reaffirmed these tendencies both in its assumption that welfare remains necessary as well as in its effort to return distributional authority and control to the theoretically more local and accountable state government. To provide certain welfare-state services, Berger and Neuhaus proposed using "alternative mechanisms," "institutions standing between the individual in his [*sic*] private life and the large institutions of public life,"[5] as mediating structures. Examples include the family, the neighborhood, the church and synagogue, and other voluntary associations. While these structures cannot solve all the problems of modern democracies, the authors believed that these structures could reconnect the largely alienating, yet necessary, political and economic bureaucracies to the personal values of individual life such as meaning, fulfillment, and identity. They write that if mediating structures "could be more imaginatively recognized in public policy, individuals would be more 'at home' in society, and the political order would be more meaningful."[6]

The absence of mediating structures imposes a bleak existence on individuals, forcing them to live under the absolute power and tyranny of that great involuntary institution, the state. Mediating institutions are

the value-generating and value-maintaining agencies in society. Without them, values become another function of the megastructures, notably of the state, and this is a hallmark of totalitarianism. In the totalitarian case, the individual becomes the object rather than the subject of the value-propagating processes of society.[7]

James Luther Adams, in his analysis of the "totalitarian case" of Nazi Germany, argues that Hitler's acquisition of power depended upon destroying organizations, particularly German mediating structures, which might have operated independently of Hitler's control. Adams writes, "We may define the totalitarian society as one lacking effective mediating structures that protect the self-determination of individuals and groups."[8] On the other hand, a "democratic society . . . is an association of associations." Individuals maintain their rights, responsibilities, and independence from the group, just as private associations maintain their rights, responsibilities, and independence from the state. Upholding order and unity in the midst of liberty and variety within and between these structures, without falling into either a dangerously suffocating uniformity or an equally dangerous societal chaos, creates an ongoing struggle in a democratic society.[9]

Mediating structures preserve democratic society because democracies, more than other forms of government, suffer particularly from the erosion of trust stemming from the people's cynicism about the government's activities. Society must institutionalize the best sort of structural mediation between the individual and the government in some way for the sake of permanency, yet this embodiment must also be able to adapt in the face of widespread change and "exist where the people are" because healthy public policy begins there.[10]

Liberalism as well as totalitarianism undermines mediating structures, in Berger and Neuhaus's judgment: "Mediating structures find an inhospitable soil in the liberal garden." Enlightenment liberalism celebrates both individual human rights and a just public order, but it looks solely to the state to protect these rights and this justice. Any institution that intrudes between the individual and the final guarantor of public order liberals consider "irrelevant, or even an obstacle to the rational ordering of society. What lies in between is dismissed, to the extent it can be, as superstition, bigotry, or (more recently) cultural lag."[11] That individual rights frequently trump the desires or "rights" of mediating institutions illustrates this tendency. Thus society needs mediating structures to place a human face on the bureaucracies in society (even big business) and a public face on the individual.

Berger and Neuhaus describe their proposals as minimalist and maximalist. They believe, minimally, that policy-makers should consider the damaging effects of legislation and policy upon mediating structures as carefully as they do their effects on the environment or ethnic groups. Maximally, they believe that public policy should attempt to "utilize mediating structures for the realization of social purposes."[12] Yet, the state should not use mediating structures as mere instruments of state power. Rather, the "goal in utilizing mediating structures is to expand government services without producing government oppressiveness." Further, Berger and Neuhaus, at the time of writing that book, did not want this decentralization of government services to raze the modern welfare state. Instead, they sought to retain the welfare state, even while finding new and more appropriate ways to sustain it through the little platoons of our common life.[13]

B. EMPOWERMENT

Since mediating structures, to some degree, limit individuals, how do mediating structures nonetheless empower people? James Madison helps answer this question and suggests more specific answers that apply to the church and the poor. Madison used as the touchstone of democracy the separation of powers.[14] Democracy requires a division of powers at every level of society: at the highest levels of government, in intermediate associations and governments, and on the private level. This separation of powers provides sufficient liberty to prevent tyranny, and sufficient order to prevent chaos. Voluntary associations, a distinct form critical to the division of powers in American society, introduce a richer and more encompassing separation of powers in the United States than the traditional constitutional division of government into legislative, executive, and judicial branches. Tocqueville affirmed this richness when he wrote, "Governments, therefore, should not be the only active powers; associations ought, in democratic nations, to stand in lieu of those powerful private individuals whom the equality of conditions has swept away." When people associate with one another in a cause important to them, they transform themselves from isolated individuals to "a power seen from afar."[15]

Madison saw both dangers and advantages to mediating structures in society. On the one hand, these groups often threatened the rights of other citizens or the commonwealth itself. "Thomas Hobbes in *Leviathan* was so fearful of threatening chaos that he described these associations, including the sects, as 'worms in the entrails of the natural sovereign.'"[16] On the other hand, these groups also provided "a protection for freedom in society against potentially tyrannical intentions of the majority." Due to mediating structures, "society itself will be broken into so many parts, interests and classes of citizens, that the rights of individuals, or of the minority, will be in little danger from interested combinations of the majority."[17]

In modern society, of course, in addition to the "potentially tyrannical intentions" of the government, we also have to contend with large-scale entities which have become transmediating institutions, such as mass media, the gigantic industrial complexes, and international corporations. All of these powers steal power from people in a democracy. These transmediating institutions pose the constant danger of "mass apathy"; citizens see themselves as powerless in the face of these all-encompassing entities, and this perception of impotence results in the transformation of their active power into "the passive power of adjustment to authority in precisely those areas which concern them most. . . . It is precisely in order to prevent self-enclosed, that is, idolatrous, commitments hostile to mutual confidence and uncoerced participation that a principle of separation of powers is required."[18]

Power, "the ability to exercise influence," confers "the ability to make decisions affecting the values of others."[19] Mediating structures allow people to participate in influencing society (empowerment) in countless ways, while simultaneously making them open to critique and dissent from inside and outside of the mediating institution itself (checks on power). This openness makes for a richly variegated society with numerous sources and avenues of power, as well as numerous checks on this power. Since social power operates through "a complex exercise in communication, in the process of influencing and being influenced,"[20] mediating structures empower by developing the complex skill of communication in citizens, thereby giving them the ability to exercise social power collectively.

Berger and Neuhaus stress "empowerment" in their proposal. Because large, powerful, impersonal institutions so often atomize and render powerless individuals, mediating structures empower individuals by allowing them to state personal values they consider important, and to offer a personal face to an impersonal process. The poor, who do not command the financial and social resources to resist victimization at the hands of a large bureaucracy, particularly benefit. "The paradigm of mediating structures aims at empowering poor people to do the things that the more affluent can already do, aims at spreading the power around a bit more—and to do so where it matters, in people's control over their own lives."[21]

Adams uses the theological language of covenant (promise making, keeping, and breaking) to account for the origin of mediating institutions and the ways in which they both empower and constrain. "The intimate and the ultimate—indeed, all parts of the inter-related world—the individual, the middle structures, the government, the society, and the divine creative ground of meaning—are held together by covenant."[22] Covenants are promises of commitment made in society, kept in society, and, because we are human, also broken in society. Covenants differ from contracts. Contracts embody agreements between equals; they only serve the interests of the persons making the contract, they don't continue in force beyond terms and time specified, nor do they always allow for a new beginning after a breach of contract.[23] Mediating institutions act like covenants; they extend obligations beyond contractual parties through time and society. Mediating institutions offer a separation of powers which reminds both individuals and institutions (unequal parties) of the strong covenants and promises they have made to each other. When covenantors break their covenants, mediating structures assume the power which makes "possible intervention in the name of the promises, intended to prevent bondage to any finite power"—a bondage theologically called idolatry.[24] As Reinhold Niebuhr might have said, humanity's capacity to covenant makes mediating institutions possible; humanity's inclination for covenant-breaking makes mediating structures necessary. The power of mediating institutions both protects against an extreme individualism, stressing the critical nature of community for human fulfillment, and also protects against an oppressive collectivism whose power threatens the justice necessary for human fulfillment. A covenant "calls for mediating structures to protect and nourish the individual and to relate the individual in responsibility to embracing structures."[25] The church, as a specific mediating structure, brings a distinct nature, and performs a distinctive function in American society.

C. THE CHURCH AS MEDIATING INSTITUTION

A current area of research, "congregational studies," has dedicated itself to study the unique qualities, histories, and social impact of congregations. Scholarly interest in congregations has developed in three phases according to Martin Marty.[26] The first phase (occurring in the mid-twentieth century) placed congregational life solely in the realm of the private—divine colonies in the world. In the second phase, exemplifying Peter Berger and Richard John Neuhaus's concept of mediating structures, congregations positively mediated between private and public activities and institutions. This advocacy on behalf of the congregation attempted to demonstrate the significance of the church in society. By identifying this mediating function, Berger and Neuhaus helped facilitate a "new charter for congregational studies." Marty criticizes Berger and Neuhaus because their "descriptions and prescriptions are more closely wedded to political interests than to inquiries concerning the nature of congregations on their own terms."[27] Most pastors and priests do not see themselves or their congregations as mediating political and social goals, even though they may in fact be doing just this sort of mediating. The third and current phase of congregational study views congregations as doing much more than mere mediation. Marty wants to develop a more adequate term beside, not in place of, "mediating structures" to express the full nature of congregational life. Deriving imagery from the Puritan tradition of calling the place of worship the "meetinghouse," he suggests the metaphor of "meeting" to supplement "mediating." The public place of meeting embodies its own integrity which does not derive from the greater public or the private citizen. Despite the hyperprivatized religion of many in the United States, described in *Habits of the Heart,* Marty views the modern congregation "to be less a mediator between spheres and more as itself an important first expression of a public commitment, albeit of a particular sort."[28]

Marty widens the meaning of "public." He identifies many kinds of publics within the commonweal. Rather than viewing congregations as private entities in a larger public world, he sees them as publics in their own right. "They are not merely mediating structures which acquire their status from the undifferentiated megastructural world to which they carry reports of private life and against which they shield private persons."[29] Public mass society is not the only public, but comprises a multiplicity of assertive and passive subpublics divided by religious, ethnic, gender, and political lines. Marty offers the image of mountains to illustrate. If we conceive of "the public sphere" as Mt. Everest, and begin from the summit, then congregations look like plains. However, if we begin on the plains of the "private sphere" then congregations appear more like public foothills—little publics.[30] In short, we should not use such a rich, complex, and multifaceted "public" univocally.

Marty, consequently, supplements the idea of mediating structures by envisioning the congregation as a public meeting place. Buber saw the meeting of human beings with each other as "analogous to the primal meeting of God as Other with people."[31] In the congregation, a person can meet people who represent other publics, namely, friends, neighbors, and strangers. In congregations, people from widely varied walks of life come together and encounter each other. Lawyers encounter homemakers; teachers, businesspeople; adults, children other than their own; the poor, the middle class—sets of people who might never meet or share each other's lives elsewhere. Regular encounters or meetings go on in churches each week between a multiplicity of publics that include a multiplicity of persons with a multiplicity of reasons for coming to worship—motives which range from personal guilt to a search for redemption, from unbroken habit to persistent familiar pressure, from obligation to do the right to an opportunity to discover the good.

Congregations both mediate between individuals and the public at large and themselves function as publics. The public meeting of the church provides the context for various mediations. Thus we can view the church as bridge-builder because bridges tend *publicly* to connect two sides of land divided by some natural or human-made object. The church acts, precisely, as that sort of institution in our fragmented and pluralistic society. The church offers bridges between a variety of publics in a variety of locations—and brings those publics together. The church by its very nature attempts to build a bridge between personal faith and public good.

Jeremiah's words to the exiles in Babylon have served to inspire many in Christian history about the public nature of the church. After the Babylonians ripped away all that was familiar to them culturally and spiritually, such as the Temple and its spiritual comfort in Jerusalem, the Jews questioned their purpose so far from home. Jeremiah exhorted them to "seek the peace of the city . . . and pray to the Lord for it; for in its peace you will have peace." The people of God in Babylon faced the temptation to ignore, or even reject, the pagan city in which they found themselves. Jeremiah confronted the false strategies of escapism, isolationism, and violent revolution and asked the people instead to seek peace—the shalom—for the *whole city*, not just the people of God. Why? Because the peace of the whole city, bringing well-being, contentment, justice, wholeness, and joy to all, must matter to the people of God: *in the city's peace you will have peace.* The church experiences a deeper shalom when the whole commonwealth has peace. Christian tradition commands the church to any number of commitments to the public at large because the prophetic word has tied the destiny of the church covenantally to the destiny of the republic.

In *The Public Church,* Marty writes about the public church, "a family of apostolic churches with Jesus Christ at the center, churches which are especially sensitive to the *res publica*, the public order that surrounds and includes people of faith."[32] This public church, which includes Roman Catholic, Protestant, and evangelical Protestant traditions, seeks to move religious faith away from issues which merely concern the personal toward a wider commitment to the public. Specifically, the congregation accepts responsibility for the common good of the wider society. To be sure, much religious activity remains private. But private activity should not automatically imply public irrelevancy. The church is not a "company of people huddled together with their backs to the world" but a group of people who face outward, open but discriminating to the world.[33] Religious institutions significantly involve themselves in public matters such as building stronger families, educating children, assisting the dispossessed, and working for better local neighborhoods. The church can even sustain and improve other mediating institutions.

In short, the church influences society, not merely privately or residually, but transformatively.[34] Mediating institutions such as churches witness and maintain human values for both individuals and the society. The great danger of the First Amendment religion clauses "is not that the churches or any one church will take over the state. The much more real danger is that the state will take over the functions of the church, except for the most narrowly construed definition of religion limited to worship and religious instruction."[35]

II. ECCLESIASTICAL ASSISTANCE TO THE NEEDY IN THE UNITED STATES

Robert L. Payton, of Indiana University's Center of Philanthropy, indicates that societal assistance to the poor draws from four basic sources: "self-help; mutual aid (families and associations); government assistance; and voluntary philanthropy (large and small gifts and donations of time)."[36] Governmental agencies already enlist ecclesiastical organizations to facilitate the distribution of large amounts of governmental funds. Furthermore, ecclesiastical charities derive a large portion of their operating budgets from governmental sources and depend upon that money. The federal government has always used the nonprofit voluntary sector[37] to avoid reduplicating efforts and to serve governmental policies. For example, Catholic Charities receives about 65 percent of its funds from federal, state, and local governmental sources. Forty-three percent of the social service field's income comes from governmental sources. Thus, while private agencies, most religiously based, deliver the majority of services to the poor, governmental agencies provide most of the funds for those services.[38] Any plan to cut the social welfare budget by turning over services to voluntary charities seems unnecessarily ironic when one considers how massively private charity depends on public funding.[39]

Half of all the money and time given to care for the poor goes through organized religion. Furthermore, those 25 percent of the population who regularly attend church "have a disproportionately large influence on all philanthropic giving and service."[40] Fifty-eight percent of Christians indicated that they donated time or money to the impoverished near them.[41] Yet, James M. Wall notes that the political shift away from government toward private charity support "does not appear to be accompanied . . . by a new willingness on the part of individuals to pick up a larger share of voluntary aid."[42] Probably the private sector cannot make up the difference created by government cuts. Independent Sector, a coalition of over eight hundred voluntary organizations, reports that from 1989 to 1993, the average annual household's giving dropped from $978 to $880.[43] Volunteerism also diminished in the same time period by about 6 percent. In fact, if giving increased by only 5 percent, it would yield about $6 billion. This amount would not have come close to making up the suggested cut of $150 billion Gingrich proposed.[44] While religious communities' aid to the needy has increased significantly (despite a drop in overall giving), David Beckmann, director of Bread for the World, estimated that each congregation would have to increase its budget to the needy by $190,000 if the nation's 350,000 congregations tried to make up just $66 billion of the proposed cuts.[45]

Furthermore, Beckmann believes that "attempts by our political leaders to make churches and charities the social safety net for the nation have only succeeded in hindering these institutions from doing what they do best. Churches are good at helping people in need take responsibility for their actions."[46] While the prospect of losing federal money might strongly motivate some of the needy to take more responsibility for their lives, federal cuts do not address the deeper causes of poverty. For example, a profound lack of self-respect manifests itself in such problems as substance abuse or teen pregnancy. The church can bring special resources for addressing the issue of self-respect. But the church needs freedom to accomplish its social purposes in its own unique way. Saddling it with such a financial burden will founder it and stop it from doing those things that it alone can do.

III. THE DISTINCTIVE CHARACTER OF CHURCH SOCIAL SERVICE AGENCIES

Capitalizing on the distinctive strengths of the church will best assist the needy and the society in which they reside. However, forcing on churches the responsibility for other activities they do *not* do well will destroy much of the good that they already accomplish.

Clear scriptural warrant that care for the poor expresses an integral part of what it means to love God with all of one's heart, soul, and mind motivates Christians to assist the needy. This attitude has infused the American church from its earliest beginnings. As a result, Christians have devoted great amounts of time, energy, prayer, and financial resources to alleviating human suffering and need. How Christians respond, however, depends upon their varying conceptions and perceptions of questions such as the causes of poverty, human nature, appropriate societal structures, and the role and duties of government.[47]

We can count the needy much more easily than we can determine the causes of their poverty. According to the U.S. Census Bureau, 15 percent of the American population, about 34 million people, lived in poverty in 1994.[48] From all over the political and social spectrum we hear widely differing identifications of the causes of poverty. Some point to structural causes (causes located outside the control of the poor); others to personal causes (causes attributed to the attitudes and behaviors of the poor themselves). We could list a myriad of causes of chronic poverty: substance abuse, racism, mental illness, physical disability, breakdown of the two-parent family, inadequate financial resources, failure of responsibility among the poor to take control of their lives, lack of jobs, lack of desire to work, lack of education, low-paying jobs, welfare programs which foster dependency, inadequate health care, and the flight of stable families from inner-city communities. The sheer number of possible causes, however, should teach us; for while economists, propagandists, and politicians variously shift blame back and forth from society to government, from the rich to the poor themselves, from internal to structural factors, in the end we cannot identify one simple cause of poverty, or even just three or four. In fact, the relative weight and pattern of the causes may individualize in a particular case. This individualization of the causes may precisely offer hope in the ecclesiastical organization. Churches and their agencies tend to match assistance to people in accordance with the individual's own specific needs, not on the basis of predetermined economic or social factors which the individual merely illustrates. Does lack of child care pose the problem? Meaninglessness? Alcoholism? Churches, uniquely situated in people's lives, can accurately determine the specific causes of hardship.

For example, Sarah Wilke, at the Wesley Rankin Center in West Dallas, told me that recipients of church social services must participate in identifying their own needs. She said that church ministries need to avoid mimicking Job's counselors (advising from a distance), and instead model themselves on Christ and listen attentively to people describe their needs specifically and circumstantially. Church agencies, on principle, must honor the dignity of the people they serve. The belief that people's individual needs and views demand a respect responsive to the dignity of the person in need distinguishes their social services and ministries (a view common to all the agency workers I interviewed). They thus treat clients as inherently worthy individuals who have distinctive needs, not just ciphers in groups.

Stephen Monsma outlines three requirements for any effective antipoverty effort. First, it must require that the poor take on specific obligations for having received assistance. Second, it calls for the extensive development of preventive programs which will discourage self-destructive behaviors and encourage a strong family life and responsible sexual attitudes. Third, and most pertinent to this discussion, an effective antipoverty program must work "with the poor on a personal, individual level to solve problems and supply the help needed."[49] Large state and federal agencies do not usually follow through on this third element because they lack the ability to give personal attention to specific needs of a particular individual. Furthermore, these agencies can easily overlook the unique familial, congregational, and neighborhood contexts out of which a poor person has come—factors which can significantly help that person overcome his or her chronic poverty. Consequently, caregivers must turn to the nonprofit sector, particularly religiously based agencies: "They have the flexibility, the community and neighborhood roots, and often the religious and moral authority needed to relate personally to those in need and to work with existing structures, building on them rather than supplanting them."[50] Church agencies can uniquely serve as bridges, linking (if not providing) poor people with the resources they need to contend with their poverty and to acquire personal power over their circumstances.

Church social service agencies can make a second distinctive contribution in the way in which they understand and deal with "dependency." Most welfare programs, many have argued, have created an unhealthy dependency in the needy upon the state. Yet, one cannot look at dependency as a sole cause of poverty. As David Heim writes, "Most of us, when we examine our lives, recognize that we have been enormously dependent, especially at certain times in our lives."[51] Dependency can serve as a necessary step on the way to independence. The trick is to transform dependency from a hammock to a transitional step in a ladder.

Yet, we deceive ourselves, I believe, if we make independence the sole goal of empowerment. Rather, we should aim at interdependence. As the Rev. Sterling Lands at the Texas Family Pathfinders inaugural conference put it, "Our mission is to move people on public assistance from dependence, through independence, to interdependence." All of us daily depend on others, daily need others, as well as trust others—even as they trust us through vocations in our communities of work, family, church, and society. The church and its agencies remind people that we all live under covenant—all dependent, all independent, all interdependent. Miss Wilke in her characteristically engaging manner disputes the distinction between givers and receivers because everybody gives . . . and everybody receives. She told the story of the man who came down to the Wesley Rankin Center to play Santa and give kids toys. He made the mistake of asking one little boy what he wanted for Christmas. Responded the lad, "My Dad." The man playing Santa thought he volunteered his time to give, and he left having received. He could not provide what the boy wanted. But, he did receive. Said Wilke, "He got a whole lot more than he bargained for!" Interdependence embodies those mystical bonds which make us aware that as we daily give and receive, we can never exactly define which role we fill at any given moment.

Churches form communities that typically understand the nature of interdependency—for they proclaim, first, that humans radically depend on the grace of God as well as upon each other. God has called congregants to accountability to and responsibility for one another. Church community should provide persons in need not judgment alone, but acceptance, love, access to the goods they need, and accountability, as they learn to move from abject dependency, through independency, to interdependency. Indeed, interdependence restores the dignity crushed by total dependency and the selfishness and pride arising from the illusion of independence.

Third, church social service agencies uniquely serve society in serving whom they serve. Ecclesiastical institutions can bring the lowest, most marginalized, and least fortunate of all back into covenant with society. As Berger and Neuhaus write, "In truth, if we are really concerned for those individuals who fall between the cracks, it is worth noting that the most anomic individuals in our society . . . are cared for almost exclusively by voluntary associations, usually religious in character. Government bureaucracies . . . demonstrate little talent for helping the truly marginal who defy generalized categories." That statement does not dismiss government help, but reminds us of those who fall outside of our common experience: for example, prisoners, the homeless, and the undocumented.

Those incarcerated for crimes committed in the United States find few advocates among the general population and even fewer among governmental agencies themselves. Religious voluntary organizations have frequently led prison reform, helping incarcerated prisoners, as well as ex-convicts in their transition into society. In most major cities, homelessness remains a vexing problem. Moreover, the homeless find few advocates. Yet, many religious groups seek to assist the silent, yet visible, homeless among us. For example, a well-organized coalition of congregations, Congregational Advocates for Homeless People (CAHP), attempts to find solutions to homelessness in the greater Dallas community. Focusing on the political, legal, and educational dimensions of advocacy, CAHP works "with and on behalf of homeless people to air their concerns and safeguard their rights."[52]

My own work as a Lutheran pastor on the U.S.-Mexico border has introduced me to another large marginalized group of people, "illegal aliens," or less pejoratively, "the undocumented." The undocumented often have only the institution of extended family and local cultural community to support them in times of crisis. Who will care humanely for these people who live in this country outside the law, thrice dehumanized and victimized, first by conditions of abject poverty in their home country, second by the *coyotes* who illegally exploit and transport the undocumented into this country, and third by an exclusion from the most basic public social services in this nation? If the state has difficulty in serving its citizens adequately, how will it serve noncitizens? The state cannot assist because it classifies the undocumented as "illegal."

The church, however, has helped and continues to help the undocumented find clothing, shelter, minimal health care, and the legal assistance necessary to gain United States citizenship. While some conservatives view the church as subversive of the common good because it offers this sort of help to "outlaws," I would contend just the opposite. By helping the undocumented gain citizenship and caring for those outside the community of citizens, the church helps stabilize society and place the undocumented back in touch with societal power. The church can freely answer the question "Who is the neighbor I am called to love?" in a way that other structures cannot. The church as mediating structure reminds society of its covenantal obligations to all people, no matter how marginalized. This same church, while seeking to obey the laws, also seeks to empower people, bringing the marginalized back into covenant with a larger society even when that larger society does not recognize them as legally and defensibly present.

Clearly, we must form new partnerships between the nonprofit sector and governmental agencies for the sake of the poor. "The debate over social services involves more than the amount government spends; it raises policy questions about who is responsible for assisting the nation's poor, who can best perform those services, and whether entitlement programs keep the poor in a state of welfare dependency."[53] Only a cooperative venture will allow both the third sector and the government to do those things that each does best. In fact, in many cases, the nonprofit sector delivers services more effectively than governmental bureaucracies.[54]

IV. The Church as Bridge and Pontifex

The metaphors of the church as a mediating structure and meeting place help explain the limited yet very necessary public function of the church in a democracy such as ours. "Mediation" evokes the picture of someone or something standing "in the middle." Mediation offers middle ground in order to bring reconciliation or settlement to conflicting parties. Christ so mediated. He stood in the middle and reconciled God and humanity, the world to himself, and each of us to one another. The church as the body of Christ also stands in the middle of a multiplicity of often conflicting parties, seeking to show how they need each other. Each party needs the other; the elimination of either diminishes the other party.

As a pastor, I have unceasingly searched for an apt metaphor, or combination of metaphors, to describe the church and its activity in the world. Because the church means different things to different people as they live and move and have their being, no single metaphor will suffice for all. Further, metaphors change as one moves from childhood (church as school), through middle adulthood (church as army), to one's golden years (church as community center). One's theological preferences also favor specific images. Some prefer to see the church as army, conquering evil in the name of Christus Victor. Others prefer the image of hospital, a place for healing from sin. Still others see the church as a bit of both, as a sort of MASH unit, both healing and battling.

To this already rich supply of metaphors I would like to add yet another image: the church as pontifex, or bridge-builder. If you will, the church is a little pontoon, not just a little platoon.[55] Pontifex brings to mind a critical role for the church in a pluralistic society: bridge-building between the conflicting interests that make up a pluralistic society. Mediation means bridging between two parties, two locations, two ideas, two people, two institutions. Meeting often leads to interaction between these parties. This mediating church offers bridges that connect people, making them aware of the covenant that binds them to each other. Let me suggest a few bridges that the church might build in its work with the impoverished.

A. A BRIDGE BACKWARD TO PAST AND TRADITION

"I believe in the communion of saints." Those churches that take seriously this article of faith testify to their interconnectedness with those people who have gone before them and have "fought the good fight of faith."

American congregations live and perhaps have always lived in paradoxical circumstances. They are simultaneously places of memory and places of amnesia. On the one hand, they bear traditions—legacies of once (still?) powerful pasts. On the other, they manifest the quintessential American penchant for freedom from constraints of the past and openness to new possibilities of the present and future. Those who belong to congregations inevitably find themselves squeezed between two contrary impulses—tradition's pressure to remember and modernity's pressure to forget.[56]

When interviewed, Elizabeth Blessing of the East Dallas Cooperative Parish commented that people, when they have run out of other sources of assistance, often call upon the church for help as a last resort. Somewhere in the past, these people have had a connection to the church, and as a result, they know they can turn to it. The individual and collective memories of many people instinctively draw them to the church to help them reconnect to covenantal communities, and ultimately to society as a whole. To no institution other than the family will people turn so frequently when in total despair. This attitude speaks volumes. The church serves as the collective memory, not merely for the members of a specific congregation, but also for the whole community.

James Gustafson writes, "Common memory makes possible common life."[57] This common memory unfolds when each person in a congregation "relives the meanings of past events in history, and makes them a part of his personal history."[58] Symbols, stories, and reenactments of past events help us relive and assimilate our communal past. The community of Christ keeps the memory of Christ alive by dramatizing the sacred narrative again and again in the liturgy. The church rehearses the acts of God in the Scripture reading and in the sacramental meal. Annual congregational events such as Reformation Day or La Fiesta de Nuestra Señora de Guadalupe make present an important part of a people's heritage. Integrating into this common memory creates and sustains a common life for each individual.

Mediating structures such as congregations and their social ministries integrate individuals into the community by reconnecting people isolated in a fragmented and individualistic society with their ancestral faith. Churches offer bridges to the recent and distant past and offer people historical foundations upon which to rebuild their lives, either complementing familial history or replacing a lost familial history. When people come to the church for help, many of them seek to relive those meaningful events of the past which have given them identity. When oppression, unfortunate circumstances, or difficult times have shattered their identities, and they feel circumstantially "pressured to forget," they renew and ground their identities by reconnecting with the church and its offer of help. The Mexican immigrants here in Texas provide a clear example of this renewal. For many of the immigrants who come here from Mexico legally or illegally, the Roman Catholic Church connects them to their past. The Mexican people have learned to distrust any state power. Hence, a connection with their collective spiritual past supplies them with a covenantal resource in this strangely individualistic land with a strangely Protestant tongue.

B. A BRIDGE FORWARD WITH HOPE

Lesslie Newbigin quotes the Chinese Christian writer Carver T. Yu as saying that two key elements, "technological optimism and literary pessimism," characterize Western society.[59] Science and medicine provide our society with an ever expanding technological power over our environment and lives. Yet, ironically, nihilism and despair fill our drama and fiction.

The church, as it seeks to live out the story of a God who loves and cares and a community that seeks to embody that love privately and publicly, offers hope for the future. The church does not direct this hope simply to "last things," that is, an eschatological hope for the coming kingdom, but to the present, a hope that inspires people to believe life worth living. The church becomes the locus of that hope. In the congregation, this hope is "present, known, and experienced."[60] This hope assumes a remarkable future for the world.

Ron Sider and Heidi Rolland firmly believe that *"spiritual* transformation must be a central component of the fight against poverty."[61] Spiritual
transformation opens up the possibility of hope, and hope gives one reason to
reject self-destructive behaviors. Some research confirms that "people with
religious faith are less likely to engage in behaviors associated with poverty—
divorce, single parenthood, drug abuse, alcoholism, quitting school."[62] In one
study, church attendance among inner-city African American males better
predicted those who would escape poverty than any other variables such as
income, involvement in sports, and family structure.[63] Many policy-makers
concur that religious faith does affect success rates among clients of religiously based nonprofits because the clients acknowledge the spiritual, not
just the physical, component of being human.

Thus, the church offers hope and the power to transform as it builds
bridges toward God. To exclude this bridge-building mediation, as do so
many secular agencies, denies many people the hope they need, that of a rec-
onciling God who offers support and help. A wholistic approach to assisting
the needy should serve the needy spirit as well as the needy body.

C. A BRIDGE OUTWARD TOWARD OTHERS

A bridge to others recalls Marty's description of the church as a meeting place
where people from all walks of life interact, communicate, and empower each
other, thus reminding one another of their bonds of covenant. Such bridges
help connect the needy to the dominant society; the common to the uncommon; woman to man; child to adult; one race to another race; infants to the
elderly. William Schambra, Director of General Programs at the Lynde and
Harry Bradley Foundation, writes that God calls Christians

> by the story of the Good Samaritan to suffer with and minister to
> the broken of this world—directly, immediately, personally, not
> through paid professional substitutes. That sort of commitment can

be effectively expressed and facilitated only in a society rich in mediating structures . . . not mediating vertically, between individual and
state . . . but mediating horizontally, between suburb and inner city,
between the wealthy and the poor.[64]

The church bridges horizontally. Sarah Wilke spoke poignantly of this image
when she described the suburbanite who left her enclosing, isolating "bubble"
in downtown Dallas to help a young child read. Rather than commuting to
another such bubble in Plano, this woman found a bridge to another person.
Said Wilke, "We embrace people and connect people who don't necessarily
run into each other. [This connection] enriches their life and the life of the
child they help."

In my own church body, a program called "Can-Do" attempts to bring
together the well-off adolescent children from suburban churches with some
of the less fortunate of all age groups from Russia, Mexico, and the urban centers of the United States. The youth that go on these "servant events" spend
time serving others full-time for a week or more during their summer or
school breaks. This program exemplifies many in American churches through
which the church itself builds bridges in our society and world. It creates
new meeting places by bringing two isolated publics into contact with one
another, and expands the worlds of both parties in the process.

Robert Bellah in *The Good Society* argues that trust supplies the critical
glue which holds democratic society together. Mediating institutions reestablish, at least, fragmentary trust among the disenfranchised in "the system." In
spite of the disillusionment caused by institutions that don't care, the disenfranchised find one institution that does care and reaffirms the possibility of
hope and faith, if not charity. While churches may hope that the disenfranchised ultimately direct their trust to the One who gives them life, they also
help to revive some trust in "the system." The order previously experienced as
disorder, they begin to see as less disorderly. Individuals in capitalistic societies
join each other by contracts. Individuals link temporarily and expediently to
exchange goods and services that gratify self-interest. The church supplies a

means of teaching and living a life that links us by more than contracts. The church, the pontifex in society, attempts to build covenantal bridges between people and remind them of their inclusive covenant with other human beings.

V. TWO PROPOSALS

Religious organizations face great dangers in accepting government funding. They may lose their spiritual identity and character as well as their ability to embody their religious faith in the programs they offer. In my view, the loss of autonomy can seriously undercut the ability of these agencies to serve the poor. First, many dedicated people serve as staff and volunteers in their group because of the religious character of a nonprofit organization; it permits them to live out their own religious commitments. As Sarah Wilke said, the Wesley Rankin Center "is a mission, not a church agency." Missions draw many people to service as a concrete expression of their faith. Second, spiritual components in many programs often determine the program's success, as in many addiction recovery programs. Spiritual beliefs affect motives and behaviors because they ground human living in God.[65] Religiously based nonprofits and congregations might enter into a symbiotic relationship with the government without the loss of autonomy and without breaching the constitutional proprieties in two ways:

A. FAMILY PATHFINDERS

The Family Pathfinders program in Texas[66] offers a creative example of how government attempts to support and utilize the church as a mediating structure in a meaningful, but not burdensome, way in order to help those on welfare. The state government utilizes the moral and social resources of the religious community (as well as other voluntary associations) in order to address the needs of people receiving public assistance. Originating out of a Texas welfare reform package, the Family Pathfinders program seeks to move welfare recipients from dependency to independence with the cooperating assistance of religious and civic groups.

The state has asked each congregation and civic organization in Texas to adopt one family in order to assist that family in acquiring some of the basic skills and resources they need to become self-supporting. The individuals acting on behalf of the adopting institutions cannot offer financial help because such help would jeopardize the benefits of the welfare recipients. Rather, the adopters offer help in the form of job contacts, skills development (e.g., mock job interviews and help on how to dress for work), child care contacts, transportation, and the like. As one pastor at the conference put it, "We are trying to give people a hand up, not a handout."

A congregation forms a team (or teams) of three to eight people who will work with a state-assigned family. The contract between a family and a congregational team runs approximately one year, but either party may, if problems arise, end the relationship at any time. Each team member must sign a confidentiality form to protect the dignity and privacy of the family assisted. Each team also receives initial training and ongoing support from the state. Family Pathfinders seeks to avoid financial handouts, which encourage dependency. Instead, this program provides a mechanism by which congregations can empower people to become dignified, contributing members of society. Furthermore, it offers a personalized approach, sensitive to the specific needs of the adopted family.

B. VOUCHERS

Ron Sider and Heidi Rolland propose another fascinating and creative way in which the government and church agencies can cooperatively assist the needy, allowing each entity to maintain an unentangled independence while respecting the dignity and freedom of the assisted. They call for an expansion of the Child Care and Development Block Grant Act of 1990 that permits states to grant families vouchers which in turn pay for child care services chosen by each family.[67] The program resembles Pell Grants, in which students may use government funds to pay for college tuition to either public or private colleges. Because people can freely utilize the grants, the government does not support religious institutions over secular ones, or one religion over another.

Sider suggests that we expand such vouchers to cover a variety of human needs. Qualified persons would receive a check they could "cash" for services at government-approved agencies, some religious. Sider prefers nonprofit entities with their own legal charter over congregations as agencies. Recipients could give such vouchers to drug rehabilitation programs, job services, medical care providers, or family counselors. Naturally, the government would have to establish guidelines both to protect the autonomy and character of the religious institution (particularly in the case of faith-based programs of drug addiction recovery) and to protect the taxpayer from paying for religious education or proselytizing.

No government has yet tried such programs extensively. Yet, they offer a way in which government and religious agencies and churches may work together for the sake of the poor. These creative alternatives open a way for the church to play a role in the *res publica* without sacrificing their autonomy and without commingling government and religion.

Conclusion

More than ever, any form of state provision for the less fortunate of society must leave room for voluntary, ecclesiastical charitable associations, for those organizations serve the impoverished in our land in ways that neither governmental nor individual charities can. Ecclesiastical social service agencies and churches are not only important, but essential, to the well-being of the people they serve and to the full flourishing of the society of which they are a part. I used to believe that a service's indispensability arose solely out of the fundamental services and goods it provided, such as food, sufficient shelter, etc. Now, however, I am convinced that a church-affiliated charitable organization offers something more fundamental out of its essential being as pontifex. It offers people a multiplicity of bridges by which they can reconnect their lives with the past, the future, other people, and God. On these bridges, on these public mediating and meeting places, people can see and meet a world larger and different from themselves, and yet a world with which they stand in covenant, to enrich others and by others to be enriched.[68]

NOTES

1. David Heim, "Are the Poor with Us?" *Christian Century* (March 1, 1980): 227.

2. Edmund Burke believed in the necessity of "little platoons," or voluntary associations of citizens, as a means for improving and increasing the public good. Benjamin Franklin also promoted voluntary associations, attributing his ideas to Cotton Mather, who had encouraged Christians to form organizations for charitable purposes. See James Luther Adams, *Voluntary Associations: Socio-cultural Analyses and Theological Interpretation*, ed. J. Ronald Engel (Chicago: Exploration Press, 1986). About voluntary associations, Tocqueville wrote, "If each citizen did not learn, in proportion as he individually becomes more feeble and consequently more incapable of preserving his freedom singlehanded, to combine with his fellow citizens for the purpose of defending it, it is clear that tyranny would unavoidably increase together with equality." Alexis de Tocqueville, *Democracy in America*, trans. Henry Reeve, Rev. Francis Brown, ed. Phillips Bradley (New York: Vintage Books, 1990), 2:106.

3. Tocqueville, *Democracy in America*, 2:108–9.

4. Peter L. Berger and Richard John Neuhaus, *To Empower People: The Role of Mediating Structures in Public Policy* (Washington, D.C.: American Enterprise Institute for Public Policy Research, 1977), 1.

5. Ibid., 1–2.

6. Ibid., 3. Writes Daniel J. Boorstin in the Introduction to *Democracy in America*: "Although Tocqueville writes about a nation and a continent, his overwhelming concern is for the individual. Haunted by a well-documented fear of the power of democracy to frighten and submerge the individual, he was a prophet—even an inventor—of individualism. The very word 'individualism' first entered our English language through Reeve's translation of Tocqueville's *Democracy in America*." According to Tocqueville, "Individualism is a mature and calm feeling which disposes each member of the community to sever himself from the mass of his fellow-creatures, and to draw apart with his family and friends." What is fascinating about Tocqueville's definition is the inclusion of mediating structures of family and friends in the definition of individualism itself! Humans as individuals are not totally, utterly alone, but find friendships and relationships in smaller associations (Tocqueville, *Democracy in America*, x–xi).

7. Berger and Neuhaus, *To Empower People*, 6.

8. Adams, *Voluntary Organizations*, 217.

9. Ibid., 218–19.

10. Berger and Neuhaus, *To Empower People*, 4.

11. Ibid., 4–5.

12. Ibid., 6.

13. Ibid., 7.

14. Adams, *Voluntary Associations*, 236ff.

15. Tocqueville, *Democracy in America*, 2:109.

16. Adams, *Voluntary Associations*, 233.

17. Ibid., 236–37.

18. Ibid., 239.

19. Ibid., 220.

20. Ibid., 221.

21. Berger and Neuhaus, *To Empower People*, 8.

22. Adams, *Voluntary Associations*, 243.

23. Ibid., 248–49.

24. Ibid., 243.

25. Ibid.

26. Martin E. Marty, "Public and Private: Congregation as Meeting Place," in *American Congregations,* ed. James P. Wind and James W. Lewis (Chicago: University of Chicago Press, 1994), 2:134–35.

27. Ibid., 2:142.

28. Ibid., 2:145.

29. Ibid., 2:149.

30. Ibid., 2:150.

31. Ibid., 2:151.

32. Martin E. Marty, *The Public Church* (New York: Crossroad Publishing Co., 1981), 3.

33. Ibid.

34. Berger and Neuhaus, *To Empower People,* 26–28.

35. Ibid., 30.

36. James M. Wall, "Give All You Can," *Christian Century* (February 1–8, 1995): 100.

37. This sector is often referred to as the "Third Sector" for lack of a better term for those groups that are neither business nor government. The third sector is not independent of business or government since its funding often comes from those sources. Nor is the third sector always voluntary or private. Instead, the third sector serves as "a locus of public discourse about the collective values of society. It provides an arena in which fundamental values, both political and nonpolitical, can be discussed, symbolized, experimented with or ritually embodied." John A. Coleman, "Religion and the Third Sector," in *In All Things: Religious Faith and American Culture,* ed. Robert J. Daly (Kansas City, Mo.: Sheed and Ward, 1990), 179.

38. Stephen V. Monsma, "Overcoming Poverty: The Role of Religiously Based Nonprofit Organizations," in *Welfare in America: Christian Perspectives on a Policy in Crisis,* ed. Stanley W. Carlson-Thies and James W. Skillen (Grand Rapids, Mich.: Wm. B. Eerdmans Co., 1996), 431.

39. Martin E. Marty, "Church and State Charity," *Christian Century* (March 1, 1995): 255.

40. Wall, "Give All You Can," 100.

41. Ronald J. Sider and Heidi Rolland, "Correcting the Welfare Tragedy: Toward a New Model for Church/State Partnership," in *Welfare in America: Christian Perspectives on a Policy in Crisis,* ed. Stanley W. Carlson-Thies and James W. Skillen (Grand Rapids, Mich.: Wm. B. Eerdmans Co., 1996), 468.

42. Wall, "Give All You Can," 100.

43. Ibid.

44. News, "Churches Worry about Welfare," *Christian Century* (February 15, 1995): 165–66.

45. David Beckmann, "Assault on the Poor," *Christian Century* (April 5, 1995): 356.

46. Ibid., 357.

47. Stanley W. Carlson-Thies, introduction to *Welfare in America: Christian Perspectives on a Policy in Crisis,* ed. Stanley W. Carlson-Thies and James W. Skillen (Grand Rapids, Mich.: Wm. B. Eerdmans Co., 1996), xiii–xiv.

48. Monsma, "Overcoming Poverty," 426.

49. Ibid., 428.

50. Ibid., 429.

51. Heim, "Are the Poor with Us?" 228.

52. Congregational Advocates for Homeless People. The Greater Dallas Community of Churches, 2800 Swiss Ave., Dallas, TX 75204.

53. News, "Churches Worry about Welfare," *Christian Century* (February 15, 1995): 166.

54. While the nation on average may have been more or less satisfied to see a welfare reform package finally materialize in legislative form in the summer of 1996, antipoverty debates should not disappear from the nation's public debate. The church and its social agencies breathed a collective sigh of relief to see the threat of an impending financial burden disappear; so also did others breathe their own sighs as they were able to avoid that nasty thicket of church/state constitutional questions, and were allowed to relegate churches yet again to the "private" sector. Monsma attributes this success to three unique factors of nonprofit agencies: (1) they have greater opportunity to

exercise creativity and flexibility in the solution to social problems; (2) those who head and those who work for nonprofits often have a deeper sense of commitment to the cause of the agency, especially if the agency is religiously based, and (3) "religiously based nonprofits . . . speak the language of morality and of religious or ethnic solidarity." Monsma, "Overcoming Poverty," 431.

55. After I settled on my own image, I discovered J. Phillip Wogaman's discussion of the ways in which congregations link people with one another, with power centers, and with sources of meaning. See J. Phillip Wogaman, "The Church as Mediating Institution: Theological and Philosophical Perspective" and "The Church as Mediating Institution: Contemporary American Challenge," in *Democracy and Mediating Structures,* ed. Michael Novak (Washington, D.C.: The American Enterprise Institute for Public Policy Research, 1980), 69–105. Even more explicitly but for other purposes, the image of a bridge was used extensively in the 1996 presidential campaign.

56. James P. Wind and James W. Lewis, "Memory, Amnesia, and History," in *Carriers of Faith: Lessons from Congregational Studies,* ed. Carl S. Dudley, Jackson W. Carroll, and James P. Wind (Louisville, Ky.: Westminster/John Knox Press, 1991), 15.

57. James M. Gustafson, *Treasure in Earthen Vessels: The Church as a Human Community* (New York: Harper & Row, Publishers, 1961), 73.

58. Ibid., 72.

59. Lesslie Newbigin, *The Gospel in a Pluralistic Society* (Grand Rapids, Mich.: Wm. B. Eerdmans Publishing Co., 1989), 232.

60. Ibid.

61. Sider and Rolland, "Correcting the Welfare Tragedy," 463.

62. Ibid., 464.

63. Ibid., 465.

64. William Schambra, "To Be Citizens Again," *First Things* (August/September, 1996): 17.

65. Monsma, "Overcoming Poverty," 446.

66. I had the privilege to attend the inaugural event in Austin, June 1996.

67. Sider and Rolland, "Correcting the Welfare Tragedy," 469.

68. Congregations in themselves are quite public in their nature and activity. James Wind in a phone conversation with me spoke of numerous studies throughout the United States which indicated that the church continues to play extremely vital, and even surprising, roles in public life, despite official rhetoric that its influence is minimal.

The Role of the Voluntary Community in the Affordable Housing Equation

Provider, Change Agent, Conscience

TREY HAMMOND

This essay explores the emergence of the voluntary community as a provider of "decent, affordable housing." Nonprofit corporations, foundations, and churches are playing an increasingly important role in building low-cost housing, both single-family and multifamily, as a tangible way of revitalizing their communities. Though nonprofits have been involved in affordable housing efforts in the past, the agenda was largely determined by government programs or the local development climate. Today's housing equation is different, in that the voluntary sector is producing unprecedented numbers of units and functions as more of a "player" in the establishing of policies and programs. In this new context, the nonprofit contribution is threefold—as provider, catalyst, and social conscience.

A historical overview of the roles the first two sectors—government and private enterprise—have played in providing affordable housing is critical in assessing the place of the voluntary community, or third sector. Arguably, the modern era of housing policy in America began in 1937, when Congress passed the National Housing Act, to encourage "the realization of a decent home and a suitable living environment for every American family."[1] Prior to this act, the government's role was limited and "market forces" essentially determined both the supply of housing units and opportunities for ownership. The 1937 legislation addressed two pressing structural problems—a shortage of housing units and limited ownership possibilities. At the time, banks made loans for only 40 to 50 percent of the cost of the house, repayable in three to five years, at 5 to 9 percent interest rates. Such restrictive financing options made home ownership difficult, not only for the working poor, but also for the middle class.

By enacting this housing policy, the government stepped in to guarantee private sector loans by creating the Federal Housing Administration (FHA). These guaranteed loans allowed financing of up to 80 percent of the value of the house, amortized for thirty years, and at fixed 5 to 6 percent rates. The result of such attractive FHA (and Veterans Administration) financing? Home ownership increased steadily from 44 percent in 1940 to 66 percent in 1980.[2] This increase illustrates the interactive relationship between the public and private sectors in the larger housing picture.

The Housing Act, in addition to jump-starting middle-class home ownership, also made special provision for housing those living in poverty, coming as it did in the wake of the Depression. In the 1940s and '50s, federal and local governments collaborated in the creation of an ambitious "public housing" strategy. The federal government provided the construction monies and the operating funds for several hundred thousand apartment units which were managed by local public housing authorities. This policy funded the large high-rise and low-rise complexes that sprang up in urban communities all across the country.

In the 1960s and '70s, the federal government's strategy changed from direct funding of housing authorities, as the primary developer of low-income units, to enticing the private sector to build affordable housing. The government offered private developers a number of economic incentives, including long-term loans at below-the-market interest rates. The Section 8 New Construction program, an especially effective incentive, produced at its peak 150,000 units annually of privately owned housing with Department of Housing and Urban Development (HUD) rental restrictions to maintain affordability. Federal incentives helped build some 1,000,000 units in the six-year span from 1976 to 1982.[3]

In the 1980s, during the Reagan administration, another sea change took place in the role the federal government played in stimulating the affordable housing market. First off, fewer dollars were allocated, as Congress slashed HUD's budget from $35 billion in 1981 to $7 billion in 1988, an 80 percent reduction. As one critic noted, "It was the decade in which the retreat from public housing turned into a rout."[4] Programmatically, the Section 8 Voucher program replaced the Section 8 New Construction program as the primary strategy. Proponents of these changes argued that by giving tenants a portable housing subsidy their options were multiplied by renting in the private market. Voucher holders, who paid 30 percent of their income towards rent, could rent an apartment anywhere in the community where the private landlord was willing to accept the voucher. The rent levels were established federally and reflected the market rents of the area.

With this voucher program at the core of HUD commitments, there were fewer incentives to build new housing and consequently government-subsidized production dropped to 25,000 units annually. This new federal policy assumed that the "free market" could and would provide an adequate affordable housing stock and that landlords would be open to Section 8 renters.

To address the needs of growing homeless populations in the 1980s, Congress passed the McKinney Act, which provided direct subsidies to shelter providers. This was a de facto type of emergency housing strategy, as the monies were used to build emergency shelter space and single room occupancy apartments (SROs). Another innovation of the period was the Low Income Housing Tax Credit (LIHTC) program that emerged from the Tax Reform Act of 1987. This incentive program targeted affordable housing efforts as essentially the last remaining tax shelter. LIHTC credits were allocated to a project, which the developers could sell to corporate investors, seeking the tax incentives, to raise needed equity.

In 1990, Congress passed the National Affordable Housing Act. The driving strategy of this legislation was to transfer federal block grants to local governments, where they could be allocated according to local priorities. The act was consistent with the growing trend of decentralizing government services and the premise that city and county governments make more sensitive policy decisions than those made according to the priorities of a national agenda.

This legislation recognized, more than any previous act, the emergence of a growing third sector of nonprofit, voluntary organizations. These voluntary organizations, generally known as community development corporations (CDCs), might originate from churches, from national organizations like the Enterprise Foundation, or from local community organizations hoping to positively impact the housing conditions in their community. Some three thousand to five thousand CDCs engage in housing or support services, generating an estimated 30,000 to 40,000 units annually. This historical background provides a context for the emergence of the voluntary sector and allows for realistic assessments of its ability to shape the housing landscape.

What is the "lay of the land" as the third sector emerges as a force? There is a daunting crisis in the availability of affordable housing. The demand for affordable housing has been outstripping the supply for decades. The year 1970 was the last year that there was adequate affordable housing for those living below the poverty line. With inflation and housing costs escalating rapidly, combined with the loss of much housing in urban renewal programs, the early 1970s saw a deficit that has grown now to over 4 million units.

In addition to availability, affordability poses a problem. Taking seriously a cap of 30 percent of total income as a reasonable allocation for housing costs, then in Dallas someone needs to earn $11/hr. to rent a market-rate two-bedroom apartment. This is more than twice the minimum wage. Today almost 60 percent of those earning below the poverty line pay at least half of their income for housing. This crisis in the cost and availability of housing intensifies as we enter an unprecedented experiment in welfare reform, whose advocates also make optimistic assumptions about the free market's ability to generate an adequate, affordable housing stock.

In the often partisan political rhetoric that characterizes the debate about the role of government and the charitable community in solving large social problems, a statement from the American Catholic bishops is helpful when it says that "the challenge today is to move beyond abstract disputes about whether more or less government is needed, to consideration of creative ways of enabling government and private groups to work together effectively."[5] Such a pragmatic approach yields these insights at the very least:

(1) Federal action, or inaction, profoundly shapes the affordable housing inventory.

(2) The free market *will not* provide low-cost housing on any scale without economic and legislative incentives.

(3) Even if the voluntary sector was completely committed to solving the housing crisis and had the technical expertise to do it, it could not generate the needed financial resources (only Uncle Sam has pockets deep enough to finance solutions to a structural question like housing).

(4) We cannot assume that the closest governing entity will "always" set the best and wisest policy; in other words, a national regulatory role for HUD is still imperative.

(5) We need new partnerships of government, business (including developers and financial institutions), and the voluntary housing sector, and all partners must contribute significantly.

Having worked in Dallas for some fifteen years with CDCs responding to the tragedy of homelessness and the provision of decent affordable housing, my experience is that CDCs can often deliver services more efficiently and effectively than traditional government programs. Note the operative word is *can*, not necessarily *do*. Effective programs, of any stripe, create something different than a client/provider relationship and strive to be empowering rather than fostering dependency. The advantage the third sector enjoys is greater latitude to engage people holistically, addressing not just physical needs but the accompanying social and spiritual aspects of their lives.

What is possible in this new time of partnership is not the same old charitable function of the voluntary community, full of heart but short on social analysis; or the same old government bureaucracies, long on social policy but lacking in the power of transformative personal relationships. What is emerging is a new brand of collaborative ventures that capitalize on the strengths of the partners.

The role that the voluntary sector can appropriately play in this new housing equation is threefold—as provider, catalyst, and social conscience. As a "provider," the voluntary sector has become a major force. Thousands of nonprofit corporations are producing increasing numbers of affordable housing units every year. The strategies and scale of third sector development efforts vary dramatically. An international organization, Habitat for Humanity, has domestically produced more than 25,000 units of single-family homes for private ownership over the past thirty years. At the other end of the scale spectrum, a large number of nonprofits and churches may build a single home or rehab a small apartment building to provide housing for a particular population of persons. A growing number of CDCs intend to be significant developers of affordable multifamily housing and generally partner with national housing technical assistance providers like the Enterprise Foundation, the National Congress on Community Economic Development (NCCED), and the Local Initiatives Support Corporation (LISC).

Governments at every level are working to stimulate nonprofit development activity. HUD has revised and streamlined its guidelines in order to make its funding more accessible to nonprofit organizations. HUD has also established an office specifically to engage the faith communities in housing-related activity. As CDCs become more skilled in large-scale production, they have to become adept at blending public and private monies, both grants and loans, to be able to keep their units affordable. Some voluntary agencies are exploring funding instruments, like loan pools and technical assistance grant programs, to help CDCs through the start-up period of a project, when funding is most difficult to secure from market lenders.

A second role of the volunteer sector in affordable housing is as a catalyst. Congregations are located in communities and may become aware of the housing needs of their neighbors or members. As a faith community, they are in a unique position to bring people and organizations together to explore solutions. Churches, foundations, and nonprofits then are called upon to provide the critical start-up resources, both human and financial, to support existing providers and to create new organizations if necessary. The voluntary sector has access to tremendous human capital in the form of volunteer time and skilled expertise.

In the current context, the voluntary sector has a chance to affect public decision-making in significant new ways. The National Affordable Housing Act of 1990 provides for the creation of a comprehensive housing plan for each community, and the nonprofits and churches have a chance to be at the table to help shape the strategies and allocate the resources.

Part of the task as catalyst is to be an advocate for progressive affordable housing policy at every level of government. The National Low Income Housing Coalition has played a pivotal role in maintaining the Low Income Housing Tax Credit over the years and in drafting portions of the Housing Act of 1990 that undergirded voluntary sector partnerships.

The third role of the voluntary community is as a voice of social conscience. In particular, the religious community occupies an important role, at both the national and local levels, to articulate God's intentions for all people to have a decent place to call home. My own religious heritage, the Reformed tradition, believes that God ordered society so that government and commerce each have a role to play in maintenance of a just society. The role of the church is not necessarily to assume the role of those partners if they falter, but to call them to task and remind them of their responsibility. At a time when some interests would want the federal government to play a decreasing role in affordable housing, the voluntary sector may be increasingly called upon to remind citizens of their social obligation, through the instrument of government, to generate the financial resources needed to address large structural issues. The voluntary sector has a crucial ethical role in acting as a voice of conscience to its partner institutions, an articulator of the dignity of people and their rights, and a vehicle by which people can as a community work for the just distribution of the basic needs of a society.

The affordable housing crisis in our nation poses a daunting challenge. The Urban Institute estimates it will cost $97 billion to construct or renovate the 36 million units necessary to meet the current demand for affordable housing. Some politicians doubt whether the 1937 National Housing Act's commitment to "a decent and suitable living environment" is even appropriate in today's social context. Still other leaders are more committed than ever to the goal of creating an adequate housing stock and know that it will take a partnership more creative than anything that has happened to date.

The voluntary sector brings vision, an ethical heritage, and human resources to the work of affordable housing. With the capacity to provide needed units, the ability to connect with people in a transformative relationship, and a voice of conscience to call our partners to fulfill their appointed tasks in the society, the third sector brings much to the table. Yet the voluntary community should be realistic and discerning as it continues to shape the affordable housing equation.

NOTES

1. Michael Bodaken, "We Must Preserve the Nation's Supply of Affordable Housing," *Shelterforce* (July/August 1995): 15.

2. Gwendolyn Wright, *Building the Dream: A Social History of Housing in America* (New York: Pantheon Books, 1981), 291; Joel Blau, *The Visible Poor: Homelessness in the United States* (Oxford: Oxford University Press, 1993), 61.

3. Joel Blau, *The Visible Poor.*

4. Deyan Sudjic, *The Hundred Mile City* (San Diego: Harcourt Brace, 1992).

5. Robert Balchelder, "Solving the Housing Crisis Pragmatically," *Christian Century* (April 18, 1990).

A Voice from the Metroplex

The following statement by Brian Burton, Executive Director of the Wilkinson Center, first appeared in the *Dallas Morning News* on August 30, 1999. This article is reprinted by permission of the *Dallas Morning News*.

Faith-Based Charities Not a Cure-All for Society's Ills

BRIAN BURTON

I listen with interest to the growing call of Democrats and Republicans to enlist faith-based charities to help solve society's lingering social problems. After years of being ignored by Washington, the attention is welcomed, but it also poses a few questions about motivation.

As director of a faith-based charity, I am proud of the effective services provided by thousands of such groups across the country. The range of social problems being addressed by dedicated volunteers and staff members is an inspiring modern-day miracle. My concern is that while faith-based charities have captured the public imagination, to expect more than a slightly greater role from them creates unrealistic expectations and leaves an illusion of effective action.

While politicians brag about cutting welfare rolls, the problems of inner-city devastation, school failure, and intergenerational poverty continue to grow unabated. Vexed by social ills with no simple solutions, confounded politicians cast a hopeful eye to faith-based charities as an antidote to despair.

On many levels, faith-based charities are up to the challenge. Freed from top-down management and rigid thinking, many faith-based charities can respond quickly to changes in their neighborhoods. Charities practice relational and holistic approaches to people seeking services which create life-changing possibilities.

199

Part of the 1996 federal welfare reform bill included a provision known as the Charitable Choice Act. For the first time, faith-based charities were allowed to compete on equal footing with other private providers for government grants. Although the charity I direct has benefited from the legislation, many questions remain unanswered in this social experiment:

- Do faith-based charities have the resources to serve, as some advocate, as an outright alternative to government programs? The nonpartisan Aspen Institute states that the total annual private social spending by religious organizations is, at most, $20 billion. State, local, and federal spending on social programs exceeded $1.4 trillion in 1994. To expect faith-based charities to expand their infrastructure to that level is like asking one's local credit union to replace Chase Bank.
- Even if sufficient numbers are available, is it realistic for volunteers to fill the wide range of special needs brought by severely addicted and abused people? While volunteers perform amazing and unselfish acts of service, they cannot provide assets like adequate housing, transportation, and child care. As author and sociologist Janet Poppendieck says, "Tutoring programs are good, but they are not a substitute for good schools. Friendly visitors for AIDS patients are good, but they are no substitute for medical care or access to pharmaceuticals."
- A typical congregation has about two hundred members and is staffed by one part-time, bivocational minister. As new congregations leap into the ring for federal dollars, are they equipped to handle the administrative reporting, follow-up, outcomes measurement, and accounting required for government grants? Will there be uniform monitoring of funds to separate the provision of social services from religious teaching and evangelistic activities?

As faith-based charities are left holding the tattered remains of a shredded safety net, politicians and community leaders must form a creative and realistic vision of prevention and fundamental action. Charities will claim their proper role and continue to heal and change lives. But government must not abdicate its role and unload a huge welfare burden onto a sector incapable of bearing it.

Inviting faith-based charities and people receiving services into the conversation to struggle with these questions is a start. Together, as mutual partners around the table, we can form an agenda that will strengthen families, transform neighborhoods, and respond to today's imperatives.

Observations on the Psychology of Giving and Receiving Money

ROY W. MENNINGER

I wish to speak here about the psychology of giving and receiving money
from two perspectives. As a psychiatrist and student of the complexities
of human relationships, I have sought ways to reduce stress and improve
interpersonal effectiveness. As a retired CEO of a 501-C-3 not-for-profit
organization, I was a seeker-of-funds responsible for a successful $25 million
capital campaign in the early 1980s, and I initiated and participated in a just-
completed campaign that raised nearly $56 million to support programs in
psychiatric education and research.

While president of The Menninger Foundation, I also received a
great many letters asking our organization for money. These letters came
from people who did not understand that we are an operating foundation
that seeks money for its own programs, not a charitable foundation that
gives money to others. So I have seen both ends of the giving and receiving
enterprise.

With grateful acknowledgment to the Hogg Foundation for permission to quote from my
published presentation, *The Psychology of Giving and Receiving: Some Occupational Hazards of
Grant Making and Grant Receiving* (Austin: University of Texas, 1988).

FEELINGS AND FANTASIES ABOUT MONEY

This bimodal experience taught me that the business of giving and receiving generates some very uncomfortable feelings. I have observed that many people laboring in the philanthropic vineyard treat these feelings at best as irrelevant roadblocks to the work, and at worst, as a shameful and undiscussable secret. Even relatively sophisticated people reveal some embarrassment when invited to talk about feelings generated by giving and receiving money. Part of this embarrassment reflects the effects of professionalism, which minimizes the importance of feelings and contributes to a persistent belief that since feelings have little to do with work, they are therefore better suppressed or shoved aside.

The embarrassment also reflects our more complicated personal feelings about asking for money, about giving money away, and about money itself. These feelings usually have little to do with the purpose for which we request money or that the donor presumably wishes to support. Few of us can claim to be wholly dispassionate about money and its many personal meanings. Merely seeking it, for example, may be associated with doubt about the legitimacy of asking, as if asking were not far removed from begging. The act of giving may also express some latent need for evidence of one's essential worth. Given such emotional realities, the presence of some ambivalence about giving and receiving money is entirely logical. What is less logical is the great variety of ways we use to disguise, to deny, to project, or to suppress these uncomfortable feelings.

We find these ambivalent feelings embarrassing, not easily discussed, and even socially unacceptable. Inevitably, they affect the development, the quality, and the effectiveness of the relationship between giver and receiver.

Much of this ambivalence originates in our very complicated feelings about money itself. The concept of money is a metaphorical freight car loaded with an enormous number of meanings almost as varied as the people who possess them. Money gives power and control; it provides influence, enables revenge or offers protection, or may supply a reason for existence. For some, money offers an alternative to dependency, a way to become independent, or, paradoxically, a means to ensure perpetual dependence. In place of otherwise unavailable or unattainable love, money allows one to buy it from others. Money enables one to have, to own, to possess, or to do, and having money is perceived by both the self and others as a sign of worth. Many of us even use the phrase "net worth" as one measure of personal value. Money may even develop an erotic quality, as in the image of the old miser caressing his gold.

We make some insidious assumptions about the power and effectiveness of money. We need money to achieve organizational goals, but a great many people, especially seekers of program-supporting grants, act as if money alone will suffice. This assumption, a fantasy, enables seekers to avoid the difficult work of clarifying project or organizational purposes, setting goals and objectives, and establishing strategies to reach them. Some organizations, for example, will very plainly say, "Look, just give us the money and we'll figure out how best to use it." Or, "No, we don't have a plan yet, but we will just as soon as we get the money." Such organizations assume that money is magic, that it can overcome all obstacles, wipe away all impediments to success, and make clear thinking altogether unnecessary.

FACTS ABOUT MONEY

We often fail to recognize painful realities about money. The prospect of obtaining or possessing money can mobilize both the best and the worst in us. Easy money can encourage sloppy thinking and mental laziness. Receiving substantial funds can alter relationships in charitable organizations, unleashing destructive interpersonal changes that split the system. Previously latent forces evoke antagonistic, competitive, and hostile behavior as large gifts awaken greed, the desire to control, or a lust for power, any of which can override the organization's commitment to its charitable mission. The organization loses the fundamental realization that money is only a means to various ends, not an end in itself.

Money can override more basic commitments of trust or equality. It can introduce a new degree of paranoia or suspicion. It certainly can stimulate selfishness. Money often stresses or distorts relationships. Look what happens in us when our own teenagers ask for a handout for the third time in a week, or consider how grandparents sometimes use money to buy the attention of a grandchild, much to the parents' dismay. When used to control relationships, money ultimately demeans them.

PSYCHOLOGICAL ISSUES IN GIVING

Conversely, giving away money is not an easy task, notwithstanding the layman's fantasy that giving is simple—and a great way to make friends to boot. Givers know that it is hard work, that it is difficult to make wise decisions among so many "good" causes, that the unexpected can undo even one's best efforts, and that giving can be awkward and can embarrass both giver and receiver, endanger friendships, and make enemies.

Several rather thorny issues can hinder the selection of recipients. A painful awareness that some people become friendly primarily because they are seeking money can deter individual donors. As one anonymous wag put it, "You never know how many friends you have until you have a cottage at the beach"—or until you have money to give away.

Within well-staffed philanthropic foundations, varying points of view and sometimes widely differing value systems can raise considerable tensions between donors, trustees, and professional staff. The donor takes an understandable proprietary interest in where the money goes—after all, he or she earned it. The understandably conservative trustees honor their fiduciary responsibility and avoid taking risks. And the professional staff members often struggle with a discrepancy between their greater knowledge of the options and opportunities, and their lesser authority to choose among such options. If not recognized and managed, these divergences can exacerbate the natural difficulty in making choices and can seriously impede good grant-making.

Consider what that great philanthropist Andrew Carnegie had to say about what John D. Rockefeller called "this business of benevolence." After Carnegie had been at it for more than 5 years, he became disenchanted with "the supremely difficult art of spending large sums of money in undertakings to be of permanent advantage to the public."[1] Indeed, this business

had proved a far more difficult task than he had ever dreamed it would be when he wrote so glibly [in his "Gospel of Wealth"] about "the man of wealth . . . becoming the . . . trustee for his poorer brethren, bringing to their service his superior wisdom, experience, and ability to administer, doing for them better than they would or could do for themselves." He had learned over the twenty years since he had written those lines that, however superior he might think his wisdom and ability to administer were, it was no easy task to do better for others than they could do for themselves, particularly when everyone he encountered felt he could do it as well as Carnegie, if not better. As a steelmaker, he had been regarded as an expert; the public listened when he spoke. But he quickly discovered that the public recognized no experts in philanthropy—there were only men with money and other men who were trying to get it away from them. He was to say repeatedly in these years that he had not worked one-tenth as hard in acquiring as he did in divesting himself of his great wealth.

For a few years it had been fun, and he had thrown himself into the game with the same zest with which he had entered business. By 1906, however, Carnegie was tired of the fame, and by 1910 he was desperately sick of it. He wrote, "The final dispensation of one's wealth preparing for the final exit is I found a heavy task—all sad— . . . you have no idea the strain I have been under." And in Peebles, Scotland, at a jubilee celebration of the Chambers Institute to honor the memory of the Edinburgh printer and philanthropist, William Chambers, Carnegie departed from his prepared text to say, "Millionaires who laugh are rare, very rare, indeed." [2]

But people do give money, and many give generously, for reasons that are not always obvious. Questioning their motives seems intrusive, if not simply irrelevant. Not everyone who gives to the same cause does so for the same reason; in fact, any single individual's rationale for giving may differ for each organization or program he or she may support. Indeed, the reasons themselves are a complicated mixture of conscious judgment about the value of the cause, and equally important compelling unconscious values about the act of giving.

Does understanding these less conscious forces matter? It should, because these dynamics profoundly affect the process for both the giver and the seeker. For the giver, some understanding of the potentially corrupting power of quasi-neurotic reasons for giving can facilitate deciding more rationally among a great many competing appeals. Promoting rational choices will, of course, benefit large givers, such as wealthy individuals and family foundations. To achieve success, the seeker of grants and gifts must understand the complex motivations for giving. Stated quite simply, three levels of unconscious motivation impel giving: (1) to satisfy narcissistic urges, (2) to meet the demands of conscience, and (3) to serve altruistic purposes.

1. *Narcissistic giving* is the most primitive, the most infantile, and the most self-centered kind. A narcissistically motivated gift is intended to magnify the image of the donor and to promote personal glory (both now and in the future) by leaving behind something concrete, something visible, something named in the giver's honor. The gift conveys several messages: "See, I existed! See, I was important! Do not forget me!" Such narcissistic motivation springs from a need for approval, for acceptance, and for recognition of one's identity and worth.

Unfortunately, the word "narcissism" often connotes selfishness, so using the word in the context of giving evokes negative images and great discomfort, especially when we apply it to an undeniably altruistic gift. Thus we must emphasize two points: first, that no one among us has ever given a gift totally free of all narcissistic elements. At a basic level, giver and gift are intertwined: the gift always conveys some part of the giver, and thus every impulse to give springs from a narcissistic root.

Second, people in whom narcissism is the primary (and sometimes obvious) motive for giving typically suffer a great deal of apprehension and doubt about their own self-worth. They suspect that they may not be truly lovable. Unfortunately, they often believe that no one would pay any attention to them if they didn't have money. Our linguistic and cultural patterns equating "worth" and "money" make that deeply rooted conviction virtually incontrovertible. Also, many honorable seekers of funds covertly sense that they might in fact not associate with some potential donors if not for the goal of raising money.

Gifts of money can increase the self-esteem of the giver, especially when the gift occurs within the context of a valued relationship that enhances the gift and extends the benefits of giving beyond the immediate event.

2. ***Demands of the conscience*** motivate a second level of giving. Obligation, responsibility, duty, expectation, approbation, and, preeminently, the mitigation of guilty feelings and relief from the tension they produce drive such giving. Our conscience, or superego, defines our personal standards and ceaselessly monitors our behavior and our choices. Much charitable giving carries evidence of this guilt-based motivation. In addition to the usual justifications about the goodness of the cause, we use the words "should," "ought," or "must" to describe this type of giving.

Sometimes these obligation-driven verbs derive from the expectations of others, and we give in an effort to avoid the shame or embarrassment we might otherwise feel. Sometimes we give to expiate real or imagined sins, the sins, for instance, by which we acquired the money in the first place. Giving to such social needs as shelters or services for the homeless, the mentally ill, the handicapped, or the poor often reflects a natural wish to share with others—but it also helps mitigate the feelings of guilt that commonly accompany good fortune and better circumstance. Some givers give because they feel guilty about having any money at all; they give, even token amounts, in a symbolic effort to redress a sense of unfairness.

3. The third level, ***altruistic giving***, might be defined as the most mature. The purpose of such giving is abstract, the reward intangible. Rather than

creating a visible monument, the contribution reflects a wish to participate in the project or program. It expresses a desire to identify with the mission and activities of the recipient organization. Such a donor becomes a part of the organization and feels some sense of ownership in it.

A quiet, unassuming man who gave most of the income from his modest family foundation to our educational program exemplified such donors. He chose to allocate his contribution to fellowships to support child psychiatry trainees. Although those fellowships carried his name, he derived his satisfaction from participating, rather than from seeing his name memorialized. From the very first award, and with each year's subsequently until his death, he personally met each of the new fellows and came to their graduation three years later to share in the ceremony. Many of them wrote to tell him how much his contribution had meant.

CENTRALITY OF THE RELATIONSHIP

Every gift reflects a mixture of motivations from all three of these levels. My brief descriptions of each level, caricatures really, illustrate some underlying dynamics of giving, but no gift ever demonstrates any of these levels of motivation in "pure culture." In practice, discerning the predominant basis of a donor's giving can lead us to provide the kind of appreciation and recognition the donor really seeks. If we assume incorrectly that every large donor wants his or her name on a building, we ignore other, more subtle interests, such as a donor's wish for a continuing relationship or an opportunity for direct involvement in the project or program. The seeker of funds who fails to recognize and deal with these varying motivations risks certain embarrassment and probable failure.

Irrespective of the underlying motivation, conscious or otherwise, the giving-receiving process embodies a transaction between two parties, each of whom has a dual interest: explicitly in the project or purpose that is the ostensible reason for the grant, and implicitly in the relationship between the parties. I cannot overemphasize the importance of this implicit relationship. No matter what variety of motivations drive either party, the ultimate success of the transaction between them will depend on the degree of mutual satisfaction with their relationship. The word "mutual" recognizes the fact that a successful relationship provides a quid pro quo: that the giver also, in return for the gift, receives something of value. Even as the giver gives, the giver has to feel given to in turn. If those soliciting gifts do not recognize the necessity of this quid pro quo, the gift probably won't come, or will almost certainly be smaller than it would have been.

The giver may receive "something of value" that is more or less tangible, but even the most concrete "something of value" matters less than the relationship that provides the context for the transaction, ultimately the most significant source of received value. The importance of such a relationship is abundantly clear, for example, to donors who enjoy welcome participation in the program, or an ongoing relationship with the initial seeker as an adviser or counselor, or even as a genuinely good friend. Not infrequently, seekers minimize the importance of this relationship and fail to acknowledge the donor's real need for intangible benefits, such as the sense of value and respect that a warm association brings. Charitable contributions depend on a positive donor-seeker relationship.[3] Certainly, large gifts originate, not in a persuasive sales presentation by an articulate seeker, but rather in the satisfaction generated by a good relationship between the seeker and the donor.

PSYCHOLOGICAL ASPECTS OF ASKING AND RECEIVING

For many of us, asking for money reminds us uncomfortably of our dependent position as kids, when virtually everything had to come from somebody else. With maturity comes independence and the capacity to do for oneself. Asking for help from others can be psychologically difficult for self-reliant people; we experience it as a regression to an earlier, less mature pattern of behavior. It is a discomfiting regression, an admission of inadequacy, a feeling of being one down. Seeking financial help to fill a need, even a vitally important organizational need, can carry the irrational implication that we—or our organization—are inadequate.

We do not easily acknowledge such uncomfortable feelings in ourselves. Though they are commonly present, we do not often discuss them. Discussion might reify our fears of inadequacy or risk diminishing the self. Such feelings generate defensive responses. Our behavior may reveal the effects of these unwelcome, unattractive feelings of inadequacy as we overcompensate for them. We may be overly aggressive, display an attitude of bravado, or deny that there is anything humbling or embarrassing about the process of seeking gifts. We may show disdain or, even more poignantly, we may defensively deny our shame for having to ask by converting these unacceptable feelings into contempt for the potential giver. Such projection conceals these unattractive feelings from our own awareness and displaces our responsibility for dealing with them by blaming the giver. This ambivalence often surfaces in the language that seekers use to describe the process and their relationship with the donor—vivid words that are often suggestive, less than complimentary, and devoid of the mutual respect so important to the process of requesting, giving, and receiving.

- Some seekers will describe the process as "a fight" or "a real struggle!" Such words suggest that they see the giving-and-receiving relationship as aggressive combat, and that they define success as overwhelming the donor in victory.
- Others may speak of "keeping score," treating the giving-receiving process as a zero-sum game involving skill and tricks, with winners and losers. Success means "I win, you lose."
- Others use words that ooze flattery: "Your participation is absolutely vital! The project will fail without your help!" Such language conveys a fawning image of exaggerated and unrealistic importance intended to exploit the common wish to be liked. The words may also convey

syrupy sweetness with erotic overtones, as if the relationship were a courtship, a love affair, or a seduction.

- Some seekers will talk about the process in a very matter-of-fact, give-and-take way that makes giving and receiving comparable to buying and selling. They focus on what they have to sell, what you have to negotiate, how you need to compromise, what sales resistance they must overcome, and so forth.

To be sure, these two-dimensional images caricature the attitudes of the seekers who use such language, but most seeker-donor relationships contain something of each. In small doses, such attitudes add charm and challenge to the exchange. But each caricature sums up certain assumptions and expectations that seeker and donor may have about each other—assumptions and expectations that obviously affect their evolving relationship, and, unconstrained, can irretrievably damage it.

A sense of entitlement poses another occupational hazard for seekers. This sense of entitlement sometimes surfaces in grant-seekers who have spent a lot of time developing particular projects. Such intense investment in the details of specific programs or projects can generate a belief that no one else—particularly a naïve, uninformed donor, however well-intentioned—could possibly understand the complexity and importance of this project. Such a belief leads to the arrogant conviction that the seeker need not explain or justify a request: "My opinion should be enough!" This patronizing attitude can very quickly turn off even an open-minded prospective donor. The seeker, of course, remains comfortably convinced that the donor's limitations, not the seeker's arrogance, led to failure.

Unfortunately, an apprehension that "my program isn't really that important" or "I am not really that smart" often lurks behind this show of arrogance. Many seekers who show this sense of entitlement or disdain for the giver are really struggling with a disturbing sense of personal inadequacy and embarrassment. These feelings must be hidden both from the self and from others.

Other complicated and potentially embarrassing feelings about fundraising can derail the process. Some seekers have commented that they see themselves as beggars; others note that asking for money, however legitimate the purpose, seems to depend on conning someone. For many seekers, a strong identification with the program or organization can lead to anger or indignation when a donor declines to contribute, as if rejecting the proposal amounts to rejecting the seeker—a response that emphasizes the common "love me, love my dog" psychology. Such rejection can also rouse secondary responses of increased self-doubt about one's role or purpose, or even feelings of unworthiness. Such feelings contribute to eventual burnout.

The unacceptable or embarrassing nature of these and kindred feelings explains why we do not commonly acknowledge or discuss them. Even experienced fund-raisers, as well as workers within many grant-giving organizations with a great deal of sophistication about the giving-and-receiving process, still fence off a large area and post it with "Taboo! Stay out!" signs. But in my view, it is a serious mistake to ignore or deny or avoid the painful reality of these sometimes inappropriate, often excessive, frequently misunderstood feelings. At the very least, unmanaged or unaddressed covert issues interfere with productivity and can seriously undermine morale. As a psychiatrist, I advocate raising, acknowledging, and discussing such issues so that legitimate feelings can be recognized and addressed, and so that inappropriate feelings can be identified and set aside.

CONCLUSION

To avoid exploiting the power position of the donor or the dependence of the seeker, we must become aware of some of the darker sides of human views of money and of giving and receiving. On both sides of this transaction, power and need affect people, as do the less attractive aspects of money. No matter how righteous the individual or how honorable the cause, these darker sides are an intrinsic part of the process. We cannot intentionally avoid them. If we do, they will only surface later in unexpected ways or at unexpected times. But acknowledging their existence lets us begin a healthier approach to a complicated business. By recognizing these troubling feelings, naming them, and beginning to understand their part in the process, we can reduce their power to exercise an influence that seems magical, covert, and incomprehensible.

In the last analysis, the quality of the underlying relationship determines the nature of the giving-receiving experience. But the vicissitudes of the irrational expectations and attitudes that both seeker and donor bring to the transaction can distort that relationship. Efforts to enhance that relationship, to give *both* parties a genuine sense of participation and value, will increase the effectiveness of the fund-raising process. A mutually satisfying relationship that persists often proves to be the most important gain for both parties.

Recognizing how easily we can bog down in the minutiae of our work and thus risk losing sight of our broader purposes, I'd like to conclude with a favorite quotation of mine. Written by Reinhold Niebuhr more than forty years ago, it helps to remind us of this larger context:

> Nothing that is worth doing can be achieved in our lifetime;
> Therefore we must be saved by hope.

> Nothing which is true or beautiful or good makes complete sense in any immediate context of history;
> Therefore we must be saved by faith.

> Nothing we do, however virtuous, can be accomplished alone;
> Therefore we must be saved by love.[4]

NOTES

1. Joseph Frazier Wall, *Andrew Carnegie* (New York: Oxford University Press, 1970), 880.

2. Ibid., 880-81.

3. Alan Radley and Marie Kennedy, "Charitable Giving by Individuals: A Study of Attitudes and Practice," *Human Relations* 48, no. 6 (1995): 701.

4. Reinhold Niebuhr, *Irony of American History* (New York: Scribner, 1952), 63.

Notes on Contributors

Brian Burton, *Executive Director of the Wilkinson Center*, a nonprofit, faith-based agency which serves eighteen thousand people each year with emergency services, including food, clothing, employment, rental assistance, children's programs and other services. Prior to his work at the Wilkinson Center, Mr. Burton served as an associate minister in Dallas for five years.

Jeverley R. Cook, Ph.D., *Vice President, Grants, Communities Foundation of Texas*, administers the Foundation's unrestricted grants program and manages charitable distributions from its designated and donor-advised funds. In 1999, with an approximate asset base of $500 million, the Communities Foundation of Texas made grants of nearly $45 million in fulfillment of its philanthropic mission.

Charles E. Curran, S.T.D., *Elizabeth Scurlock University Professor of Human Values, Southern Methodist University*, has served as president of three national professional societies—the American Theological Society, the Catholic Theological Society of America, and the Society of Christian Ethics. Dr. Curran has authored and edited more than forty books in the area of moral theology. They include most recently: *The Origins of Moral Theology in the United States: Three Different Approaches* (1997) and *The Catholic Moral Tradition Today* (1999).

The Rev. Carl Lee (Trey) Hammond, *Coordinator for Urban Ministries at the General Assembly Office of the Presbyterian Church U.S.A. in Louisville, Kentucky,* accepted his national post after working as a pastor in Dallas for sixteen years. He has served as President of the Oasis Housing Corporation and Dallas City Homes, Chair of Congregational Advocates for Homeless People, and a consultant to the Downtown Dallas Family Shelter and the Interfaith Housing Coalition. In 1994, the Greater Dallas Community of Churches honored him as "Minister of the Year."

Leon R. Kass, M.D., Ph.D., *Addie Clark Harding Professor at the University of Chicago,* has also taught at Georgetown University and St. John's College in Annapolis, Maryland. He is a Founding Fellow and former Board Member of the Hastings Center and has served on the National Council on the Humanities of the National Endowment for the Humanities. An active, award-winning teacher of undergraduates, Dr. Kass is the author of *Toward a More Natural Science: Biology and Human Affairs (1985), The Hungry Soul: Eating and the Perfecting of Our Nature* (1994), *The Ethics of Human Cloning* (1998) co-authored with James Q. Wilson, and *Wing to Wing, Oar to Oar: Readings on Courting and Marrying* (2000), co-authored with Amy A. Kass.

Robin W. Lovin, Ph.D., *Dean and Professor of Ethics at the Perkins School of Theology, Southern Methodist University* since 1994. Dean Lovin is a member of the World Methodist Council and an editor-at-large of *The Christian Century.* In addition to experience in the pastorate, Dean Lovin has taught at Candler School of Theology at Emory University, and for thirteen years at the Divinity School of the University of Chicago. He is the author of *Christian Faith and Public Choices: The Social Ethics of Barth, Brunner, and Bonhoeffer* (1984), *Reinhold Niebuhr and Christian Realism* (1994), and *Christian Ethics: An Essential Guide* (2000).

William F. May, Ph.D., *Cary M. Maguire University Professor of Ethics, Southern Methodist University,* also served as the founding Director of the Maguire Center for Ethics and Public Responsibility at SMU. Earlier,

Professor May founded and chaired the Department of Religious Studies at Indiana University and served as President of the American Academy of Religion. A Founding Fellow of the Hastings Center and an award-winning teacher, his writing in professional ethics includes *The Physician's Covenant* (1983), *The Patient's Ordeal* (1991), and *Testing the Medical Covenant: Active Euthanasia and Health Care Reform* (1996). Forthcoming is *The Beleaguered Rulers: The Public Obligation of the Professional.*

Curtis W. Meadows, Jr., *former President of the Meadows Foundation, Consultant on Philanthropy, Of Counsel to the Dallas law firm of Thompson and Knight, and visiting faculty member at the University of Texas, Austin.* After practicing law for seventeen years, Mr. Meadows served as President and Director of the Meadows Foundation from 1980 to 1996. Mr. Meadows's civic and community activities include service on boards or committee leadership positions with the Council on Foundations, the Conference of Southwest Foundations, the Center for Nonprofit Management, and more than sixty charitable community organizations.

Roy W. Menninger, M.D., *Chairman of Trustees, The Menninger Foundation, Topeka, Kansas.* Dr. Menninger was elected Chairman of Trustees at Menninger in 1993 after serving as the fourth president there from 1967 to 1993. The Menninger Foundation is a nationally known center for treatment and prevention, research, and professional education in psychiatry. Before his election as President and CEO in 1967, Dr. Menninger was Director of the Division of the School of Mental Health and Director of the Department of Preventive Psychiatry.

Waldemar A. Nielsen, Ph.D., *President of Nielsen Consultants of New York, Inc.*, served in the public sector as a planner and administrator for the Marshall Plan. His work in the voluntary sector has included service as an officer of the Ford Foundation, President of the African American Institute, and adviser to the Ford Foundation, the Rockefeller Brothers Fund, and Ewing Kauffman Foundation. He is the author of *The Big Foundations* (1972),

The Endangered Sector (1979), *The Golden Donors* (1985), and *Inside American Philanthropy: The Dramas of Donorship* (1996).

David H. Smith, Ph.D., *Professor and former Chair of Religious Studies at Indiana University in Bloomington*, has taught since 1967 at Indiana University in Bloomington, where he received distinguished teaching awards in 1979 and 1986. Professor Smith directs Indiana's Poynter Center for the Study of Ethics and American Institutions, which has studied the social responsibility of professionals, research ethics, ethical issues in human genetics, and the social role of trustees. He is the author of *Health and Medicine in the Anglican Tradition* (1986) and *Entrusted: The Moral Responsibilities of Trustees* (1995).

A. Lewis Soens, Jr., Ph.D., *Emeritus Professor of English at the University of Notre Dame*, has also taught at Drake University, University of Colorado, and Smith College. A Fulbright Scholar at Magdalen College, Oxford and editor of *Abstracts of English Studies*, Professor Soens is the author of several books including most recently *I, the Song: Classical Poetry of Native North America* (1999).

Steven Sverdlik, Ph.D., *Associate Professor of Philosophy, Southern Methodist University*. Before coming to SMU in 1982, Dr. Sverdlik taught at Virginia Commonwealth University. He now teaches chiefly in the fields of ethics and aesthetics and received the SMU Rotunda Teacher of the Year Award in 1991. Recipient of three seminar grants from the National Endowment for the Humanities, Dr. Sverdlik has published fifteen articles in his fields of specialization, including essays on "The Nature of Desert," "Justice and Mercy," "Hume's Key and Aesthetic Rationality," and "Collective Responsibility."

Carl C. Trovall, *Campus Pastor and Assistant Professor of Religion and History, Concordia University at Austin*, also served as pastor for an ethically diverse congregation in South Texas for seven years. He currently is working on his dissertation in religious ethics at Southern Methodist University titled *An*

Analysis of the Political and Moral Implications of "Mestizaje" for Michael Walzer's Conception of Civic Community in the United States.

Steven C. Wheatley, Ph.D., *Vice President of the American Council of Learned Societies*, previously taught history at the University of Chicago. At Chicago, he also served as Dean of Students and Assistant to the Dean of the Social Sciences Division. Dr. Wheatley is the author of *The Politics of Philanthropy: Abraham Flexner and Medical Education* (1988), as well as a new introduction to Raymond Fosdick's *The Story of the Rockefeller Foundation*. He has served as a consultant to the Ford Foundation, the Carnegie Corporation, and the Lilly Endowment Inc. and as a member of the Doctoral Fellows Advisory Committee of the Indiana University Center on Philanthropy. He is a member of the Academic Advisory Council of the Rockefeller Archive Center of Rockefeller University.

James P. Wind, Ph.D., *President of The Alban Institute*, a non-profit organization serving congregations and denominations. Dr. Wind's earlier experience in the voluntary sector includes twelve years in the pastorate; extended service as Program Director, Religion Division, at the Lilly Endowment; and as Director of Research and Publications at the Park Ridge Center for the Study of Health, Faith, and Ethics in Chicago, Illinois. He is the author of three books and co-author of five more including *American Congregations: New Perspectives in the Study of Congregations*, Wind and Lewis, eds. (1994).

Susan M. Yohn, Ph.D., *Associate Professor of History, Hofstra University*, has written on the tensions between volunteerism and professionalism, the shifting contributions of women in time and treasure to voluntary organizations, and the complexities of volunteer work in multi-cultural settings, especially in the Southwest. An associate professor at Hofstra University, Dr. Yohn has also taught at New York University and Princeton University. Her book, *A Contest of Faiths* (1995), received the Stessin Prize for Outstanding Scholarship from Hofstra University.

Index

Abrahamic tradition, and giving, 60–61
Adams, James Luther, 161–62, 165
Addams, Jane, 145
Affordable housing, and voluntary community, 191–98
African charitable traditions, 73
Agape, 72
Albanian Orthodox Diocese in America, 122
Alcoholics Anonymous, 51
Alinsky, Saul, 130
Altruistic giving, 208–9
American Catholic Bishops, on solving social problems, 194–95
American charitable tradition: appeal of nonprofit system to feelings and emotion, 74–75; association with others to address social problems, 73–79; scope of individual giving, 74; trust as basis of voluntary giving, 75
American Law Institute, 100, 101
American political culture: antimonarchical impulse, 82; republicanism, 85
Angell, James, 87
Annenberg, Walter, 58
Antipoverty programs, 172–73
Applied ethics, xxx
Approbato, Tom, 127
Aquinas, Thomas: *Summa theologiae*, 38–39
Aristotle: on the good life, 61–62; *Nicomachean Ethics*, 51 n. 1; on pity, 30, 47, 51 n. 1, 52 n. 2; on relation of virtue to compassion, 46
Armenian charitable tradition, 73
Asian Pacific Law Center, 125
Asking, psychological aspects of, 210–13
Aspen Institute, 200
Autonomy, respect for, xxx, xxxi, xxxiii

Bacon, Francis: "Of Goodness and Goodness of Nature," 2; scientific understanding of nature, 12

Baptism, 126
Beckmann, David, 170–71
Bellah, Robert: on good practices of life, 78; *The Good Society*, 181
Beneficence, principle of, xxx
Benevolence: conflicts with other norms, 28–29, 32–33; eighteenth century notion of, 27, 46–47; as a norm, 28–29; and prudence, 47; as a virtue, 28; vs. complacence, 27–28
Bentham, Jeremy: "An Introduction to the Principles of Morals and Legislation," 30, 34 n. 8
Berger, Peter, 117, 160–63, 165, 166, 174
Bill of Rights, 74
Blake, Alice, 143–44, 145–46
Blessing, Elizabeth, 178
Board members. *See* Philanthropic boards
Bradley (Lunde and Harry) Foundation, 180
Bread for the World, 170
Buber, Martin, 167
Burke, Edmund, xxxvi, 160, 185 n. 2
Burton, Brian, 199
Butler, Nicholas Murray, 90, 92

"Can-Do," 181
Capacity responsibility, 23
Caritas, xxvi
Carnegie, Andrew: creation of Carnegie Corporation, 83–84, 96; on the difficulty of foundation management, 206; on foundation trustees, 98–99, 102; "Gospel of Wealth," 98; leadership of Carnegie Corporation, 87; on the perpetual foundation, xxxvii, 107; spirit of philanthropy, 101–2
Carnegie Commission on Higher Education, 105–6
Carnegie Corporation of New York: under Carnegie's direct management, 87; as case study in philanthropic ethics, xxxvi–xxxvii, 96–107; conflict of interest of early board

221

of, xxiv–xxv; modern meaning, 2–3; nature of, 35–41; pluralism of values, 66; political attacks on, xxii–xxiii; and preferential option for the poor, 39, 45; and prevention of suffering, 18–19; question of how to serve, 10–12; question of whom to serve, 4–10; relationship between giver and receiver, xx–xxi, xxv, 68–70; and sense of community, 72; and shared power, 152–54; support of human excellence, xvii–xviii; two levels of service, xvii

Philanthropy—CHURCHES: aid to undocumented, 175–76; as alternative to government welfare programs, 199–201; as bridges backward, 177–80; as bridges forward, 179–80; as bridges outward toward others, 180; centrality of in American life, 117–18; challenges facing, 131–35; changing leadership ecology, 134; changing public roles, 123–25; confusion about treasure, 135; contributions to common good, 119–20, 123, 159–60; creative coalitions and partnerships, 125; dangers in accepting government funding, xxxiv, 182; decreasing role of denominationalism, 133; ecological concerns, 132; economic challenges, 134–35; individual giving to, 123; institutional reconfiguration, 132–33; as mediating institutions, 166–69; number of denominations, 122; number of in U.S. and Canada, 121; participation levels in, 121–22; patterns of self-serving and vindictiveness, 120; public nature of, 166–69; shaping of leaders, 118–19; social service agencies of, 171–77; symbiotic relationship with the government, 182–84; tradition of charity, xvii, xviii, 3, 60–61, 170; unrecognized contributions of, 136 n. 2

Philanthropy—FOUNDATIONS, 64; community, 112–13; and conflict of interests, xxix–xxx; establishment of priorities, 108–14; grant-making process, 151; as means to an end, 70; political tension surrounding, 84–85, 86–87; as public agencies, 85–86; staff, xxxvii, 83, 84; symbiotic relationships with recipient organizations, 109, 112–13; tensions between donors, trustees, and professional staff, 205

Philanthropy—OTHER VOLUNTARY ORGANIZATIONS: and affordable housing, 191–98; balanced representation on boards of, 113; collaboration with government, xxxiii–xxxiv; community service

organizations, 74; competition for support among institutions, xiv; contributions of treasure and time, xix; effects of receiving substantial funds on, 204; and ethics, 96–107; government funding for, 169–70; moral constraints on giving, 66–68; moral problems, xxix–xxxi; need for experiment, xxviii–xxix; partnerships with governmental agencies, 176; public responsibilities, 113; small-scale, xxvii–xxviii; support of service bureaucracies, xxviii; as "third sector," xiii, xxix, 187 n. 37, 191, 194

Phillips, Kevin, xxiv
Pifer, Alan, 105–6, 107
Pity, 7, 30, 32, 47, 51 n. 1, 52 n. 2
Plato: *Republic*, 24
Pluralism, 64, 132
Poor, preferential option for the, 39, 45
Poppendieck, Janet, 200
Poverty: American view of as temporary condition, xxiv; causes of, 171–72; and religious faith, 180
Powell, Colin, 140
Preaching, 126
Presbyterian Woman's Board of Home Missions, 141–49
"President's Summit for America's Future," 140
Preventive programs, 173
Prison reform, 175
Pritchett, Henry, 100–101
Private property, 37
Private wealth, 109, 111
Pro bono publico service, xxvii
Progressivism, 149
Promise Keepers, 51
Protestant women's missionary movement. *See* Women's missionary movement
Prudent compassion, 23–24, 28, 30, 32, 33, 45, 48
Psychology of giving and receiving, xxv, 202, 205–9, 210–13
Public Broadcasting Act, 105
Public disclosure, xxx
Public funding. *See* Government
Public needs, structure for meeting in U.S., 63–65
Public-private partnerships, 65, 133, 140, 169–70

Racial segregation, 31
Racism, 130